MIKE DOUGLAS
MY STORY

MIKE DOUGLAS
MY STORY

G. P. PUTNAM'S SONS ● NEW YORK, N. Y.

SBN: 399-11963-9

Library of Congress Cataloging in Publication Data

Douglas, Mike.
  Mike Douglas: my story.

  Includes index.
    1. Douglas, Mike.   2. Television personalities—United
States—Biography.   3. Singers—United States—Biography.
PN1992.4.D58A36   791.45′092′4   [B]   78-2694

Grateful acknowledgement is made to Michael Leshnov for
providing many of the photos reproduced in this book.

My sincerest and deepest thanks to
Carroll Carroll for his assistance
in the preparation of this manuscript
—Mike Douglas

CONTENTS

(I)
CONFESSION

I belong to a group of people who believe that confession is good for the soul. Being able to say, "I was wrong, I made a mistake, I'm sorry, forgive me," will always make you feel better about yourself and your fellow man. It makes me happier.

Happier each day than the day before is the way I will always want to be. I want to make every tomorrow better than any yesterday.

My goal is bringing pleasure and entertainment, refuge from worldly problems, to others. That's what keeps me going. And this could be the answer to that banal question interviewers are always asking me, "What is your philosophy of life?"

"Philosophy of life" to me is just a heavy phrase for two more simple ones: "life-style" and "your own thing."

To find out what that is you must watch a person at work and play. Observe your fellow man. Personality can't be explained but it is well worth studying.

I know this: if I tried to put into words how and why I live

9

the way I do, what I'd probably come up with might seem to be a rewrite, a sort of comic book version of the Golden Rule and the Ten Commandments. So I won't try to articulate it; I'll just keep on doing my thing.

I major in people. It's a form of going to school; it could be called "The Mike Douglas Show." . . . I sing along with people, talk with them, play games with them and, to a degree that surprises me, I often supply them with a little free couch time that would cost them about fifty bucks at their neighborhood shrink.

It's true and it's fascinating. Some people (including a rather large TV audience) tell me things they withhold from their family and closest friends. How far to let them go is my responsibility, my job. That's how I spend most of my time.

Time (to coin a cliché) is our most precious possession. We only have a certain amount of it and every minute we waste leaves just that much less in the bank of life.

I guess that's why I come down hard on people who keep me waiting. I'm a bug on punctuality. Make a date for me at 10 o'clock, I'll be there—probably a few minutes early. True, I may be wasting some of my time that way. But I'd rather do that than waste someone else's. I want to be in control of my time. So to have someone else keep me waiting and waste it makes me furious.

One of our wits said once, and I wish I knew who, so that I could give him credit, "There's no use being on time because no one is ever there to appreciate it."

Well, I'm always there and I appreciate it. Possibly this is because I've been in the broadcasting business so long. Obviously, we run on a strict schedule. So I not only don't think it's *chic* to make someone wait for me, I know it's not good business.

My proof that I'm right is simply that the real VIP's in my line of work, the pros who have reached stardom and gone on to become legends are seldom those who keep people waiting. They succeeded because they knew that making it is, in part, being where you are supposed to be at the proper time.

To give you one shining example, Bing Crosby, according to all those who worked with him, was what he might have called "the very personification of punctilious punctuality." Or, put another way, Bing was the personification of good manners.

I've unwittingly drifted away from the point I was trying to make—that confession is good for the soul. I hope it's also a good way to start a book.

Rummaging through my memory and my files for a way to get this gig on the road, I came across a letter written to me in the summer of '76 (that's 19' not 17').

It's from Rev. Leo J. McKenzie, director of the Eucharistic Congress, and it's addressed to "Mr. Michael Douglas, Independence Mall East, Philadelphia, Pa., 19106." There's more to this letter than meets the eye.

Dear Mike,

Please accept my sincere appreciation for your participation in the Eucharistic Congress. It was kind of you to be with us as commentator at the opening mass.

We are also thankful to you for having Mother Teresa appear on your show. We all feel that she is a woman with a message and thanks to you, her message will be heard by many.

Time magazine called Mother Teresa a "living saint." That's about the best rating a person can get. It makes me want to try a little harder.

I know I felt like a better person after merely shaking hands with Mother Teresa. She's dedicated her entire life to underprivileged children the world over . . . . in the most crowded, the most remote, the most plague-ridden spots on the face of this earth. I felt I had touched a person whose selflessness was, to me, a kind of holiness.

At the time we met I had reason to believe she was in her

early sixties. But because of the rigorous and dangerous life she'd led, she looked much older. Her face was so deeply marked with lines put there by other people's troubles that it brought tears to my eyes.

It must be a miracle that she's never fallen prey to the many diseases that ravaged the countries she visited to help the children. She must be bathed in a spiritual antiseptic.

I asked, "In all your travels, in all your experience, what do you think—besides understanding one another—is the biggest problem in the world today?"

Softly and thoughtfully she said, "Loneliness."

Being on television, bringing pleasure, knowledge and entertainment to many who are lonely, giving them a little companionship and love, seems to me one tangible way of helping solve this loneliness problem.

But to get on with it, and since Father McKenzie obviously doesn't know the truth about me, I'm here and now about to confess.

In addressing me as Michael Douglas, Father, you could only be referring to a motion picture producer by that name who told me when he co-hosted the show that he gets a lot of my mail, as I get a lot of his.

My professional name is Mike Douglas, just Mike. How that came about is one of those show biz secrets that I will explain later in this exposé and disclose what can happen to a run-of-the-streets neighborhood kid from the West Side of Chicago, if he's lucky, and has a Mom and Dad and a big brother and a big sister who, each in a different way, put him and keep him on the right track.

Everybody knows that what your parents impart to you gets you out on the fairway. But take it from a good Sunday golfer, you have to bring a little something of your own to the approach shots. And to get your whole game together, everything depends on how you come through in the clutch on the green.

The more or less mechanical part of my luck was that I was born with a good ear; two of them, as a matter of fact, hung neatly on each side of my head. Mom said I used to hum myself to sleep listening to Fritz Kreisler recordings that she liked to play. They made doing housework easier.

As I grew older my musical education extended to the radio. That was my postgraduate course in music. I was an avid radio band listener. And of all the bandleaders I listened to over and over again, the one who fascinated me the most was Kay Kyser and his "Kollege of Musical Knowledge."

"How y'all?"

Kay's personality and music made such an impression on me that years later when I was playing at the Texas Hotel in Fort Worth with Bill Carlsen and His Band of a Million Thrills (yes, alas—that was the name of it), a strange prophetic thing happened. I was sitting in the coffee shop with Carlsen one morning. Bill sort of protected me because I was the "baby of the band." One of Bill's sidemen whose name I've forgotten (but I remember he played the trombone) was with us.

Suddenly the whole world lit up for me. The legendary Kay Kyser walked in and sat down at a nearby table. My hero in the flesh! He was with Harry Babbitt and a couple of other stars of his organization.

For a few seconds my sixteen-year-old jaw hung open. When I could get my tongue untangled and make my jaw work I said to the two men with me, "Kay Kyser just came in. See." I pointed. "He's sitting right over there. Someday I'm gonna sing for him."

"Yeah," chuckled the wisecracking 'bone player, as he tried to sip his coffee without getting the spoon handle in his eye, "but will he listen?"

Bill Carlsen didn't say anything. He just smiled indulgently.

"You don't understand," I tried to explain—funny how you remember conversational trivia—"I mean it! Someday I'm going to sing with his organization. I mean, actually work for him."

In retrospect I can see that it was a mighty strange way for a kid to talk. It was ambition—or destiny—at work, and that's how it turned out. A few years later I was actually singing on the radio show "Kay Kyser and his Kollege of Musical Knowledge." My fantasy realized!

I always have been a positive thinker, thanks to Mom. She used to say to me, "The word 'can't' is for failures."

I don't want to race ahead of my story but I must introduce here the fact that not only did Kay Kyser give me my first real break, my first show business recognition, he actually gave me my name, "Mike Douglas."

You see, my real name, my name to my wife, Gen, and to my three daughters, Kelly Ann and the twins, Christine and Michele—and also to the IRS—is Michael Delaney Dowd, Jr. But if I'd signed that name to this book, you never would have bought it.

I realize I'm a pretty big guy to be toting around a "Junior" at the end of my name but at this writing, thank God, Michael Delaney Dowd, Sr., is still around confounding men many years his junior with his physical and mental agility and snapping one-liners off the top of his head as if he were Henny Youngman's prompter.

I'll never forget talking to Dad long distance, one day late in the Great Depression. I was working for peanuts (that was before they became our national fruit) in some cheap night spot out in the boonies. I was worried about how he was getting along.

After his cheery hello, I asked, "How are things in Chicago?"

"Bad, son," he told me in his musical comedy Irish brogue. It was almost as if I'd asked, "How bad are they?"

for he moved right along with, "Things are so bad here that midgets are trying to get into the orphanages."

So it is as an honor to my Dad that my legal name still includes the "Junior." I retain it as a show of pride, proclaiming myself his son.

Here's to you, Dad!

(II)
AND SO IT BEGAN

I want to make it clear at once that the following series of anecdotes and recollections is not the product of advanced planning. It is merely a gathering of random readouts from that most complicated of computers, the one most of us are born with but fail to use often enough or well enough: the mind. Which is to say, it is less an autobiography than it is a volley of short flashes, often out of sequence, from a frequently short-circuited memory.

If I'd known how to make this book more cohesive, I could have called it an autobiography. As is, it might accurately be titled "Excerpts From A Diary I Might Have Written But Didn't."

I think it takes a different kind of ego from mine to write a diary, to sit down each day and laboriously record what you said, did, and thought about. (The laughs at lunch with Pearl Bailey or the tips on diet from Carol Channing.) Particularly if you've been too busy to think about much, or, as in my early years, too worried and depressed to give anything a second thought. Now I have a 90-minute, 5-day-a-week

TV show that takes care of most of my conscious minutes, plus some of my unconscious ones and probably a few subconscious ones.

But, inevitably, there are things that make an indelible imprint, and there they stay (like invisible tattoos) until some fleeting sight of something, or a chance phrase, motivates the power of suggestion, which punches them up for you.

I was once interviewed by a reporter in Los Angeles who told me the only notes he ever made were the date, the time, the address and the correct way to spell the name. As for all the rest, details on background and color, he left to memory. "What's worth remembering will stick in my mind," he said. "Everything else is garbage." So was the story he wrote.

Of course, everyone has a few events in his personal history he'll never forget. For me, one of these happened on Thursday morning, January 3, 1962.

I got up earlier than usual and left for work sooner than usual.

Instead of going directly to the studios of KYW-TV in Cleveland, as I'd been doing every morning for about three weeks, I went straight to the newsstand in the Statler Hotel.

The Statler was home to a great many theatre people stopping over in Cleveland. So naturally the newsstand carried *Variety*, the widely acclaimed "Bible of show biz." It traditionally hit the streets in New York on Wednesday. It took an extra day to reach Cleveland. (It had taken me thirty-six years.)

The price of *Variety* was then 35¢. I walked up to the newsstand, trembling with excitement, handed a ten-dollar bill to the girl and asked for ten copies of *Variety*.

"I can't sell you that many," she said.

"Why not?" I argued. "I'm here and I've got the money."

"We only get eight copies a week." (That was show biz in Cleveland.)

"I'll take them."

"I can only sell you six. A man was here a few minutes ago and brought two. What's going on?"

I took my six copies and my change, sat down in one of the big leather chairs in the lobby, put five copies on my lap and opened the sixth, leafing through it until I came to a full page ad that featured a reprint of a television review and a headline above four familiar photographs.

The headline said:

> DOUGLAS DOES IT!!
> Mike Douglas Show Puts
>   Cleveland On TV Map!
> Celebs Using Format As
> Proving Ground For
>   New Untried Material.

Then came four photos. Under the top one the caption read, "Jerry Lester Clowns for Tony Pastor, Mike Douglas and Johnny Desmond on the Mike Douglas Show." In the early days of TV, Jerry, who became the Daddy of television talk show hosts (well, the stepdaddy) when he took over "Broadway Open House" from Morey Amsterdam in the 50's, was quoted as saying, "This format and the KYW-TV crew are great. I've been able to test routines I've been thinking about for years."

Under the second picture appeared the following caption: "Lovely Carmel Quinn had a full 90 minutes daily to work out new and 'pet' routines during her week in Cleveland. Of the program she said, 'The Mike Douglas Show is delightful. I loved working every minute of it, and I know others will. . . . I really mean that.'"

The third picture was captioned, "Joe E. Brown convulses Elaine Malbin of the Metropolitan Opera and host Mike Douglas." (There's a picture of me, doubled up, with my mouth open so wide it looks bigger than Brown's.) "Joe's week-long performance drew equal response from audience and critics. Of 'The Mike Douglas Show' the famed comedian commented, 'The audiences seemed to enjoy it . . . I know I did.'"

The fourth picture showed Jim Moran, the eccentric publicist who had leaped to fame selling refrigerators to Eskimos, or something like that; me (with curly crew cut), Gretchen Wyler and Dick Patterson. Under this one it says that they are looking at a fright mask which could mean me.

The ad also says, just beside the photos, "See *Variety* review which is quoted in full." The ad concludes, "If you have a yen to spend a full week in Cleveland working to an audience of a quarter of a million, contact Woody Fraser, KYW Television, Cleveland, Ohio. Telephone SUperior 1-4500."

I sat and read the *Variety* review over and over again. As my friend Jackie Gleason, "The Great One," would say, "How sweet it was!" Then I tucked my six copies under my arm and went happily off to contact Woody Fraser as the ad suggested. I found him in the first place I looked—my office—reading one of his two copies of the ad and review.

George Washington must have been one of my forefathers. I find I cannot tell a lie. I did not find Woody in my office. I did not have an office. None of us did. We just had desks and worked as hard as if we each had a room with "a nameplate in the door and a Bigelow on the floor." Maybe harder.

"Stand perfectly still, right where you are," Woody said to me the moment he caught sight of me. Then he started to read me the review, which we both knew by heart.

"I've read it! I've read it!" I said, using my best Jack Benny delivery. "But go ahead anyway. I like the way you read."

Here is what Woody read just as it was printed, word for word.

THE MIKE DOUGLAS SHOW
With Ellie Frankel Trio, guests.
Producer, Woody Fraser
Director, Ernie Sherry
90 Minutes—Mon.-Fri. 1 PM
KYW-Cleveland.

Judging from its first week's output, KYW-TV's daytimer, "The Mike Douglas Show" should quickly work up a following and perhaps a steady niche in local television. It also has syndie possibilities since the regional angles are kept to a minimum and also since the Westinghouse Broadcasting Co., station owner, has been scouting for something to get it off the "old-movie" hook.

Douglas is bright and brash with a solid 16-year career in show biz including several years of network TV, big band and night club singing and emceeing. He came here via Los Angeles and Chicago, where he did well on NBC originations.

Carmel Quinn was co-host the first week, except that she missed Monday and Tuesday because of a Christmas radio tape commitment with Arthur Godfrey in New York. This week it's Joe E. Brown. Jerry Lester is due next week.

The second string talent on the first programs was equally impressive. The opener, for example, had Gretchen Wyler and Dick Patterson of the touring company of *Bye Bye Birdie*. Miss Wyler sang "Spanish Rose" and "Lola" and also chatted a good bit about show biz and the people in it.

Patterson, who must have a future as a single, did everything but tear down the studio and was working on the rugs when the management gently removed his microphone. Since he is not a pantomimist, he quit at that point.

The settings, camera work and production in general were smooth and professional, giving even more substance to the syndie possibilities here.

Ellie Frankel is the town's leading pianist (jazz type) and she and trio performed admirably, particularly considering that they also work all night at the Theatrical Grill. Kai Winding brought along his trombone and blasted a couple of numbers. Jim Moran, the super press agent, was also there booming a new movie, and Father Joseph Dustin, the banjo-playing priest, was along on the opener for some solos and sing-a-longs.

The show was designed particularly as competition for "The One O'Clock Club" on WEWS-TV, and they run head-to-head. There is a distinct difference so far, however. Club is built around the personality of Dorothy Fuldheim and Bill Gordon, its co-hosts, plus regular local guests, book reviews and much table-hopping chatter interviews. "The Mike Douglas Show" leans more toward show business with a heavier ration of guests, either passing through town, per-forming here or hired particularly for the program.

Whether it can stand the pace, only its budget director knows.

The review was signed *Russ*

Thanks, Russ. And you were right, we're still having trou-ble with the budget director. Reading what you wrote and looking at "The Mike Douglas Show" as it is today tells the world why *Variety* is "the show biz Bible." They called it pretty good.

There are a lot more people to thank. First of all, Woody Fraser, for sticking to an idea he believed in and for believ-ing in me.

If it hadn't been for Woody and his solid gold chutzpah (which I will fill you in on later), today I might be in the real estate business in Southern California.

Naturally I owe an awful lot to my wife Genevieve, and al-though this book is going to focus on my work life, not my family life, I want to make a bow of gratitude, right here, to Gen, who was willing to change her mind and give up an important decision we'd made to get out of show business and go into something more comfortable.

Things looked very iffy. We had decided to give up what looked like a dead-end career of two-bit jobs that gave me neither satisfaction nor enough money to live on comfortably and instead to go into the real estate business. After all, we reasoned, real estate was selling and selling was a part of show business so we weren't making such a radical change. What was even better, we reasoned, selling real estate in California kept you out in the sun a lot. I even worked up a repertoire of sales approaches. I could sing songs to my clients: "There's No Place Like Home," "This Ole House," "Just a Cottage Small by a Waterfall," "A Little White House at the End of the Lane," "Home," "Penthouse Serenade," "A Shanty in Old Shanty Town," "That Tumbledown Shack in Athlone" and "My Little Grass Shack in Kealakekua, Hawaii."

I also saw selling real estate as a wonderful chance to play lots of customer golf, which is a version of the game that has you trying to outslice and outhook your opponent and letting him outputt you on every hole. (Sometimes this is tough. It takes a lot of practice to miss a two-inch tap-in.) But lots of lots are sold that way.

Gen had already enrolled in school and was studying for her license as a broker. I was planning to do the same as soon as I finished the gig I was on.

Having made the decision, we talked it over with Gen's brother, Charles, who at that time happened to be writing for the syndicated astrologer Carroll Righter.

The next morning Charlie phoned. "Hey," he said, "I hope you and Gen change your minds about going into the real estate business because, according to the stars and charts, at the end of the year you're heading for a real bonanza."

That's what Charlie told us but that's not what stopped us from going into the real estate business. On the other hand, who knows, maybe the real estate business was the big bonanza Charlie saw in the stars. At this writing the little G.I. homes like the one Gen and I built in Burbank for $15,000 when I got out of the Navy, are going for around $55,000 to $60,000.

If you really want to know what steered us off selling dirt, you'll have to stick with me till I get to it.

Naturally I did want to add here a few thoughts about Westinghouse Broadcasting Company, Group W, for having faith in me, and before this gets to sour d too much like the last ten minutes of one of my friend Billy Graham's "little talks," let me quote the following letter I received from a viewer, Mrs. Karen J. Howard:

Dear Mr. Douglas, I have recently enrolled as a student in Orange Coast College in Costa Mesa, California.

I was immediately sympathetic because I, too, am a college person, an alumnus of "Kay Kyser's Kollege of Musical Knowledge."

We in our English composition class have been studying and analyzing words that we feel have special meaning for us. Our assignment is to choose an individual of national prominence in order that we may ask him if there is, indeed, a word that has strong, singular meaning for him. I have chosen you.

Would you please reply at your earliest convenience, indicating the word that has special significance for you, and a brief paragraph outlining the reason for choosing that word. It is necessary that the letter be signed personally by you.

Thank you for your help.

Very truly yours,

(signed) Karen J. Howard

I have a photo-copy of that letter before me and at the bottom of it I have written in long hand the one word: "Faith."

By way of explanation I added, "Since success came rather late in life for me (36), the word is meaningful. It took faith on the part of my wife and everyone who helped me, coupled with my own faith in myself, to get me over a lot of rough spots."

Let me add one more letter from the file. It was written to me by a man who was one of the biggest names in radio decades back, in its so-called Golden Age, when I was a disk jockey in Oklahoma City and he was writing the much acclaimed thriller serial "Lights Out" and other radio plays. His name . . . Arch Oboler.

Arch was on our show during a visit to Philadelphia and wrote me:

> Dear Mike,
> A quick word from my moutain top to thank you for a most interesting interlude. I can well understand your increasing popularity. You're a top-flight showman.
> I would be remiss indeed if I didn't comment on those of your amazing staff whom I met. Starting with Penny Price, Amy Hirsch and then Susan Solomon and Stuart Crowner. I never met people more dedicated to a project since I invented NASA.
> May we meet again in good laughter and high ratings.
>   Cordially,
>   Arch Oboler

So, you see, things haven't changed a whole lot in fifteen years. Things around the show are still, as I've heard my German friends say, *gemütlich*.

What I didn't know was that Arch invented NASA. Although he *did* tell me he invented radio. That's all we spoke of, the so-called "good old days," the Golden Age.

During that talk Arch reiterated the great rule for success on that medium; one that I'd heard from such other qualified experts on success in radio as Bob Hope, Jack Benny, Bing Crosby, Red Skelton and Edgar Bergen. . . . "Tell 'em what you're going to do, do it and then tell 'em what you did."

Well, I don't have to tell you what I'm about to do. You're reading it right now. This testifies that I did it.

(III)
THE PLAINS PEOPLE

The winter of 1976 and '77 will long be remembered by most people as a very cold and unfriendly one to almost everybody in the country except the Carters of Plains, Georgia.

Because of this we took our cameras and lights and went down there to spend the day, not long after James Earl Carter was elected to the Presidency of the United States, thrusting his mother, Miss Lillian, and his daughter, Amy, into the national spotlight.

It had been many, many years since one of our Presidents had a mother who was a veteran of the Peace Corps. So she was really the one we went down there to meet and have lunch with.

As our regular viewers know, we frequently make trips to various places for various reasons—we call them remotes—they add interest, timeliness, spice and diversity to our show. I don't know of any remote we've ever done that I looked forward to with more enthusiasm than I did to our day in Plains. Or look back on with more warmth and satisfaction.

As luck would have it, we were there the same day Henry Kissinger was to have lunch with the President-elect. It doesn't take long for news of that nature to spread around a town the size of Plains, even a town that had suddenly become accustomed to the daily arrival of celebrities and crowds of visitors larger than the town itself.

The only one who wasn't at the train station to greet our little group was Mr. Kissinger. He hadn't arrived yet. But there were plenty of locals and tourists milling around to catch a glimpse of the remarkable lady we'd come to talk to. They kept pressing in closer and closer—in spite of the polite help from the police and Secret Service—to get a better look at her, to touch her, to get her autograph—or mine, or the cameraman's or someone's.

We were trying to make our way to the security of Miss Lillian's home, the Pond House, where our interview was to take place. I was walking beside her, trying to get to know her and to help keep people at a suitable distance. (I suddenly appreciated what a job those Secret Service people have.)

"Do these crowds bother you?" I asked.

"I don't mind. I don't mind people asking me for things," she said. "But I just don't like people to touch me. Really! One of those men had the *coldest* hands!"

She told me something on the walk to the Pond House that made me feel good. She said, "You know, I had to make a choice today. Jimmy invited me to have lunch with Mr. Kissinger and him and I chose to have lunch with you."

You can imagine how proud that made me feel. I like to think it was the imp in that free-talking lady that made her decide she'd have more fun with me.

There was a lot of setting up of cameras and lights at the Pond House so Miss Lillian came over to The Plant—that's where they exalt the common goober into a national food—and had hamburgers with us, us being the President's brother Billy, the workers in the plant and my crew. I couldn't help wondering as we sat there on big bags of peanuts, munching our burgers, what they were serving Kissinger over at the Carter house.

After lunch the crew split and went back to setting up for the interview, while the rest of us went on and toured the peanut warehouse, an elephant's paradise.

Finally—since nothing is rushed in Plains—we wandered back to the Pond House to tape the interview with Miss Lillian.

All the tourists who'd been at the train station had now flocked to the Pond House. The TV lights could be seen shining through the windows. It was common knowledge I was in town. The crowd thought that maybe even Kissinger might be present.

Finally everything was set up in the living room and Miss Lillian said to me, "I want you to know this. I've never been nervous in a television interview."

It flashed through my mind that this was because she was an honest person. Honest people don't have to fear the TV cameras.

"I'm not the least bit nervous now. So you just relax."

"I'm not nervous," I told her. "I'm only nervous when I'm worried whether my guest is going to look good or not. I have no such anxieties about you."

We talked for a little while about things that have since become well-known about her life, her Peace Corps tour of duty in India, her personal interests; then she noticed that the crowd had gathered around the house and that some were actually peering in the window. At the first break, she excused herself, got up and walked calmly over to the window and drew the drapes.

When she came back she said, "You know who I saw? I saw that man with the awfully cold hands."

When I'd interviewed almost everyone in the family—Billy, Amy, Rosalynn's mother (Rosalynn was in Americus buying Jimmy a suit)—I finally expressed my one great concern to Miss Lillian, the one thing that bothered me about being in Plains when Kissinger was there. "Do you mean to say that I'm going to have to leave Plains without meeting your other son?"

Without a word but with a twinkle in her eyes she left the room. When she came back she said, "You will meet my son before you leave today."

Suiting the action to the word, at the proper time she led us over to the President's house, took us in and called, "Jimmy . . ." (Most people say Jimmy as if it were two eighth notes. She makes it two half notes with a hold.)

From another room, Jimmy called back, "Just a minute!"

Miss Lillian smiled, turned to me and said, "You see. He goes in there, too." She waved her hand idly toward a door that was obviously what is now politely referred to as "the powder room" although it wouldn't surprise me if Miss Lillian thought of it as "the company two-holer."

Finally Jimmy emerged wearing a pair of slacks and a beige sweater, probably the very one he wore in that first fireside chat he made after the inauguration. What surprised me was that he was wearing a necktie. Generally a guy in a cardigan sweater has an open collar. It struck me that he must have worn formal attire for Kissinger, and afterward doffed his suit coat in exchange for something more comfortable.

He sat down and motioned me to take a chair and right off the bat I put one of my favorite questions to him. It's just one word, but an important one for an interviewer. In most cases it's an interesting starting point.

I asked him, "Why?"

There was a pause.

"Why in the world does any man want to be President today?"

There was another pause.

"Why do you want to be in front of the cameras five days a

week instead of off in a corner somewhere, perhaps sweeping the floor?"

"Now wait a minute, hold it. We're in two different ball parks. What you're doing and what I'm doing cannot be compared in any way, shape or form."

So he explained that all through his Navy career (I didn't tell him I was an old Navy man, too), when he got a promotion, he wouldn't let his mind dwell on that. He'd be thinking about the *next* promotion. He just has this tremendous drive—and dedication—and that's what it takes for the job he's got and that's "why," and "why he got it. . . ." Which I don't suppose is any big scoop.

Amy was the only member of the family who seemed a little uptight talking to me. She's bright, she's alert and she must be a lot of fun to play with when you get to know her. But like most kids in an interview, she has a tendency to give one-word answers that suggest she might wish you'd get lost.

"Are you anxious to live in the White House in Washington?"

"No."

I have a feeling that a kid who'd been briefed would have said, "Yes."

She had a lot to experience, to digest in a very little while. But I really ignited something in her when I spoke of her trip to Canada. I told her our show was seen by a lot of Canadians and she became quite enthusiastic about the country. It was an entirely new world to her, a world of red-coated constables and endless drifts of snow. She enjoyed the trip. We talked quite a lot about it but it had to be cut from the show to allow all possible time to Jimmy and Miss Lillian. The interview must have been at least 18 minutes long, come to think of it. I wonder if my secretary knows Rose Mary Wood?

I'm sorry we lost it because at that point Amy became

more than just a nice little President's daughter. I mean a nice little daughter of the President. She became a person with something to say. And it made me feel good to have drawn her out of her juvenile reserve.

Billy was a happy surprise and an enormous help to us when we were in Plains. He and I got to like each other a lot; and I don't even drink beer. He came back to Philadelphia to appear on the show and spent the night in our home. I think I was privileged to see the real Billy Carter.

He seems to be playing a role. I don't even want to try to guess why, for fear of being way off base. But I have a gut feeling that's what's happening. And I'm not even sure what the purpose of any such role might be. But he's making more money at it than the Prez is making.

In our company he showed himself to be charming, friendly, likable and very bright. He was frank, widely informed, extremely well-read, probably as well-read as the President.

He told us that he sleeps very little. We know he gets up at the crack of dawn—as every good farmer should. Most of his time he spends reading. That can't make a man dumb. He's totally unlike the public image of Billy Carter.

Driving down to the studio the next morning he seemed a little tense. Finally, during a break in the taping, he turned to me and said, "I've never been afraid of being on television or nervous. But today I am. Because I like you a lot."

I could only interpret that—and I could be all wrong—as being because he felt I knew the real Billy.

I'll always be grateful for that day in Plains, talking to a different kind of First Family.

(IV)
A MATTER OF ROUTINE

I spend time that averages out to 450 minutes a week (7 1/2 hours) just talking to people and listening to people, trying to find out what there is about my guests that my audience—my viewers—would like to know. It sounds complicated to write. It looks simple to watch. It is, of course, both.

To help me get on with this simple complicated job there is no owner's Manual or Guide to refer to, there are no guidelines beyond the stream of my own curiosity and the hope that, because we are all of the same species, my interest runs down the same hill as that of my audience.

So I ask myself, as I try to write about this daily chore: What if the tables were turned? What would they ask about me if given the chance? Again it's more or less a matter of guesswork except for two things. One: There's a feature on the show in which members of the audience can ask questions. Two: Three or four times a week, more times than it pleases me, I find myself being interviewed (for me an uncomfortable experience) by some journalist for some magazine or newspaper, or by some graduate student writing a doctoral paper called, "The Psychology of the TV Talk Show—A Phenomenon."

Parenthetically, I'd like to throw in here that it is just a matter of writing convenience that I allow myself to permit "The Mike Douglas Show" to be classed as a talk show. The show is actually booked and routined as a variety show and should correctly be called a variety-talk show. So much for that.

One of the first questions most interviewers ask is, "What is your routine? How do you hold together doing a show as long as the average TV special five days a week?"

Well, for openers: I sometimes do six 90-minute shows a week, but make it my policy to reserve Friday as a day of rest. This is one reason why I'm able to carry what some seem to consider an unnecessarily heavy and probably monotonous work load. I'll come back to that word "monotonous" later. It shouldn't be there. I'm allowing it to stand for negative emphasis.

The six-shows-a-week schedule puts me a whole week of shows ahead every six weeks for R. and R. How many other people can arrange their jobs that advantageously?

"Don't you get sick of the routine?" I'm asked.

No. Because it's NOT monotonous in the sense that doing almost any other kind of a regularly recurring TV show becomes monotonous. I do similar but not identical shows. Sometimes they're not even similar. Sometimes the show we planned has no similarity to the one we actually tape. I don't rehash the same routines, with the same cast day after day. Just as you don't know what surprises or disappointments lie in wait for you when you put your feet on the floor in the morning and go groping with your big toe for your slipper, neither do I.

I have one hope, and nothing more, and if you're a run-of-the-mill person such as I am, it's probably the same as yours. That is, that before I close my eyes on another day, I've gained some knowledge, some information, learned something new about something or someone—and there's no way of knowing what that will be. Could be I talked with Orson Welles or Kreskin about magic or ESP and what goes on in a world which few of us can get in touch with. Or maybe I've watched and wondered (but never really found out, although he explained it clearly) how Uri Geller bends a spoon that I can't bend.

(Incidentally, Kreskin offered to prophesy the number of the page in this book on which his name will appear—a cute way of assuring that I'll mention him. So stay tuned. I'll let you know how close he came.)

The world and its people is, I think, the brightest and best textbook a man can turn to for an education. College will give you facts—the world will give you wisdom. You don't need diplomas hanging from the fingers of your two hands to prove you're educated. All you need are eyes and ears and the know-how to use them.

There is an old show biz adage, "The best ad libs are those you wrote down the night before." This is no more than a glib way of saying that you can't get by without doing your homework. When something seems completely spontaneous, generally there has been a lot of careful planning somewhere—by someone.

For this preparation, to do my homework, which I myself will test out for the first time on the air, we have a magnificent staff of producers and assistant producers, talent coordinator and assistants, directors and technical people, musical director, floor managers and secretaries.

No writers. The writing is as simple as any set of questions can be. Beyond that, the answers are the responses they draw from me.

To oversimplify, many trained professionals combine their experience to present for my approval each morning a cooperative effort that, because of their skills, talents and diligence, turns out to be 99 and 44/100% perfect 99 and 44/100% of the time. And every afternoon it floats.

The workday actually begins in my office at about 10:30 A.M., and because the worst person to describe how a job is done is a person who does it day in and day out, I'm going to quote from two pieces, one by Starkey Flythe, Jr., written for *The Saturday Evening Post* and one by Bill Hickok of *TV Radio Talk.*

Egotistical as it seems for me to quote, this is how Mr. Flythe opens his piece. (I wanted to ask him if that was really his name but I was afraid he'd ask if Mike Douglas was mine.)

> Mike Douglas emerges from the swamp gas of American talk shows a pertinent, perspicacious, poignant (when he sings) performer who fields the slightly baggy-waggy chatter of show people on his ninety-minute afternoon program with the strong right glove of a golfer who shoots in the low seventies and won the Low Celebrity in the Jackie Gleason Inverarry Classic. . . .
>
> "I'm absolutely uncomfortable sitting here being interviewed, instead of interviewing," [Douglas] tells me.
>
> He's no Simon and Garfunkel [which kind of dates the article, but I'm still no Simon and Garfunkel], but he's der Bingle, Perry Como, Andy Williams and those crooners who stumble around within the limits of perfect pitch. Singers who look at you. The notes come out of their eyes instead of their throats.

If someone wants to pick me an epitaph, that can be it, "The notes came out of his eyes, not his throat."

Writes Bill Hickok:

> Mike Douglas's day starts when he walks into a new bronze colored building, part of Philadelphia's refurbished Independence Mall.
>
> The long, narrow lobby is filled with folks waiting quietly and contentedly to become the show's audience—about 150. They have usually been waiting up to 10 months to get their tickets.

He enters his Mediterranean style office, decorated by his wife Gen, and tells a visitor, "That lion up there over my head was Gen's idea. I'm Leo."

The guest says, "I can't imagine you roaring a lot." His producer Woody Fraser says, "He's been known to. After all, he's Irish." Then he adds, "But every time he blows off steam, we have a better show.

"Our ratings go up with his adrenalin. So no one minds very much because as quick as he is to pop off, he is even quicker to forgive and forget. And," Woody added, "you know it's always better after a fight."

For a while in his office he reads his mail and then the meeting takes place. The show's coordinators go over with him what they've planned, show him the questions they expect o put on cue cards (which he may ultimately ignore) and, in general, brief him on what's ahead. Invariably, I'm told, he complains that there's nothing new or exciting in the questions. But you feel that he's secretly aware that what's "new and exciting" can only come from the answers to the questions and whether the gimmicks that are planned (when they are) will work or, as he occasionally suggests, should be scrapped. The staff makes frequent trips to the "bar" for soda, coffee, tea or milk. There is nothing else. Mike likes tea with honey.

Before everything is agreed upon, Mike will ask about whether something is "in good taste" . . . whether it will offend anyone.

It's true. *I* ask that. But my guests never consult me. Let me tell you about an incident with a well-known movie star whose name my attorneys have asked me to withhold. Before the show started I had seen a little boy of about 9 or 10 months toddling along the hall and I stopped to talk to the very attractive young lady who was urging him to take a few more steps.

"You have a great kid there," I said.

"Yes, he is. But he's not mine," and she told me he was my guest's.

(I wish I'd had such an attractive nanny when I was a baby. I might have decided not to grow up.)

When we got on the air, my star guest spoke of her child and I mentioned having seen him. A few complimentary remarks were exchanged and then the little boy was brought out to his mother.

Without further explanation, excuse or request for permission, this beautiful picture star unbuttoned her blouse and proceeded to give her son his lunch.

Don't get me wrong. I think there's nothing more beautiful than Mother and Child. But I also believe that there are many people who believe it should be a more private matter, not something for an afternoon of entertainment on a TV show. I tried to cover my confusion and the director moved the cameras around quickly. The interview continued as if nothing had happened.

The only point is that while I worry about how guests and audience might react to what I say, my guests seldom give the matter any consideration.

Back to Mr. Hickok.

When everything is finally agreed upon, Mike leaves his office, walks through a dressing room alcove with make-up, past a wardrobe that could outfit the entire Eighth Army.

I have to cut in here to add that they'd all be put on report for being out of uniform. I'm not that big a clothes horse. But when you're putting on around 250 shows a year you need more than that old sweater you wear when you paint the house.

So I leave the wardrobe problem largely up to Gen. She generally picks out the styles she thinks are current: vests or no vests, wide lapels or no lapels, leisure suits or blazers; and she also selects the fabrics. It's hard when you have to wear as many outfits a year as I do. So when we find a fabric we like that comes in several colors, she orders an outfit in each of the best shades.

Ties are no problem. I now have my own line of neckwear so Gen picks out the one that goes best with each outfit. Occasionally, depending on the weather, I wear a turtleneck; that doesn't thrill my tie people!

But shirts. It's as if all the shirt manufacturers got together and said, "Let's see if we can make a shirt that won't fit Mike Douglas." And they succeeded.

If I find one that fits me right in the neck and shoulders there'll be enough cloth in the body to accommodate a few more people. And the collars are never comfortable for me. I like to show a little more linen in back and have them cut lower in front. It makes it easier to sing. So all my shirts are made to order, too. And that is also Gen's department. In fact, to be honest, *I* am Gen's department. I worry about the show and she worries about me.

She has the perspective to decide what's good and bad because she's not in on the planning. She has good taste and knows what's right for me to do as well as to wear. A big responsibility off my mind. Actually, she's the only person qualified to give me an honest opinion about anything because she's sure I wouldn't think of firing her if she's negative on something.

So I value and treasure her ideas and opinions and it's worked out perfectly and I have no plans to change anything for at least a hundred and eight years.

But I interrupted Mr. Hickok. He had just moved—

. . . past the wardrobe and through the drafting room where some of the work is done on the sets, down a private elevator used by half the people on the show, then out to the studio where the white chairs are still covered in canvas, the stage yet unset. He listens to the band wood-shedding the music for the day, runs quietly through the numbers he knows and learns any new ones. Then he rehearses a little gag. Henry Lee Tang mothers Mike, Tony Curtis and James Coco through a simple dance routine which Mike gets perfectly the first time. Later, on the shows he stumbles around to get laughs.

After that it's off to Bookbinder's for a late lunch and back to repeat the whole process for the second show.

What no interviewer ever really understands is that each show, to me, has the same dangers as a search and destroy mission through a mine field. You step gently around political problems. While my feelings might be able to sway votes I don't think they should. I'm not that smart politically and besides, when you take sides you lose everyone on the other side and no performer really likes to lose any part of his audience.

So I talk to Robert Blake, a free-thinking, free-talking, free-swinging soul who has lived a lot of life in a short time and who has some thoughts that are seldom catholic with a little "c," or orthodox with a little "o," knowing that I'll find it interesting but wondering if my audience will.

At one end of the political spectrum there comes John Wayne, who makes no bones about the fact that he's so far to the right that he feels only "right" can be right. And John, who during the campaign for the Presidency in 1976 made it clear that he did not support Ronald Reagan's concern for winning the election by wooing the liberal Republican vote, said "I'm a right wing extremist Republican. I don't think eighteen-year-olds should be allowed to vote, and that goes for some of the twenty-eight-year-olds too," he added. All I thought was, "right" can also sound wrong.

On the other side of the fence along comes a guest like Gore Vidal, who I feel doesn't think any of us, of any age, are qualified to vote. Nevertheless, I'm sure he would insist on our right to do so. When the red light pops up on the camera focused on him he becomes that "perfect political comic," juggling one-liners about those he feels are running the country into the ground.

Sometimes, complications in booking are not apparent or are overlooked during meetings. On the surface nothing sounds wrong with having Harry Reasoner as a guest. He's a strong, charismatic man in a fascinating branch of our business. But when he actually came on stage and we began to talk it seemed a little fatuous for me to be interviewing him. He felt the same way, apparently. He felt he should be interviewing me. It was like a steam fitter interviewing another steam fitter. I felt it could become a Mexican stand-off so I mentally assessed the situation and hitting on a possible solution, I asked Harry if he'd ever been called on to interview an important political personality on a moment's notice, with no time for preparation.

Harry said, "Yes. Of course. Many times."

"Then let's see how you do it," I suggested and introduced our next guest, Senator Hubert Humphrey.

Then I shut up and let them have a go at one another. There is no evasive action in the world like a politician answering the simplest question, such as "How do you feel?" And the Senator was feeling well then.

When the time came for me to step in and break it up, I recalled a surprise invitation to a White House dinner and my astonishment when Mrs. Johnson, after shaking a long country mile of hands, said to me, "At last a familiar face." It was very flattering. Later on at that same dinner the President remarked, apropos of something, "Take Hubert Humphrey, for instance. He can make a speech as easily as you can take a breath."

The line stuck in my mind so I mentioned it to the Senator.

Harry laughed.

"Did the President say that?" asked Humphrey.

"Would I lie to a United States Senator?" I asked.

"Then it's true," said the Senator, still going down the straight party line. Then *he* laughed.

"You mean it isn't true?" I asked, prompted by his laugh.

"No," he said, "I was laughing at your answer. 'Would I lie to a United States Senator?' A man who could say that has a great career in politics."

Which reminds me of an invitation we received to take

our cameras to Hubert Humphrey country. It was a treat and a thrill for all America, as well as ourselves, not only to see that beautiful Minnesota countryside in which one of our great Americans grew up but also to enjoy the friendly hospitality of the home where Hubert and Muriel Humphrey spent so many happy years, when they were not in Washington, and where he kept in touch with the feelings of the people he represented.

But it was not the Vice President of the United States that I saw and our cameras photographed, tooling a 1924 Model T Ford along a country road, it was a proud grandfather taking his four granddaughters for a ride in the kind of car he rode in when he was their age.

It was hard to tell whether he was prouder of the kids or the car that he himself had put in condition and of which he said, "Gets thirty-five miles to the gallon, runs like a Swiss watch and was the major attraction the year before at the Minnesota State Fair."

I knew he was telling the truth about its running like a Swiss watch because I saw him wind it.

As for his grandchildren, I told them I was going back to tell mine that the wife of the Vice President of the United States had baked me a chocolate fudge cake. They just giggled. Because they knew it was their grandma who baked it.

Of course I asked Muriel if it came from an old family recipe and she assured me the recipe had been in the family for years . . . the Betty Crocker family.

But that kind of kidding came as no surprise from Mrs. Humphrey. Earlier in the day she had glanced at a monitor and seen a shot of her husband sitting in a rocking chair and said, "Doesn't he look like Whistler's Mother?"

And when we all went for a cool dip in the Humphrey pool, it was Mrs. Vice President herself who took to the water with a jackknife off the board that made it look so easy we all wondered why we couldn't do it.

What a gallant man Hubert Humphrey was. He provided

us with strength and inspiration as he fought with all that great American heart of his a battle he could not win against cancer.

Maybe Humphrey was onto something. Perhaps I should have been a politician. In 1967 when our show became the first non-network show ever to win an Emmy, *Business Week* described the award as having been given for "limitless blarney and baby blue eyes."

Time magazine said on the same occasion that I was "the all-American Mommy's boy . . . avoids show biz patter . . . viewers empathize with him as one of them. . . ." They called me (and this was 1967) "a homespun hippy who can parry with Stokely Carmichael or Jack E. Leonard" (the late Fat Jack, the man who seems to have pointed a direction to Don Rickles).

And *Newsweek* took the Emmy occasion to say our show was "for the housewife who's interested in serious things." (That was because we'd given Ralph Nader the first serious TV forum for his battle with General Motors.) "The Mike Douglas Show," *Newsweek* said, "gives her something to talk to her husband about when he comes home." *Newsweek* failed to point out that it also proved that she'd stayed home all day watching TV.

Sometimes the staff scolds me for self-indulgently asking them to book someone they don't think "my audience" really cares much about. Generally it's a big name in sports. And I get this kind of a reaction, "Who the hell in our audience cares about Jack Nicklaus except Mrs. Jack Nicklaus?" Then they have to develop an angle.

I get flak like that with almost all the sports stars I like to book. "Okay, Mike, what's to do with Julius Erving?"

"Have him shoot some baskets and then let me try it."

"You two standing side by side would look like he could slam-dunk you."

"You're excused from the meeting."

But the problem was solved. That's what we did. And it's what we can do with almost all sports characters. We generally book along with them a Gabe Kaplan or a Kevin Dobson, both pretty good athletes who can also participate.

Or we go somewhere with a baseball team or a football club and fool around with them in practice. When the home team looked as if they might win the Pennant, we shot some tape at the ball park, had the players on, along with their wives.

"How do you explain a Philadelphia man like you," I was asked by Jack Reilly at one meeting, "having Sparky Anderson and some of the Cincinnati Reds team on the show? And not only that, walking around here in full view of everyone wearing a Reds practice jacket?"

To begin with, Sparky's an old and respected friend, and he's also a very big name in baseball. The Cincinnati Reds are one of the county's finest baseball teams. I got to like them when we were in Cleveland. Bob Hope had the Indians so I had to take the Reds. I've had the Phillies people on, and some of the Dodger people. Tom Lasorda of the Dodgers is a good friend. Maybe I just like ballplayers. They wear funny clothes. So the answer is, yes. It is indulgent for me to book athletes. I like them. It's also good booking. Know why? You'd be surprised how many bars and barber shops tune in "The Mike Douglas Show" in the afternoon.

As for wearing a Cincinnati Reds practice jacket around Philadelphia I can only explain that by admitting that I must have a death wish.

Actually, Sparky gave me that jacket and it's the second most valuable memento I own. The other is a half dollar Gen gave me after one of our very first dates when she suggested we "go Dutch" for a soda.

As for self-indulgence, maybe you might call it that, when I insist on booking Jack Nicklaus on a show that's seen mostly by homemakers. But some of them play golf and most of them have men who do, husbands and sons.

Hearing about it through me may make them understand the game better.

Hearing about golf from Jack makes *me* understand it better. I'm a golf nut. The game taxes my mind as well as my muscles. It's an exercise in self-control. I imagine this is true of any contest in which you're pitted against yourself. And how many of those are there? Solitaire doesn't do much for your biceps. It's humbling to play a lousy game and know there's no one to blame but yourself.

Maybe the one positive thing golf does for me mentally is to help me release my aggressions. My temper used to be a real steamer. Whoever was close when she blew, got burned. But now it's controlled. Now I play golf. The ball becomes my enemy. It's whatever thing or person made me mad, and I punish it.

All this is, I guess, an explanation why, when I got the chance to receive five lessons from one of the finest golfers I know—and one of the greatest guys—the superstar of golf—Jack Nicklaus, I headed right for Dublin. That's Ohio, a suburb of Columbus, Jack's hometown, where he went to school and college and, I guess, where he first started to play golf. Obviously he wanted future kids of the area to have a better golf course to start on than he had.

We met at that "better" course, Muirfield Village Golf Club, the fulfillment of Jack's great dream. What a golf course! And why not? If Jack Nicklaus sets out to build a golf course you'd better believe it's not going to be any old pasture. It took him eight years to get it all together—the land, the financing and the building.

Jack's dream is now called the Memorial Golf Course because every year around Memorial Day, it's the site of the Memorial Tournament, honoring a different golfer on each occasion. The first one, of course, was in honor of the immortal Bobby Jones.

During my five lessons, which we spread over five shows, I got to meet Jack's two assistants, Angelo Argee, who's been caddying for him for eleven or twelve years (probably more by the time you read this). And Willy Peterson, who marks the holes for him. Golfers will know what that means and it's too dull to try to explain, but it's an important job in a tournament.

Too bad there's no way I can explain the lessons Jack gave. It's also too bad they don't show up in my game. But as things are and as I told Jack, I only get to play once or twice a week during the season and occasionally when I get a few days off in Florida. I never seem to have time when I'm in California: work, work, work. Nevertheless, if I do say so myself, I manage to keep a fairly low handicap, helped by some tips Jack has for Sunday golfers like me. His advice is to take it slow and easy. Be deliberate. Relax. Think about each shot. Line it up. Give it your full attention and when you swing, follow through.

Hey! If I could really stick to that advice and add it to my naturally fair-to-middlin' game, I think—with enough playing time—I might eventually play scratch golf.

Jack's the greatest golfer since Bobby Jones (better, of course, just as Hank Aaron was a better home-run hitter than Babe Ruth).

I never concentrated harder, nor played better than I did in that match with Jack. Nor was I ever as tired by the eighteenth hole.

Playing against yourself is tough but when your mind is also playing against Jack Nicklaus, well, two against one ain't fair.

Another Jack in my life and also a great golf enthusiast is the Great One, Jackie Gleason. I'm very solid with Jackie. He's not "on" all the time, like most professional comedians. And he's not all hardy-harr and ho-de-ho.

The first time I was in his home he was showing me around. His pride and joy was the library. It could have loaned books to Carnegie. "And I've read every one of them," he said proudly. "I'm now reading them for the second time."

"Didn't you understand them the first time?" I asked.

"Hardy-harr," said the Great One sarcastically.

But all the sports people we booked are not a lull to the large distaff audience we enjoy. Take Billie Jean King. Her, they liked. She was not a kid when she beat Chris Evert. Although, in athletics as in life, time turns the tables and youth prevails.

It's not my game and I never spent any time at it but in a fun match with Billie Jean I was able to hit the ball with the middle of the racket, which in the tennis business ain't eatin' peas with your knife. Billie Jean told me I was amazing for my age. I'll bet she said the same thing to Chris Evert.

What she actually told me was something I found out for myself when I was a kid boxing and playing hard ball, and later as I came to play golf. I have a good eye. That's great, very important in any game.

Boxing, hey, if you don't have a good eye somebody's going to ruin whatever it is you have very quick. Ken Norton, Muhammad Ali, Joe Frazier will all tell you that, at least that's what they told me.

And in team games, it's not only your eye that counts, it's also your head. You've got to understand and remember the plays—when to use them, how to use them. Very tough.

I think I'll stick to what I'm doing.

(V)
MY REMOTE LIFE

There have been a lot of feature stories about me, dwelling on what their authors called my "remote way of living", in the suburbs of Philadelphia. They claim that for someone in show business there is nothing more remote than that.

Well, here are the facts about my "remote" life.

When Westinghouse Group W started "The Mike Douglas Show" in Cleveland, it was not with the intention to fail. They expected a money winner. They expected a success. Fortunately for all of us, this happened faster than anyone could imagine.

Several factors were involved. One was Cleveland's need for television entertainment that really belonged to Cleveland and yet was not too provincial. From the very start, with the Broadway and Hollywood talent that we brought in—and that caused us considerable problems—"The Mike Douglas Show" had a "big-time" feel. It was in Cleveland but it was not just living on Cleveland. It was bringing something in, people, stars, excitement, all of which meant business. A lot of civic pride was involved, and this was very gratifying to all concerned, particularly Westinghouse. They had a big investment in us.

Naturally, the success in Cleveland attracted a lot of attention in the trade and in a year and a half we began to be syndicated nationally, and soon after, with maybe twenty stations to our credit, we embarked on our first trips away from our home studio, our first remote. This, for us, was what a baby's first step is to the baby. We were very brave, very uncertain, but very anxious to get going.

We went to Boston. With its Irish population, how could a guy like Mike Douglas miss? And for insurance we took along as co-host Pat O'Brien, who has always been just a little bit more Irish than Brian Boru, in spite of the fact that he comes from Milwaukee.

For more insurance there was some tie-in between Westinghouse and the Prudential Life people, who had just opened a fine new building in Boston. It contained an auditorium that they wanted business people and societies around the country to know had a seating capacity of 5,900. As Pat described it, "That's a lot of souls."

Aside from all the normal mechanical problems connected with taking a 90-minute show away from its home base, that 5,900-seat auditorium presented a problem, which was—how to fill it? To give you an idea how big a problem, I'm the kind of guy who when he sees one empty seat in the house tends to panic. So I took this up with a man named Joe Ryan, who was handling arrangements in Boston. He assured me there was no need to worry.

His exact words were, "Don't worry. We'll fill it."

I was reminded of a story about a mother taking her four-year-old into the surf for the first time. Her husband sat on the beach and watched as the two walked slowly into the sea. When he saw that the water was well above his wife's waist, he called to her, "Where's Junior?"

His wife turned and asked what he said. By this time the ocean had risen to well above the woman's chest.

"Where's Junior?" her husband repeated in panic.

"Don't worry," she called back. "I've got him by the hand."

I don't like people to tell me not to worry unless they fully understand why I am worrying. So I explained my concern to Ryan and again he told me not to worry. But this time he explained that three weeks ahead of our arrival they planned to mount a P.R. campaign that would certainly guarantee the filling of all the seats.

It certainly did. Moving the tickets proved to be a cinch. They had only been advertised for three days—and this was two and a half weeks before show time—and already 95,000 requests had poured in. And these ducats weren't free. You bought admission to one of their regular events—the Flower and Garden Show—and that included a seat to see our show.

This was very gratifying and ego-building but I still had a problem I didn't know about. My staff had a tendency—and still has it—to sit around and try to figure how to get me in trouble on the show. They think it makes for excitement.

Well, for this Boston date they came up with a beaut. It seems the Boston Fire Department had a drill team that did fantastic things in connection with fighting fires. One of these was putting up a pair of 120-foot ladders so that they formed a triangle with the ground.

It wasn't putting up the ladders that was the trick. Any volunteer fireman can do that. The trick was, they'd take a person on their shoulders, run him up the 120 feet and run him down again on the other side. But I mean run. I watched them fascinated. That hundred and twenty feet of ladder looks like forever.

When I was told that a fireman was going to take me on his shoulders and run up and down the ladder with me, I said what I always say before I finally wind up doing something silly. "No he's not!"

The truth is, I'm not happy with heights. I tried Adler elevator shoes once and they made me a little giddy. But I've got my pride and I'm not going to admit in front of a bunch of firemen who run up and down ladders that I'm afraid of that kind of a game. So on that first remote in Boston, Dopey Douglas set a pattern of doing things that men have been put into upholstered rooms for doing.

Okay. The cameras are rolling. The tape is running. The fireman grabs me in that fireman's hold that every Boy Scout has to learn and when he gets a little older tries to demonstrate to his girl friend. All I'm thinking about is, "How did I get into this and how do I get out of it?" I could see headlines, "Mike spits up on Prudential Plaza." Something had to be done and I did it. Not only that, in my panic I even got a laugh. The camera's following me up and at about a 15-foot elevation I hollered, "Get me down. Quick! I have to go to the bathroom!"

This, of course, made a heavy impression on the fireman who was carrying me and, even though he was wearing a rubber coat, the prospect wasn't the pleasantest. So he brought me down, and we cut to a commercial. And I went to the bathroom.

Our show has been the travelingest one in its field. Group W Productions board chairman Dave Salzman encourages us in doing these remotes frequently. The company's Frank Miller, Jack Wartlieb and Ron Little, among others, are often checking sites and making all the unusual arrangements since every location is different. And Owen Simon, George Sperry and their promotion and press people are busy letting everyone know that we're "Going Places." But perhaps the most "remote" of all the remotes we've ever done were the ones we taped in our own studio in Philadelphia, co-hosted by what *Variety* called "the husband-and-wife sexperts," Dr. William H. Masters and Mrs. Virginia E. Johnson, co-authors of *Human Sexual Responses* and *Human Sexual Inadequacy.*

I call those shows "remotes" because nothing could be more remote from the so-called "typical" Mike Douglas show than those no-singing, no-holds-barred rap sessions on sex.

On the first of our three shows, Dr. Masters and Mrs. Johnson just talked with me and answered questions from our nonprofessional audience. The questions were frank, unabashed and totally healthy.

It was that way, too, with such professionals as Peter Lawford, Alan Alda, Meredith MacRae, Maureen Stapleton, Bob Cummings, Susan Strasberg, Patty Duke Astin and her husband, John Astin, and other couples like Anne Jackson and Eli Wallach, and Valerie and Bill Mooney.

Naturally, before as well as during each of the shows the TV audience was warned of "adult material" and the advisability of "parental discretion." That was important because the talk faced right up to such things as orgasms, erections and all the physical and psychological aspects of sex.

To write about the subject tends to make it seem either prurient or heavy. Believe me, the shows were neither. *Variety* reported, "There were frequent smiles and laughs but not snickers."

This was because, as Mrs. Johnson said, "We were convinced you wouldn't make sex a dirty joke." This was why, she said, "We finally decided, after not appearing on entertainment shows for many years, to co-host 'The Mike Douglas Show.'"

At this point I suggested that I'd just been awarded the Mr. Dull Award of the Year. Mrs. Johnson shook her head no. She said they felt ours was a "comfortable" show and would know how to make people who might not ordinarily be relaxed talking about sex, feel at ease.

Alan Alda, star of TV's "MASH," said he was never embarrassed about sex because of his early show business background. "I was three years old," he explained, "when my father was in burlesque before he went on into musical comedy and films. You gotta break in somewhere, you know. And I'd stand in the wings and watch the comics and the strippers. They took off their clothes on stage but covered themselves up chastely on the way back to the dressing room. It brings up an important point about nudity and sexuality. Intent! Maybe that's why most people don't mind disrobing in front of a doctor."

So I asked how it was with Dr. Masters, if he ever brought his work home. "Do you and your wife ever look at each other . . . er . . . " I paused, at a loss for words.

"Clinically?" he asked, helping me out. I nodded. His answer was that anyone who brings his work into the home is asking for trouble. Then he laughed. "I don't mean to say that some of us don't carry our work home . . . but it's in a little satchel. There are all kinds of homework. Some I like better than others."

Mrs. Johnson said she wouldn't have made any different answer, that it never occurred to her to think, "What's happening?" "When I'm home I never think like a textbook," she added.

When the subject came around to parental attitudes, Meredith MacRae said her father, singer Gordon MacRae, was very strict. "He'd say," she reported, "you don't have any pimples this week. Have you been making out again?"

This didn't sound too strict to me. So I asked Dr. Masters what his parents had taught him. And he told about getting his first sex lecture from his father in a day coach on a Pennsylvania Railroad train going from New York to Trenton. It's about an hour's ride.

"I was on my way to enter prep school and my father thought I should know something about what every young boy entering prep school ought to know. The trouble was, the more involved he got in his sex lecture the louder he got. A mother and her young daughter were sitting on the seat in front of us. The daughter kept leaning her head back and the mother kept leaning forward. Finally she got up and took the girl into another car. The lecture ended abruptly and unfinished as we pulled into Trenton and I had to get my things together and say good-bye.''

Apparently he, too, learned about life, as it says in Irving Berlin's song, from "doin' what comes naturally.''

Maybe the most important thought the two "sexperts" left with me and my viewers was the information that after their second book was published, between 3,500 and 5,000 "sex clinics" opened around the country, of which 50 *might* be legitimate. Dr. Masters said, "Maybe the public is being duped.''

I say, "Be careful.''

When something unusual happens in show biz, every TV show on the air wants to get in on the action, from the evening news to "Hollywood Squares.'' So what's surprising about our picking up our gear and traveling to Dubuque, Iowa, so that Sylvester Stallone could be our co-host?

The biggest news to hit Hollywood in the Spring of 1977 was Sylvester and the picture he wrote and acted in, *Rocky*. What Hollywood calls "a sleeper" was this story about a third-rate club fighter who gets a chance to box the champ. Knowing he can't win, he trains his heart out just to go the distance and does. In so doing he wins back his self-respect and the girl. And *Rocky* became an immediate box-office smash and won an Oscar, elevating Stallone—just another broke and struggling Hollywood writer—to superstar status and riches almost overnight.

Stallone's "heart" and self-confidence rivaled that of the hero of *Rocky*. He had turned down a $300,000 offer for the screen rights because the bidders wanted to cast someone other than himself in the starring role. He held out, taking a gamble that paid off, and wham! Presto, everybody in the film business was beating a path to his door. Producer-director Norman Jewison, famous for such films as *Fiddler on the Roof, Jesus Christ, Superstar* and *In the Heat of the*

Night, was the man who got him and, before you could turn around, Sylvester Stallone was in Dubuque, Iowa, shooting a film called *F.I.S.T.*, in which he also starred. The MDS headed west to ask Sly (as his friends call him) one question, "Why Dubuque?" His explanation? Because it looked like Cleveland in the 1930's, the locale and period of *F.I.S.T.* (As everybody by now must know, the initials stand for Federation of Interstate Truckers.) The old-car buffs who went to Dubuque with us to tape Stallone were delighted when Sly and I drove onto the set in one of the vintage cars that Norman Jewison said cost a fortune to restore.

The interesting thing, as I'm writing this, is that you, the reader, will know how *F.I.S.T.* succeeded as a picture while I only know that as we watched it being made, it looked good.

Noteworthy about *Rocky* was the fact that it not only won an Oscar for Best Picture, but John Avildsen also got an Oscar for directing it, and Stallone himself received the gold statuette for Best Original Screenplay. Ironically, the one award that eluded him, in spite of a fine dramatic portrayal, was for Best Actor. All he really derived from the film was fame and money, but about that, he said, as we sat under a bright springtime Iowa sky, "I haven't made a nickel yet on *Rocky.*"

"With the picture headed for a worldwide gross of over $100,000,000 at the box office, I wouldn't worry," I said.

He nodded. "It's expected to bring me about two million but I haven't seen a penny of it yet. I think it's lost in transit."

"And another thing," he went on, "since *Rocky* nobody shakes hands with me anymore. They give me a body punch."

Everybody was calling him Rocky and I asked if that bothered him. He said he didn't mind the strong identification with the role he wrote but that he thought *F.I.S.T.* would probably change that. "Rocky," he explained, "was a character who was led by men. In *F.I.S.T.* I play Johnny Kovak, a trucker who is a leader of men."

I said, "It'll be interesting to see if they're calling you Rocky or Johnny or Sly after this picture."

"I don't care," he said. "Just so they call me."

Everybody in show business knows that feeling of mingled hope and insecurity that gets you down even as it buoys you up and is so much a part of being an actor.

When I think of some of the screwball things I've done and had done to me, I have to believe it's a miracle that somebody hasn't gotten hurt, namely me.

We did a remote in Savannah, Georgia. My co-hosts for the week were Mike "Mannix" Connors alternating with Burt Reynolds.

So the staff thought it would be fun to open with me in the middle of one of Savannah's quiet, charming little squares, describing its placid, old-world beauty, only to have everything I was saying upstaged by a wild car chase—the kind featured in Mike's "Mannix" TV show—while I looked on aghast, my face expressing the natural amazement of anyone who finds himself the centerpiece in a mini-Indy 500.

The camera picked me up as planned, standing in the square talking about the peaceful Southern charm of old Savannah, when ZOOOOM! Two speeding cars, chasing each other, are coming right at me. Burt Reynolds seemed to be in one of them. Roaring after him in the inimitable "Mannix" manner could only be Mike Connors. Careening around the square, the two cars narrowly missed me. Having failed, they roared back for another try.

Circling the square (if that's possible) are hundreds of people from the surrounding area who had come to watch the taping of "The Mike Douglas Show." I'm stammering, not knowing what to say but also knowing it won't make any difference because my words will probably be drowned out by the racket of the engines.

Suddenly the Reynolds car spun out of control into a zig-zag skid. The spectators scattered helter-skelter and it's a miracle that no one was hurt. The vehicle straightened out and headed for a grand old magnolia tree that, hit at that speed, would have totaled it. And it wouldn't have done the tree much good either. But the auto pulled to a screeching halt.

Burt Reynolds started to run toward me followed by Mike Connors, gun in hand and shooting at him. Cut!

Then everyone rushed over to the car by the magnolia tree, Burt Reynolds, Mike Connors, my cast and crew, the Savannah police who were acting as crowd control for us, and almost the entire population of Savannah. "Marvelous! Sensational!" was the consensus.

"Thanks," said the driver, Burt's stunt man, Hal Needham, who was sitting there pale and shaken. "I wasn't kidding. That really happened. I wasn't trying to do that. The car actually got away from me. I'm lucky to be talking to you. Did you get the pictures?"

That was the first stunt to go wrong during our week in Savannah.

Figuring if you have a stunt man around it's a waste of money not to use him and having brought Mike Connors' personal fill-in, Dick Ziker, along with us for the auto chase, the staff decided on another little surprise down at the harbor where we went one day at 6 A.M. to watch the shrimp boats come sailing in.

I'm standing there looking across the misty water and I'll bet I was singing "Shrimp boats are acomin'/Their sails are in sight," when I see a guy in yellow oilskins, hat, coat and pants waving to me from the crow's nest of one of the boats. He's not only waving, he's hollering, "Hey, Mike!"

Then came the clever gag they'd worked out. They held

up a card for me to read, "Hey, it's Mike Connors! Come over here, Mike." This was one of the dumbest things I've ever said because the boat was about a block and a half away and the crow's nest was 40 feet in the air.

Ziker—as Connors—started to climb the rail of the crow's nest as he hollered back, "I can't! I'm. . . ." He broke his speech by falling off his perch.

Remember that old movie story about C. B. De Mille shooting *The Ten Commandments*? Thousands of extras were to come pouring through the Red Sea in a scene that could only be shot once.

C.B. gave the signal for the scene to start and it was going great, in fact it had gone great, when he heard from his head cameraman, "Ready when you are, C.B."

The same thing happened to us. Our cameraman was asking the director on the intercom, "Where do you want me to be? Where do I pick him up?" when the only spot he could be picked up from now was the deck of the boat.

I'm glad I wasn't the one who had to tell the guy we'd missed the shot, that he had to do it over. At 6:30 in the morning. Before breakfast. Forty feet. But that's the sort of thing that happens to stunt men, and it's one of the reasons that line of work could never be my cup of tea.

Not all the shows we did in Savannah featured that kind of slapstick violence. We did capture the city's charm, and the highlight was our visit to that writer of wonderful lyrics, Johnny Mercer. Like Jack Benny, he was one of the majors in show business that you never heard anybody put down.

Johnny was a native of Savannah, and although he lived in California remained one of her cherished citizens. So though he wasn't at all well, he made the trip by train from Los Angeles to be with us and his mother on her ninety-fourth birthday and to show us the handsome old restored Williams House that was built for his granddaddy. Sad to say, it was shortly after this visit that Johnny was fatally stricken.

But we recorded on tape some wonderful memories of Johnny and Mike Connors and me on the lawn in front of the old house. Unfortunately, it was not the kind of a day the Savannah Chamber of Commerce features in its advertising. Clouds and intermittent showers interrupted the shooting and forced us indoors "till the clouds roll by."

Johnny made light of this tiring inconvenience, even though it wasn't easy for him to get around. "Too bad we can't make this rain and these delays into a song," he said.

"You write it and I'll sing it," I promised. And we spent the time having some nostalgic talks about the music business, and Johnny thanked me again for having introduced his hit "Laura" on the radio in March of 1945.

And when we finally got to shooting, Mike Connors and Johnny and I wound up the afternoon on the lawn, doing an old-fashioned sing-a-round of some of Johnny's hits, "Days of Wine and Roses," "Lazy Bones," "You Must Have Been a Beautiful Baby," three or four other classics and, of course, "Laura," "Tangerine" and "Moon River."

The sincerest tribute to Johnny that I can think of is what happened when we arrived at his former home. We were all in a happy frame of mind, horsing around, trying to top each other—Mike Connors, the staff, the crew and I. But the moment Johnny's wife, Ginger, greeted us and welcomed us into that grand old house, an awed silence enveloped us. Our eyes and ears were all for Johnny, one of the few men who had written songs we'd all been singing all our lives.

I think the Johnny Mercer portion of our Savannah remote was one of the few on which I did not become a bad insurance risk. On the other hand, on one of our trips to Miami, the thought was born in the diseased minds of my co-workers that it would be funny to have co-host Jerry Lewis and me engage in tag-team wrestling with a couple of professionals. So they set out to find two and must have dredged the Everglades because they came up with two monsters. Either of them would have made King Kong cringe. Next to

Jerry and me they looked like two city halls.

One of these behemoths (he's dead now) took a bronze medal in the 1972 Olympic Games. I'm not sure whether he got it for wrestling or bulk. He tipped the scale—and by that I mean tipped it clear over—at 450 pounds.

They topped this by booking a second man who looked like a piece of land-moving equipment with a face. His name was André the Giant. He was a 7-foot-5 Czechoslovakian who weighed so much he'd been asked to leave that country because when he walked he caused it to tilt.

The American could be sort of cued by Jerry Lewis as to what he should do to allow Lewis the most latitude to do his shtick so they saved the big Czech for me. One problem was that he spoke no English and had to be talked to through an interpreter who also spoke no English, or so it seemed.

As a result, our producer, Woody Fraser, left Jerry and his Olympic champ free to work out whatever Jerry wanted to do, and he huddled with André to see what they could cook up for me.

Woody Fraser, the man responsible for many of these Katzenjammer tricks, asked André what his specialty was. This took about 45 minutes of gibberish and jargon among Woody, André and his manager/interpreter. It was finally determined that what André could do very well was pick me up, hold me over his head as if I were an applause sign and whirl around with me.

"Then," Woody told me later, "we had to figure out a signal for when he should do this." Just thinking back on it got Woody hysterical and for a few minutes it almost got him severed from the show he'd worked so hard to create.

The maneuver they came up with was this, when Woody held both arms in the air over his head it would indicate to André that he was to do the same but holding me and whirling around. At the proper moment Woody held up his arms, but André only thought he should imitate Woody, so he faced the audience like a victorious gladiator. Woody, in back of the camera, kept trying to signal André that he was supposed to hold me high in the air. I'm watching this whole charade with interest, wondering where it's going, when suddenly André remembered the bit and I found out. I'm high above André's head spinning around like an insane windmill. At that moment, Woody realized something. He'd forgotten to invent one of his ingenious little signals to tell André when to put me down, or how.

"For a terrible minute," he told me later, "I could see you flying through the air being shot at by the Air Force as a UFO." Finally he hollered "Enough!" The interpreter got the message and screamed a whole string of Slavic words and I came gently to earth. Everything was fine except for the balance fluid in my inner ear, which had been turned into a banana daiquiri. For the next twelve hours I didn't dare turn my head for fear it would fall off.

Then there was the incident behind the Hilton Hotel in Las Vegas. Sounds like a duel and in a way it was.

For reasons best known to the management of the Hilton, there was a whole corral of ostriches behind the hotel. So we took a remote crew around back to have a look at them. I did a little interview with the man who handled the big birds and then suddenly he asked me if I'd ever handled an ostrich. How do you answer a question like that? I told him I wanted to when I was a little boy but my mother wouldn't let me keep it in the house. He just smiled as if he knew something I didn't know. And that's exactly why he was smiling. He did.

The next thing I knew, Dom DeLuise, my co-host, and I are being briefed on how dumb those big birds are, how fast they can run and how if one of them kicks you with one of those long tough legs you could easily become the longest punt in the history of either football or ostrich kicking.

From this information on the I.Q. and power of an ostrich, the man segued into the gentlemanly sport of ostrich racing.

"The driver," we were told, "sits in a little sulky like at the trotters. The birds are brought to the starting point, blindfolded. When the blindfold is removed, the birds just take off and they can accelerate from a standing start to about 50 miles per hour in 2 seconds. What's more, they'll just keep running until someone at the end of the track grabs them. If he doesn't, the bird will keep going till he falls down or runs into a wall or sees a McDonald's, whichever comes first.

"The only way the driver has of steering his bird is with a broom," the man explained. "If he wants to turn right, he holds out the broom on the left side and the shadow in the ostrich's eye will cause him to swerve away, thus turning right. A regular kitchen broom like this is used," he went on, and handed the broom to me.

"It's a nice clean sport," I said.

"Oh, yes. If you're careful you won't get hurt."

"Me?" It suddenly dawned on me what this was all building to. I was to be the first Philadelphia talk show host to race an ostrich.

The guy then handed a broom to Dom DeLuise, who is one of the world's foremost chickens, and one of its most naturally funny individuals. And then Dom knew, as I knew, what was happening to us. "No," he screamed. And Dom's a fairly good screamer. "I won't do this. It's crazy!" Then he turned to me and said, "I don't care if you get two million dollars for doing things like this, I won't do it. I wouldn't do it for four million." I bravely said something about its being a world's first: "The first time a chicken ever drove an ostrich." And by clever misdirection while we were protesting that we wouldn't go along, we were maneuvered into the sulkies behind the blindfolded ostriches.

The cameras were hot, floor manager Bill Freeland threw a cue, the blindfolds were snatched from the ostriches and away we went, each waving his broom in sheer terror and causing the birds to swerve from side to side, suggesting the chariot race scene in Ben Hur, when the villain purposely bumps chariots, trying to knock Ben's wheels off.

Fortunately, the run only lasted about 8 or 10 seconds, over which I was supposed to dub a "call" of the race. But for the entire time of the running nothing could possibly have been heard on the tape over Dom's screaming.

A man stopped *my* bird but the guy who was supposed to grab Dom's missed. If they hadn't had a back-up stopper about a hundred yards farther on Dom DeLuise would at this moment be on his 4,976th lap around the world in a sulky pulled by an ostrich.

This would be a good point to mention that when there has been genuine danger to my life or limbs—and it has happened to me many times in our studio and on the road—I can always count on our crew to come through. What a loyal, hardworking group they are. Nothing could have pleased me more than being made an Honorary Gold Card Member of Local 804 of I.A.T.S.E.

One of the things that makes co-hosting on "The Mike Douglas Show" a great adventure is that occasionally the leprechauns who plan the shows devote their midnight revels to devising little tricks to pull on the co-host, freeing me of everything but the awesome responsibility of explaining that it was "all in fun."

There's a place in New Jersey where people take their children to fill them full of hot dogs, cotton candy, popcorn and soda to test their stamina against internal attack. It not only offers fun and games for kids but also for adults. It is called Great Adventure.

It was here that George Hamilton, my co-host for the week, developed a more or less meaningful relationship with a group of resident dolphins. They are friendly creatures that seem to long for the companionship of human beings. Because they do not get a lot of it, they trust us.

There is a pool full of them, all yearning to get closer to us

Homo sapiens, at Great Adventure. Having heard George Hamilton sing, one of my program planners thought it would be nice to have him sing to the dolphins and, perhaps, cool them off on their dreams of closer ties with the human race.

It was all good fun and carefully rehearsed. George was to walk out on a little pier to which the dolphins came in the hope of closer communion with man. He was then to sing to them. It all looked faintly amusing to me and, innocent of all wrongdoing, I went to bed that night a happy man.

What I slept through was the action of my elves who cut away some of the planking at the end of the pier and covered it with heavy wrapping paper painted to look just like the solid portion. George, of course, was as innocent of this little maneuver as I was. He also did not know that at rehearsal his song had been taped.

When it got to actual shooting time, they told George they were running a little late and that he'd have to do the scene on the pier with the dolphins without any more rehearsal. "No problem," said George bravely. "I've got it down cold." So they went right ahead, handed him a dead mike so he wouldn't electrocute himself and started to shoot.

The expected happened, of course. George approached the paper part of the pier and before you could say Jacques Cousteau he was under water and the dolphins loved him.

The pay-off to this damp little joke was the expression of rage mingled with surprise on George's face as he surfaced and heard himself still singing as he had been doing all the while he'd been submerged. And that was the way the show went out over the air.

Although this happened months ago, George Hamilton is still getting fan mail from adoring dolphins who want him to come back and sing for them again.

Not all our mishaps are suspect of being "inspired" to add a little extra surprise and fun to the show. In Hawaii, which I consider one of the most beautiful places in the world, something went wrong that could only come under a heading the insurance people call "an act of God."

We went to the Islands to open the Hawaiian Regency Hotel at a time of year that is late winter in some places, early spring in others and the windy season in the Hawaiian Islands.

Plans were made to do the show on the roof of the hotel. But the part of the roof they assigned to us wasn't part of the building. It was a covering over a breezeway between two wings. It turned out to be more of a wind tunnel.

The audience was expected from all over the Islands, because we'd made arrangements for tickets to go only to locals instead of to tourists. We knew the people who lived in Hawaii were big fans and this would give them their first chance to see us in the flesh.

The windy season was going great by the time we were ready to hit the sack, early because we had to get ready for taping the following morning. Outside our window gusts of wind blew hard enough to carry sparks clear from the fires of Hell to the Gates of Heaven.

Then the telephone call came. "Hello, Mike?"

"Yes?"

"You awake?"

"Wait. I'll see."

"Guess what."

"You woke me up to play games?"

"The set just blew down."

"The whole set?"

"The whole set."

It had taken two weeks to build so there was nothing to worry about—it just couldn't be rebuilt in time.

Setless, we did the show against the panorama of Hawaii's beautiful green hills, one of the prettiest shows we ever shot. But it was a little late in getting started.

Just as the audience was filing in, another gust of wind

swept the rooftop and down went row after row of empty chairs, clattering like a chain of dominos. This was followed by the incoming audience's trying to help set them up again, each in a place the person thought would provide the best view of the show.

Watching the chaos, I felt like the Nebraska farmer who saw two trains run head-on into each other and said, "That sure is a helluva way to run a railroad."

But we did have a very serious mishap at Cypress Gardens. We'd booked a blind skier. While it doesn't sound like sense to have any kind of skier in Florida, this did. Having mastered conventional skiing, the man had decided that he wanted to try it on water.

We have had all sorts of overachievers like this on the show, and we were confident he would come through okay. So after a couple of show practice runs, we went for a take.

The boat got up to about 35 miles per hour and he went around the island with great skill and ease. It was so wonderful that he began to shout for joy and the man who was running the boat thought, "If it was so great, why not try it again?" But the second time around our skier miscalculated or lost his bearings and went smack, head-on into a tree.

A collective gasp rose from the crowd and for the next moment the world was as quiet as it will ever be. Everyone thought the man was dead. But miracle of miracles, he was hardly more than bruised. I still don't understand it.

And I still dream about that blind man crashing into a tree. It makes me worry about how some of the stunts we do *can* backfire.

On one stunt I almost lost my buddy Burt Reynolds. It was during one of our Miami Beach remotes worked out through Hal Cohen and the Tourist Development Authority to spread the Florida sunshine around the country. We had some circus people on the show and were working outdoors. Burt was to do a little trapeze swinging and, on command, let go and drop into the net.

The trapeze artist, the flyer, who does that sort of work for a living, was standing beside me to give Burt the command to let go. But Burt decided to do it on his own and smacked his head right on the edge of the net. The flyer who was standing next to me gripped my arm so tightly he almost broke it. A few inches over and Burt would have had it.

I'm a little crazy, too, about doing stunts. With my fear of heights, I still let them take me to the top of the training tower at Fort Bragg, where half the parachute candidates flake out. I don't know how I ever got through that. But I did, and what's more I agreed to make a free-fall parachute jump with Major Pete Dawkins. I strapped on the two chutes and we went up together but at the last minute they wouldn't let me jump. And was I glad!

In Puerto Rico, working out with some frogmen I had a go with the wet suit and flippers at dropping off into the water. And it wasn't too soft at 30 miles an hour. If you don't do it right you could break one or two of your bones. And then, when the time for the pick-up came, they missed me. There I was paddling around the vast blue sea and not a sail in sight. I never felt so alone, so abandoned.

It seemed hours before they came around and got me. It was probably only about 15 minutes. But that's the kind of stuff that gives a man gray hair, and the gray hairs you get that way, you've earned.

Then they tried to get me under water in scuba gear but with my claustrophobia there was no way. Although I did try it under controlled conditions in the studio some years later.

But enough about me.

One of my dearest friends is Marty Allen, the comic, and the last thing in the world I would want is for anything to happen to him. So when he was co-hosting with me at a theme park called Sea World, in Aurora, Ohio, and said he didn't want a second ride in one of the park's speedboats, I replied that I wouldn't ask him to do anything I wouldn't do myself and I didn't want another ride either.

Here's what happened.

Marty and I were to ride with one of the expert speedboat drivers in a try at going over a water ski jump. You've seen it done a million times and I thought it would be fun to add to all the other stunts my co-hosts and I have tried.

Well, we rehearsed it and everything went fine except that Marty emerged from the boat with a bruised knee. Then I tried it alone and when I came ashore I had a black-and-blue mark on my hip that looked like a Hawaiian sunset.

Finally, one of the show's associate producers, Merrill Mazuer, decided it was time to try the stunt himself and find out what Marty and I were doing wrong so we wouldn't hurt ourselves when it came time to tape the show. Several minutes later, the jump completed, he sported what was diagnosed as a broken nose.

So that's why Marty didn't want to take another ride in the boat and neither did I. The boat jockey had to go it solo.

To show what a good friend Marty is, he's co-hosted with me many times since then. And I counted his lovely wife "Frenchy" my friend as well. She succeeded in helping him become one of the most recognizable of all stars. I know because I have walked through airports with him all over the country.

Among all the remotes, no place we ever visited was more fun than Disney World. Aren't we all really kids at heart?

Being in Florida, we asked Anita Bryant to co-host for a week. There wasn't a dull moment as we explored that whole magnificent lay-out of fun and games and rides.

The fun increased with the appearance of Phyllis Diller. Then an embarrassing incident occurred. Anita and Phyllis and I were loitering in front of one of those dark rides in which scary figures pop out at you. Phyllis was wearing her usual outfit and fright wig when suddenly a man walked up to us and said, "I beg your pardon, I'm the manager of this ride and I'd be obliged if you'd talk to this lady somewhere else." He pointed to Phyllis.

"Why?" I asked.

"Well, sir," he said, "I'd rather the kids weren't scared *before* they take the ride."

On all our remotes Gen is a constant companion. I'm not sure whether it's just because she likes to go places and see things, because she loves me and wants to be near me or because she feels someone has to be around to protect me. One thing I know for sure, she's my eyes, looking around, taking care of things, observing, getting ideas.

But if I had to vote for one of those reasons, I'd opt for the notion that she loves me. I'm grateful, too, for her frankness in telling me what I did wrong or what I could have done better or what I should never have done at all, after the fact.

There was a time in San Diego, however, when I wish she'd taken a stronger position *before* the fact. But she has her code. It's one of noninterference in the show. Though she's told me time and time again that being married to me is like being hooked up with a fireman, a cop, a bullfighter or a test pilot. She never knows what's going to happen when I go to work in the morning.

In San Diego, where I wished she'd interfered, I was a bullfighter.

For a long time Woody Fraser had been thinking about a bullfight segment. I was automatically against it for two reasons: 1) I knew I'd wind up in the ring with some bull who didn't mean well by me; 2) There are an awful lot of very vocal people who eat steak any time they can get it but think it's cruel to kill a bull.

However, the idea became an obsession and during the

week of shows we were doing in San Diego and its environs (only 12 miles from Tijuana) it started to fester. Everybody figured with Trini Lopez, who is a bullfight aficionado and amateur torero, as my co-host it was a natural . . . an idea whose time had come.

One of our talent coordinators was put on the problem and came back enthusiastically announcing that she'd found a bullfighter, a bull, a bullring, everything in fact, only a few miles out of San Diego.

Thinking about it as I write, I wonder how she did it on such short notice. Where do you start looking? The Yellow Pages? Or do you look in the "At Liberty" ads in *Billboard* for something headed "Matador Available—Have Bull— Will Travel"?

One way to book talent is the way our head talent coordinator Vince Calandra does it. He learned his magic working for the never-to-be-forgotten "Ed Sullivan Show," for which he booked all sorts of acts at specially arranged prices by beating their agents at either golf or tennis and then settling for an appearance on the Sullivan show in lieu of whatever cash was involved.

Booking for us is harder. In the first place I make it hard for Vince by insisting that he try to get acts that kind of mesh, that have some artistic or personal relationship one to the other. Another hardrock part of booking our show is that like all talk shows it's what's known as a "scale show." This means we pay the union scale, which is somewhere around $400. Vince gets us people by pointing out that they not only can plug whatever their latest enterprise happens to be—a new TV show, a picture, a book, a charity—they will also find that their honorarium will in no way upset their tax structure. What argument was used to get the bullfighter and his paraphernalia, I don't know. Probably vanity. Having booked this whole lash-up, they finally told me about it and, good scout that I am, I okayed it.

When Gen learned of the plan she as always went right to

the point and had the good sense and good judgment to suggest that they tell me what sort of animal I was going to face. So they got in touch with the bull's owner and sparring partner and asked what kind of animal he worked with.

The response was most reassuring. He was one of the top amateur bullfighters of the world (whatever that means). The bull was a young one, not full size, whose horns had been filed down. All in all it would be as safe as playing with a puppy in your living room.

It did develop that there was no regular ring. They were setting one up specially for our event. That didn't sound too healthy. On the other hand, in the final analysis, it was the bull I was going up against, not the ring. So what difference could it make as long as the background looked legit?

In short, I went along with the whole scheme, rationalizing that God takes care of children, drunks and singing talk show hosts named Douglas. I should have known better because I could still see Gen had reservations. I attributed this to some false ideas she got from seeing Ricardo Montalban in too many bullfight films.

So the next morning about six we left San Diego on the longest "12-mile" drive I've ever been driven. Finally we arrived where we were supposed to find the mocked-up bullring. What we found was something that looked like a miniature version of Chicago's old stockyards. The place looked like nothing but a bunch of cattle pens. Because that's what it was.

It then turned out that what they had done was to take one of these pens and drape canvas all around it. There was a chute through which the bull was to make his entrance. The bull himself was in a truck; the matador, waiting in his dressing room.

To simulate the stands, they'd built a sort of temporary bleachers that Trini and I had to climb a 10-foot ladder to sit in. The whole lash-up looked like a junior high production of *Carmen*.

Trini and I were supposed to sit up on our perch in the "stands" all wired up with RF—that's radio frequency—mikes, not even a cable connecting us with the outside world, and chat about the action in the ring as our amateur matador and his friend, Mr. Bull, did their stuff.

Then, having seen how easy it all was, I was to go down, get into the ring and prove that you, too, can be a Dominguez with just a few hours' practice every afternoon at your neighborhood abattoir.

While we're up on this perch, rehearsing, a question popped into Trini's head. "When Mike goes into the ring, if the bull chases him, how does he get out fast?" he asked the director.

This was the answer. "Just climb the ladder."

That brought violent protests from everyone, led by me. So the bull's people got an ax and, right before our very eyes, cut another way out. It was at this point that Trini excused himself and asked Woody if he'd seen this animal I was to be involved with. The one with the filed horns, remember? The little young bull?

Woody saw Trini's point. But he was told this was impossible. It was out of the question for him to go into the truck, him or anybody. And if they took the animal out they wouldn't be able to get him back. So the show must go on. But before it did, Trini again pointed out that there was a total lack of the traditional barrier of heavy planking around the ring, behind which a scared torero can hide when he's in real trouble. The lack was taken care of by surrounding the ring with bales of hay. The final construction was what you might call your standard, early morning San Diego makeshift bullring.

I could see that Gen, who'd been quietly watching all this, was becoming more and more uneasy. Clearly she didn't like any part of what she was seeing or what was going on and neither did I. But we'd passed the point of no return.

The taping started. I had a little chit-chat with the amateur matador and wound up asking to see the animal he was going to spar with. Trini and I climbed the ladder and sat in the make-believe "stands." They opened the gate and the next thing I saw was this "baby bull" with the "filed" horns charging out of the chute like Mario Andretti in a rocket car on the Bonneville Salt Flats. He weighed between 350 and 400 pounds. The baby bull, not Mario. There was nothing little about him nor were his horns filed. They could have been a couple of King Kong ice picks.

When we'd asked about this detail earlier, we were told, "Señores, we cannot file the bull's horns. Too expensive. Bull no good then."

Make a note of that. If anyone ever gives you a bull and his horns are filed, he's no good. If they're not filed, you may end up no good.

The bull's boss faced up to the animal and did a few sloppy veronicas with his cape, while his helpers stood by with capes ready to divert the bull if he began to indicate serious interest in the little man with the big red hankie.

It all began to look very simple and I started to wonder why I had been so worried. This meant that when my turn came to play bullfight I walked into that ring with the confidence of a Cordobès.

Meanwhile Gen was having a hard time controlling herself. Somebody heard her say to herself, "Mike should not be doing this." She was right but it was too late. The action had started. But all fears, mostly mine, were laid to rest when it began to look as if the whole face-off with the bull would be a piece of cake . . . bull cake. I waved my cape and he, figuratively, waved back. He had suddenly become Ferdinand. We'd been sold a housebroken bull, I thought. This gave me courage. I got braver and braver and more and more active with the cape. I moved in closer. Who was afraid of the big black cow?

I faked a little comedy by running behind the bales of hay and peeking out. The bull peeked back. I ran back into the ring waving my cape. I was great! I was getting laughs from the crew.

Not from Gen. Suddenly all her fears became truths. Just when I thought I was going great, the bull apparently thought otherwise and came at me in what was clearly a very mean frame of mind.

I think I flew to the barrier and got behind the hay about one wingflap ahead of El Toro. They came with capes and worried the animal away before he could toss the bales aside and get at me. Then the cameras were cut and everyone rushed toward me to say how "terrific" I was.

I humbly told them that they had seen my last bullfight, that I had suddenly decided to retire from the sport. If that's what it is. And I apologized to Gen for having done a foolish thing.

All she said to me was, "Mike, please don't put me through anything like that again."

Perhaps the apparent danger of the bullring might not have affected her so intensely if she hadn't been so terribly shaken up by what had happened a few days earlier when we were taping aboard an aircraft carrier off San Diego. Actually, it had knocked us all for an emotional loop. I really don't think I've ever been quite the same.

We were steaming from San Diego to Long Beach Harbor. And having terrific technical problems because the ship's radar scanner, which they are required to keep going all the time, was preventing us from sending a proper TV signal. We finally got the Navy to loosen the regulation and give us a break by turning off their radar. That wouldn't have meant much if we hadn't been cruising in a heavy fog, which slowed us up so that we were about four hours behind on our shooting schedule and in danger of losing our light before we finished. Finally, about noon, the sun broke through, and with it came another problem.

The carrier had to be in Long Beach harbor by 4:30 that afternoon because a ship that size isn't allowed to enter the port except in full daylight. This was the captain's problem. Our problem was that we were trying to do one of those Bob Hope–type shows for the crew on the deck.

We had marines landing in helicopters. We had hovercrafts. We had fighter planes zooming around. It would have made panic at a three-ring circus look like a quilting bee in a home for the terminally old. But the real problem was that in order to do this show on deck, the ship had to move with the wind at wind speed. This would neutralize the wind factor and enable us to shoot the show.

But having been delayed by the fog, the captain couldn't permit this slowdown. He had to maintain faster speed in the direction of Long Beach to meet that 4:30 harbor deadline. Thus, our crew was forced to set up and prepare for a "take" in a 40-mile gale, reinforced by the forward thrust of an aircraft carrier moving at flank speed. Cameras were blowing over. Heavy cables were whipping in the wind. A bass drum took off for Baja, California.

In the booth, Dick Creque, our technical director at the time, was having troubles as a result of all this confusion. But typical of Dick he remained calm, and it wasn't because he didn't understand the problem. What he understood was that you could only fight panic with coolness under fire.

Dick, like Ken Philo, the art director responsible for the show's innovative graphics, had been with us since the show's inception. And we relied on his colossal cool under all conditions.

He was a very religious man and this aspect of his character was evidenced in his magnificent way of keeping peace in the company. A lot of tempers are lost doing a TV show and a lot of things are said that aren't really meant. Dick straightened all this stuff out among the members of the staff and crew. He was truly loved by everyone.

Well, Dick had come up from the mobile unit, five decks down in the plane storage area of the ship, for a meeting with Woody about how to solve one of the zillion nuisances

that confronted them. He'd been up and down the five
flights of ladders between the unit in the bowels of the vessel and the flight deck, God knows how many times. I saw
him take off on a dead run for the down ladder. He only got
a few rungs down the ladder when he slumped over and
fell. He was dead when he hit the deck and there was nothing the Navy could do, with all the emergency equipment
they have aboard a ship like that, to bring him back.

Whether it was good or bad, I don't know, but Dick's wife
happened to be aboard. She hadn't planned to join us until
the next day but Dick had urged her to come along because
how many civilians ever get the chance to watch the working of one of those floating airports. Gen was with Lee,
that's Mrs. Creque, when the ship's captain (it was his job),
followed by Woody and me, came to tell her what had happened.

She seemed to know everything before he had a chance to
say a word. The tears in my eyes must have told her something. I had trouble, as I always do in such situations, controlling my voice. Dick to me was someone special. He was
like a member of our family. It was a good thing Gen was
there to comfort Lee . . . and me. When things go wrong,
she's strong.

Obviously, that was the end of the shooting. I think the
incident made quite a change in my life. Up to then I'd not
thought of anything much each day but getting the show
on. That's what Dick had been doing. His ironic reward for
dedication to his job made me wonder if there wasn't more
to life than just "another opening, another show." It was unacceptable to me that we'd, in a sense, sacrificed a life to a
trivial purpose.

And yet I think about it a lot, that "trivial purpose." In its
small way it gave work to hundreds of people all over the
country, helped support a lot of performers and technicians
and musicians. Still, when I see anyone pushing himself too
hard, trying to get too much done in too little time, I try to

do something to slow him down. I never want to lose anyone else the way I lost Dick Creque.

To continue this odyssey of remotes on a brighter note in another part of California, if you ever get to San Francisco ask the tour guide to show you exactly where Tony Bennett left his heart. You'll find mine right next to it.

I think it's one of the finest cities in the world, beautiful, spectacular, a panoramic complex of great views, great food, good manners and charming, cosmopolitan people who seem always to be handsomely and appropriately dressed for whatever the occasion.

There's a warmth about San Franciscans, a down-to-earth friendliness born, perhaps, of holding each other on the running boards of cable cars or trying to catch the VW they parked too hastily on a 45-degree hill, which has taken off like a lemming for the waters of the Bay. I have never been in San Francisco either for work or play or both that I didn't hate to leave.

I met Karl Malden in San Francisco (on the streets, of course). An old hand from my home town, Chicago, he was in the radio scene there a few years ahead of me, when the best of the soap operas poured out of there from the mills of Irna Phillips and the Hummerts.

We hit it off perfectly, not only because of our Chicago backgrounds but because we each were enjoying a long and happy marriage that kept our heads together when thousands upon thousands of couples were losing theirs.

Our being at the Golden Gate made it convenient for California's then governor, Ronald Reagan, to appear on the show, an appearance that gave us one of the best of those once-in-a-lifetime, you-can-never-repeat-it bits—the kind I love.

Jim Nabors was also a guest on the show, and after we'd talked a little while we went into a number together which we performed like an old-time two-man vaudeville team in blazers and straw boaters. We finished with the typical exit, strutting off with straw hats held high, then came right back, taking a bow in rhythm. And this time Ronald Reagan followed us, mimicking what we were doing. I doubt if he ever got a bigger reception in his entire life.

This is how we worked it. While Jim and I were taking our first bow, a couple of stagehands walked on stage carrying a flat with the Governor behind it. So when he came out to join us it was a complete surprise to everyone.

Reagan was at first very undecided whether or not to do the actor bit, cute as it was, because, after all, he was the Governor of California and had to maintain his dignity. But then California has never been widely known as the Dignified State. And Ronald Reagan has long been known as an actor.

There's nothing in our law that says an actor can't be a governor or a president—an actor, a peanut farmer, a millionaire—anyone at all—if enough people agree on it.

Luckily, the Governor's savvy as an actor on how showmanship can pay off overcame his reluctance to participate in our stunt. After all, dignity is not so much what you do but what you bring to the doing of it, which is part of the meaning of the word "professional" as we use it today.

Moving right along to another exciting city, let me tell you about our Mission to Moscow.

We were given a warm and gratifying welcome by a people very much like ourselves—neither sinister, suspicious nor hostile, but on the contrary, sincere, trusting and receptive. Our audience was among the most enthusiastic we've ever had.

We had been in Moscow less than a day, among people we anticipated would be withdrawn and stand-offish; instead we were greeted by smiling, waving crowds. Most of them had never even heard of us let alone seen us. Yet there they were, doing their best to make us welcome, to greet us, to communicate their interest and their affection in every possible way human beings have of overcoming the language problem.

It was clear that they were longing for something new in their lives, something they hadn't seen before. But how did they know us so quickly? The government saw to that. Without bothering to tell us, or maybe nobody bothered to tell me because we were pretty busy, they broadcast the show we'd been taping during the day, in prime time on Channel 1.

Not knowing this, it hit me as a big surprise that those who could handle the language were asking if I'd made a recording of "Love Story." There has never been a more conclusive proof of the efficiency of television to give instant recognition to any person, thing or concept.

This was why our journey to Moscow was undertaken at the request of the Soviet government. It is no secret that a drinking problem exists among the Russian populace. To beat the problem the government hit on the idea of importing a form of after-hours recreation that is healthy, good exercise and almost impossible to get hurt at—bowling. This, they figured, would give the workers something to do on their off hours besides knocking back vodka.

So a deal was made with the Brunswick-Balke-Collander Company to put a bowling complex in Moscow and try to get the people off the streets and into the alleys. Brunswick then made a deal with us to take the show to Moscow and do some shows that included the grand opening, as well as some of the other sights, sounds and activities of the great city of Moscow.

It struck me as funny that a country which prohibits strikes should try to introduce bowling.

We arrived at the Hotel Intourist, which, I was told, accommodates all Russia's VIP visitors, and I was informed that ours was the same suite Kissinger had occupied. I'm sure this was true because I found a note in the desk drawer saying "Pick up a few words in Arabic. In Israel it's Hebrew NOT Yiddish."

The show we finally did for the opening of the bowling lanes was a lesson in high diplomacy. As part of the opening ceremonies, some high Russian officials were to demonstrate the fine art of rolling a ball down a strip of wood and knocking over a bunch of solid wood bottles.

My co-host Joe Adamov, who speaks Russian (and English) better than I do, tried to convince the politicos that a little practice never hurt anyone. But there were a lot of visitors to the run-through and they didn't want anybody to witness a member of the Russian government being shown how to do anything. So we had to confine ourselves to a demonstration of how the fingers are inserted in the ball, the best way to throw the ball and what it is best not to do. But no actual practice.

It is almost impossible to describe what happened when we began to tape. Jerry Lewis, Charlie Chaplin and Willie, West and McGinty all working against each other could not have come up with such a demonstration of bowling. But we finally got enough footage acceptable to both the Brunswick-Balke-Collander people and the Russians.

It is equally impossible to convey all the problems of producing a TV show in Russia. We, who spoke no Russian, were provided with a crew who spoke no English. Everyone became very adept at sign language. Getting the simplest thing done looked like a class in wig-wag at the Navy School of Communications that I attended before I shipped out as a radio operator. (Apparently they taught me wig-wag because they really didn't feel safe just relying on radio.)

The technical problems weren't formidable once we got across what we wanted. Cooperation was marvelous, but discipline, as we know it, was something different. Maybe we fell down in telling what we actually wanted. But people would go off on a lunch break and never come back. Or go home and take a nap and come back hours late. Complete confusion prevailed.

Take, for example, what happened in the Moscow subway, truly a sight to see. Every station clean, neat, spacious and a veritable gallery of art. I thought of the graffiti-scarred subway cars and station walls in New York and Philadelphia. Nobody dared try anything like that in Moscow. They had too much respect for the beauty of the stations.

We worked out a segment where I'd enter a Russian station, look around and comment on what I saw while a camera followed me. When a train came in, the camera took me to the door. I entered the train where there was another cameraman who caught me coming in. All this went fine. The cameraman on the train followed me to the door at the next station, where I got off and was picked up by a third camera that stayed with me as the train pulled out.

Only one little thing went slightly wrong. Instead of getting off at the station after I did, the camerman on the train stayed aboard and went home. It was his train. It took a whole day to get the tape and equipment back. But who cared, we were in no hurry. We went sightseeing, got a lot of great picures and interviews and were finally taken to the Tomb of the Unknown Soldier, where we were lucky to catch a most unusual Russian ceremony. A newlywed couple arrived, fresh from the wedding, and laid a wreath at the tomb. The symbolism was touching—two people who had joined their lives dedicating themselves to their nation by paying homage to one who had given everything for Mother Russia.

When I was introduced to the happy couple I told them it was a custom in my country to kiss the bride and asked permission. The groom seemed reluctant to allow me this privilege but after some negotiation with Joe Adamov he consented. After kissing the bride and complimenting her on how attractive she was, I asked permission to kiss her again. What I got from the groom was a solid "Nyet!" Perhaps there was some matter of morals involved. I never found out. I know that physically I presented no threat to the husband, who was young, strong and handsome—which I decided early in life I didn't want to be, as it was sort of pretentious.

In several of our shots of the streets and markets and showplaces of Moscow, Gen made some of her rare TV appearances. Although she is a lady who really looks great on TV, I feel more confident if she's somewhere keeping an eye on the things that fall in her field of expertise, namely matters of good taste and me.

As a comparison between the new order and the *ancien régime*, we were taken to a cathedral that was commissioned by one of the czars. He instructed the architect to erect an edifice entirely different from any that had ever been built anywhere. I must say that it looked as if the architect fulfilled the assignment. When the czar saw it, he asked the architect if he could duplicate the feat somewhere else.

"Of course, sire," was the answer.

So the czar had him blinded. This story may be apocryphal.

Our last evening in Moscow we were having a late dinner with our Brunswick friend Hal Meyers and our producer. We'd all had a hard day and wanted nothing more than to get to bed.

The orchestra leader came over and asked me if I'd do the number they'd heard me sing on television—"Love Story." My throat was tired, and I was tired. My heart wasn't in it but I was trapped.

The response made the effort rewarding. The applause that followed was loud and heart-warming, and grew more emphatic because their custom is to applaud in unison as if there were a cheer leader (or Tony Orlando) encouraging them.

They were calling out a word, the Russian word for "encore." The translator with our party said, "They want you to do it again."

I pulled the old one, "Why, didn't I get it right the first time?" It was a mistake. They thought they'd insulted me.

Finally I was able to beg off explaining how tired I was after working all day taking pictures of their beautiful city and country.

When we left, the whole room full of diners rose and formed a double row—an aisle—we had to walk through to get from our table to the door. As we passed they crossed their arms over their chests. The effect was similar to a cavalry officer's wedding, where his fellow officers make a canopy of their sabers for the couple to march under. It was a beautiful end to a happy week.

About a year later our friendly call on the Russians was reciprocated by the dramatic appearance on our show of the Russian film star Victoria Fedorova. She is the daughter of the Soviet actress Zoya Fedorova, who fell in love with United States Admiral Jackson E. Tate when he was stationed in Moscow. Theirs was a five-month romance before the Soviet government learned of the affair and arranged for his recall. Eighteen years passed before the Admiral discovered he had a daughter.

Miss Fedorova said she first found out about her father, as a little girl, when her mother told her he had been a pilot killed in action.

Years after he first heard of his daughter's existence, Admiral Tate had open heart surgery and while recuperating asked to see her.

Henry Gris, roving editor of the *National Enquirer*, flew to Moscow and made the arrangements for Fedorova to come to Florida for the reunion. Afterwards, she took the time to stop in Philadelphia to be on our show.

When I asked her what she especially liked about America she answered instantly, "Father!"

She went on to describe the meeting, in her own words as translated by Henry Gris: "It was my first dawn on the American ground. I am very long flying to this country. I see through the window the eyes of my father and I understand that I must make the first step toward him. I saw eyes that look so much like my eyes. And they are telling me, 'Come, come to me.'"

We called him during the show and on the phone from Florida Admiral Tate said, "She came up with the rising dawn, the light behind her and she just fell into my arms. It was a case of such nostalgic reachback that it's very hard to explain. I thank my lucky stars that it was in a peaceful place where we had a little bit of privacy and understanding."

While the Admiral listened, I sang the Russian song "Dark Eyes" to his daughter. Then Victoria and I (she in her very limited English) did "If I Give My Heart to You."

The whole meeting with Victoria and her father was a very touching and poignant one for me and, I've been told, for all our viewership and, I feel sure, that in some very small way it helped on the people-to-people level, to ease the tensions that exist between the Russians and ourselves, tensions bred largely of misunderstanding I think, because, like us, they are warm, outgoing and friendly.

When we said good-bye to Fedorova I gave her something she said she's dreamed of having ever since she was a little girl, and "Now I am a big woman and it's still my idea."

Her dream was to have an American car, and it was driven right into the studio for her.

As she inspected it she said, "I can only drive a Russian car." But she seemed ready to hop right into the Vega and take the first turn on the Pennsylvania Turnpike, to Russia.

(VI)
THE UNLOCKED DOOR

The Dowds were what I like to think of as a friendly family. We still are, what's left of us. We not only love each other, we like and trust each other. I always wondered whether we were closer than most families. In retrospect and from observation, that's how it seems to me.

Most of the neighborhood kids I grew up with seemed anxious to get out of their homes and "be free" and "have fun." For the Dowd siblings—me, my sister, Helen, and my brother, Bob, it was different. We had fun at *home*. We felt free.

Mom sang a lot. She sang for the pure joy of it, a pleasure only singers understand, a joy that comes from hearing a sweet sound come out of you. She had a lovely high soprano voice and had she been born in a different day she might have had a wonderful career on the stage. But when Mom was a girl, show business was considered—to use the word of the times—"racy," nothing for a "nice young lady." So any thoughts she might have had about a theatrical career were heavily frowned on. Her voice was limited to bringing happiness to family and friends. And that she did.

But times were hard and to raise us kids the way she felt such wonderful children as hers should be raised, Mom had to go to work to supplement Dad's income. Her work went to other women's heads. She made hats.

Later she learned by trial and error how to be a beauty operator.

I think I inherited Mom's voice and her gift for improvisation, her knack for learning how to do things by doing them. I also got a great big hunk of her enormous energy, which she squandered too freely.

As for my father, Dad had that kind of Irish wit that reached a flowering in George Bernard Shaw, Brendan Behan and such men who brought wise laughter to the world. He laughed a lot, too, and we all laughed along with him. There was blarney in his soul and the love for us that shone in his eyes lit up the whole house.

I don't know why I wrote "there was" blarney in his soul. He's still with us, still at it, as snappy and sassy and sparkling at the age of 86 as he was when I was a kid.

Dad's early career, before he went with the Canadian Pacific Railway, a job that only lasted 40 years, was managing prize fighters. He was a prototype of the average Irish immigrant kid of his day who grew up facing four possible career choices. He could be a fighter, a fight manager, a cop or a priest. Dad chose to be a manager because he figured that being a manager was the smartest way to be in on the excitement of the fight game without having to worry that sooner or later someone would come along and rearrange all your best features.

Naturally, Dad's admiration for the manly art of self-defense extended to me. He taught me all the moves and never to let anyone push me around. To Dad the fist was mightier than the word, although he was a pretty handy man with his tongue when it came to telling a story or telling a belligerent exactly who he was, what he was and where he could go.

If it ever came to Dad's attention that I hadn't done likewise, taken care of some kid who tried to take advantage of me, Dad would let me have it, with a warning that I was never, never to let anyone shove Mickey Dowd around.

As a result of this I beat up a lot of kids. I was fast. I was lithe. I was strong. And as a result of all *this,* I was cocky. And I stayed that way until my late teens, when an incident in Oklahoma City, where I was working for a radio station, had a remarkable effect on me. It turned my whole personality around. But we'll come to that. Let me tell you about my brother and sister.

We three kids got along as well, I think, as any three siblings possibly could. My sister Helen was so fond of me, the baby of the family, that she almost "big-sistered" me to death. And she's still in there doing it. She's the biggest fan I have. She watches the show every day and writes to tell me that I ought to be more careful about how I tie my tie or button my coat or comb my hair.

She's happily married now to Robert Keeler, lives in Fox Lake, Illinois, and is the mother of five beautiful children; two boys from an earlier marriage and three girls with Bob Keeler. Having Helen as a sister is one of the great joys of my life.

As for my brother Bob, he was my elder by five years and grew up to be the one man in the whole world I have ever envied. Bob was never a great success as most of us measure it in terms of money. But he was a success in the area of human relations, love of life, love of family and kids and in an eagerness to help anyone he could to make this a better world.

The best way I can tell you about my relationship with Bob is to quote from something I wrote about him for the September 1971 issue of Norman Vincent Peale's magazine, *Guidepost:*

Some boys grew up resenting an outstanding older brother. That isn't the way it was in my family. My brother Bob was a star in everything that he did and he was my hero. He was my special champion and protector.

My father who worked for the Canadian Pacific Railroad was away from home a lot which may be one reason why, early in the game, Bob assigned himself the job of watching over me. I never thought I needed watching over but he did and there were times when I wasn't sorry.

Bob was big and tough and kind and had a wild temper that could work to my advantage or disadvantage. One of my favorite memories is of the day a big English bulldog charged at me as I was walking home from school. The dog's owner was sitting on his porch and I went up to him and told him he ought to keep his dog on a chain. This made the man so mad he slapped me.

Boy was it exciting when I told Bob. He did some charging of his own. I can see him standing on the man's porch, that terrible temper steaming, the man peering out the window but refusing, wisely, to leave the house.

There was another time when some pals and I were out joy-riding and we dropped into a honky-tonk. Somebody saw me there and told Bob and the next day Bob got hold of me and shook me and sat me down and told me exactly why I was not to go into such places. He added that if I ever went in again and he found out, the shaking I'd gotten would seem like child's play. The point was well taken.

Bob was directly responsible for the greatest thrill of my childhood. He was 17 and a basketball star playing with a team called The Question Marks. I have no idea why. I was 12 and sitting on the side lines during a big tournament. The Question Marks came down to the final minutes with a decisive lead when suddenly Bob left the game. He came over to where I was sitting on the bench and shoved me onto the floor in his place. The ball was passed to me. I took aim and scored. Most kids just dream of things like that. But Bob had the touch for making them come true.

We were a sports-mad family and athletics were the big thing in my life until one day Mom took me downtown to the

Chicago Theater to see a vaudeville show. That was the day the show business bug bit me. Before I was out of my teens I was working at an Oklahoma City radio station, WKY. And it was there in Oklahoma that I met Genevieve and we were married. She was in high school and I was 18.

The years passed and although I was only intermittently in Chicago and our life-styles were utterly different Bob and I remained close. He married, fathered five children, worked as a tile salesman. He became a most effective and popular member of society, as I knew he would, and a strong member of the church. I looked with great respect on the way he conducted his life.

On the other hand, like so many show business people, I spent the years struggling, hoping, angling for that one big break.

Eventually it came but not until I was 36. From 19 to 36 is a lot of years of waiting; a lot of years of food cooked in hotel rooms and a lot of pants pressed by Gen in cramped backstage areas. It was a lot of maneuvering to keep my twin daughters, my wife, and me together as a family, the way Bob's family was.

Once "The Mike Douglas Show" came into being, however, I worked like a demon to make sure that what I had achieved for us did not get away.

I seemed to be living on a treadmill. I was exhausted. Life as a TV star wasn't that rich, it wasn't that enjoyable or satisfying, even though in subtle sneaky ways I began to be pleased by the power that TV success can bring. Yet I was to learn that it can be a deceptive power. I was to learn it suddenly.

In September 1969, I faced one of those crises that most people think happen only to other families. Bob went into MacNeal Memorial Hospital in Berwyn, Illinois for an operation. The doctors suspected cancer.

Mother and Dad were on the way to his bedside when their car was struck by a mail truck. Mother was hurt seriously and the ambulance rushed her to the hospital where Bob lay gravely ill. And so it was that there in the MacNeal Memorial Hospital, Mother on one floor, Bob on another, the family gathered. It became a time for quiet whispering, for deep thoughts and long silences, a time for looking hard at life and at oneself with fresh and serious intensity.

The word came that mother would be all right. She was in traction and she was in pain but she was safe. Bob was not. He was dying.

I paced the halls of the hospital in confusion. I was fully aware that this was my chance, at last, to reverse our roles. This was my chance to be Bob's champion and protector. But I was powerless.

During that night I came to terms with some of the subtleties of success and power that I had been grappling with. The very day I left the show in Philadelphia to fly to Chicago, I honestly had the feeling I could do something. I would get the best surgeons, I had money and connections.

But I was powerless. . . .

I can't remember how it happened but somewhere, some time in the middle of those long walks down antiseptic corridors, I began to pray. It had never been like me to rush to church and light candles, church had always been Bob's department. He had always tried to make me take religion more seriously but I had resisted.

My prayer, fumbling expression that it was, was not a begging one. Somehow I just wanted to feel, wanted Bob to feel, the presence of God. I wanted God to know—as if he needed my help—what a fine man Bob was and how grateful I was for having him. Strangely in the imminence of death mine was a prayer of gratitude.

Bob died. As soon as I could, after his funeral, I went back to Philadelphia and went to work again. But it wasn't the same. From the outset I discovered I had changed. Seeing Bob's wife and kids and feeling once again the texture of his life made me look more closely at my own. I found more time, surprisingly lots of time, to be alone with Gen and with the only daughter still at home, our little Kelly.

In learning to enjoy the blessings at hand, no day has passed since then that I have not said my prayers and thanked God for my family and my health and my job.

I am new to it and I do not understand the great ramifications of its power, but today I would not live without prayer.

I find it intriguing that ever since I stopped running so hard, ever since Bob died, people have stopped me repeatedly to say, "Mike, you never looked better." I think I have always looked calm in front of the camera but it has only been in the past years that I have discovered that I am calm. Even my golf game has changed for the better. Are all these things a coincidence? I doubt it.

Before every show there is always a moment when I go off into a corner for a very private prayer. Then is when I remember that it was Bob who really taught me to pray. When this thought comes to me I smile because, you see, he's still watching over his little brother.

That's the end of the piece. But reading it now, I feel I didn't say enough about Bob. I wrote only of his love for his own five children. He taught them to be good people and good little athletes as he coached their Little League teams. And they responded to him.

His guidance and counseling were eventually extended to a lot of youngsters who needed it and were so appreciated that years after his death, with all those kids grown into men of dignity and substance, they worked to raise money and bring into being a recreation park and playground dedicated to, and named for, their teacher and friend—and mine, Bob Dowd.

I will always continue to think of Bob as my *successful* brother. And if my sense of loss at Bob's going was great, my mother's must have been almost unbearable. In fact she never quite came back from the accident that put her in the same hospital with Bob. When she finally did seem to be back on her feet physically, senility came prematurely and very fast, possibly due to some head injury that was never properly corrected, or even discovered. Or it may have been that the loss of Bob was more than she could take, or wanted to.

But, of course, before that time came, as life grew better for me I tried to think of things I could do for Mom and Dad.

A memory that has stuck with me to this day was Mom doing washing. I don't suppose we were any more dirty than any other family. It was just that there was no money to send things out to the laundry. Everything had to be washed at home and by hand.

So one of the first major gifts I gave to Mom was a washing machine, washer/dryer, one of those sophisticated jobs that does everything but go through the pockets of your work pants to see if you left anything in them before you put them in the hamper. Mom was simply fascinated by this. She'd sit and watch the wash go swirling around, totally puzzled by how the whole thing worked, turned itself off, turned itself on, got things clean and dried things at just the right temperature and saved her all that work.

Larger gifts that came later couldn't compete at all with this miracle machine that did so much to cure her "nagging backache," the kind you get leaning over a wash tub. As I ran out of machinery to make her life easier, I was able to buy her and Dad the first house of their own, from which they derived a great deal of happiness.

I think I'd give up all the worldly success I've had if it would bring her back.

But Dad's still reasonably healthy for a man of 86, living comfortably in a condominium in Fort Lauderdale surrounded by absolutely everything he needs and wants except Mom.

The reason I'm sketching out what kind of family we were and what kind of family we grew up to be is to offer it as an explanation for why I didn't lock the door to my bedroom one afternoon when, as a little boy, I was sitting on my bed counting an assortment of quarters and dimes that would suggest to anyone who was hip that I'd been mixed up in a very low-caliber neighborhood crap game. This was not the case. But I felt instinctively that the true source of that money wouldn't make Mom or my brother Bob very happy. On the other hand, I took no pains to be secretive about it.

I counted the coins very slowly and very lovingly because ours was not a wealthy family. We weren't destitute, the way it was possible to be in the depression days, but we had to count our pennies and there I was just a kid, counting quarters and dimes.

As I did so it soon became clear, to my dismay, that I'd have in the neighborhood of nine bucks, which isn't a bad neighborhood, as any gag writer will tell you, for a little boy who operated his life on a very tight budget based on an allowance that was frequently deferred. Considering how easily the money had been earned it took no great imagination to see the nine-dollar flurry snowballing into a blizzard of money.

On the basis of a five-day week, it came to $45 weekly. This times 52 weeks a year with maybe a little extra on Christmas, New Year's, Easter and St Patrick's Day could easily run up to $2400 annually.

The amount gave some substance to a story a kid in my class told me about his sister, who was going with a guy who danced in some kind of a show downtown in The Loop. He made so much money she was going to marry him. She had plans for them to go to Hollywood, where he'd become a big movie star.

It crossed my mind that maybe I could enlarge my operation and, in time, go to Hollywood and replace Dick Powell. All this was pretty advanced dreaming for a kid they tell me was so shy that—when urged by his family and visitors to sing for them—he'd only do it through the crack in an almost closed door. I don't remember that, nor do I think I was shy. But Mom told me and Mother knows best.

And speaking of Mother, my bedroom reveries of financial and artistic triumph were terminated by her sudden presence. She took a long slow look at the chicken feed on the counterpane.

"Why, Michael," said Mrs. Delaney Dowd, Sr., showing genuine surprise and feigning delight, "where did you get all that money?"

This was a question I didn't want to answer. I knew instinctively that it was loaded with all kinds of problems, one of which might mean the sudden termination of my windfall new income.

I hung my head and held my tongue trying to think of something to say that wouldn't be too incriminating. I never learned how to lie.

Mom waited a minute, then said, "Michael Delaney Dowd, Jr., where did you get all that money?"

Have you ever noticed that when a mother is really teed-off and about to come down heavy on a kid, she calls him by his complete, full name?

I tried to buy a little more time before answering by just hanging my head and sort of hunching up my shoulders as if to ward off a heavy blow.

"Did you steal it?" There was unbelief and fear in Mom's tone. But she knew that there were kids in the neighborhood, as there are in all neighborhoods, who did steal things; some just for the fun of it, others because they needed the money and a few just because they were bad.

The moment of truth was fast approaching. Mom had pounded into me the glory of the great American work ethic. You were supposed to *earn* money. What could I do? There was only one thing to say. And I said it.

"I earned it."

As I said it I knew the talk I'd so often heard on how important money would become to me (and how I'd learn to value and take care of it once I'd earned some of my own) was coming. It would be told with a smug sort of "I-told-you-so" pleasure. I hoped the inquisition would then be ended. It wasn't.

"You earned it doing what?" asked Mom in the quiet,

"I've-got-it-made" tone of voice that a skilled prosecutor uses when he's leading a defendant to a confession.

"Singing," I said, flashing my "typical Irish" smile, the one I'd seen Dad use to melt the hearts of all around him.

"How nice," said the voice of F. Lee Bailey, issuing from the throat of my mother. "Where were you singing?"

Suddenly I realized I heard in her voice the fear of a probability that she didn't really want verified. Around where we lived there were some pretty raunchy resorts where they might find it amusing to hear a little Irish lad sing songs of love and of the old sod.

"Rafferty's," I confessed, knowing the jig was up. This was the sort of institution of good fellowship and bonhomie that is known in Great Britain as "the local" and to Americans as "a saloon," although when the 18th Amendment was repealed that word was supposed to disappear from our language.

Dumbfounded, Mom said, "You went to Rafferty's alone?"

"No, I was with Loren."

Loren Eminger and I were, in the manner of little boys, pals, buddies, chums. We stood against the world, and thanks to the training and tips on the manly art of self-defense which Dad taught, we generally won.

"Let me get this straight," Mom reviewed, "you two children were singing in Rafferty's?"

"No. Only I was singing. Loren doesn't sing good enough."

"Not even for Rafferty's?" asked Mom, becoming just a little bit amused.

"All Loren had to do was throw the quarter."

Determined to pursue her investigation to the end, no matter how awful that end might be, Mom asked, "What quarter?"

"My quarter."

There was a long pregnant pause. I'm sure Mom had more than a sketchy idea of what went on in spots like Rafferty's that won them their place in society as "the working man's club."

She learned this from Dad, who knew a lot about such places, which were all close to his heart as headquarters for good talk, good food, good drink, good fellowship, wit and laughter, in all of which he shared generously.

At the start of this confrontation I had risen and was standing by the bed full of money, partially in its defense, I think. But mostly because I'd been taught it was polite to stand when addressed by a grown-up, particularly your mother.

"Michael, why don't you just sit down and tell me exactly what you and Loren were doing at Rafferty's, just exactly how you got all that money?"

I obeyed instantly and sat on the bed. This caused the mattress to tilt and a major portion of my wealth went avalanching off the counterpane and onto the bare wood floor.

I started to pick it up.

"Pick it up later, Michael. First tell me how you earned it."

"Well," I began, taking a deep breath and graciously waiting for Mom to conquer the smile I saw creeping around the corners of her mouth (I figured it was no time to embarrass her), "well, me and Loren . . ."

"Loren and I."

"That's what I said. We went into Rafferty's and I just started to sing. Then when I'd sung most of 'When Irish Eyes Are Smiling'—just as I'm going for that high note at the end—Loren, in the back of the room, tosses a quarter onto the floor in front of the bar."

"How appreciative of him," said Mom. This time she was giving herself time to suppress her laughter. "And where did Loren get all that money?"

"From me. I gave it to him."

"You gave Loren a quarter? Why?"

"To throw on the floor in front of the bar." Suddenly the surprise and wonder of it all came flooding out of me. "When the quarter hit the floor, all the men in the bar reached down into their pants pockets and threw some more money onto the floor just the way it happened in that movie we saw. That's where we got the idea. You see this kid's mother was sick and needed an operation."

"You needn't tell me anymore, Michael. I think I can guess the rest. What did Loren get out of this little show you put on?"

"I always give him his share."

"Always? Then this wasn't the first time?"

"No ma'am."

"Well, it's the last time."

She came over and put her arm around me and drew me to her. "You sing very well, Michael, but really I don't want you singing in saloons." She paused and then added wistfully, "Not yet, anyway." It was as if she saw the handwriting or, at least, the vocalizing on the wall.

I think it was right there in my bedroom, with small change all over the floor and her arms around her youngest son, who had taken his first step into the real world, that my mother realized that her Michael was destined for some kind of singing career.

"How much did you collect?" she asked, her curiosity getting the better of her.

"About nine dollars," I said. "Do you want some of it?"

She laughed at what sounded like an offer of a bribe and said, "Oh no. It's all yours. But no more of that kind of singing. Now pick up your money and put it in a safe place."

She started to go out, then came back and kissed me and said, "You must have been pretty good."

These words and the wonder of the heavy money that could be made just by singing, I think unlocked the door to my decision to enter show business.

(VII)
WE GET LETTERS

Back in the early days of television, the guy who is now my neighbor down in Florida, Perry Como, had a feature on his TV show, which he introduced by singing the title of this chapter. The second line was, "We get lots and lots of letters." He would then read some of them. I don't think that custom should be allowed to die.

Newspapers and magazines print some of the better letters they receive. Why shouldn't we, on TV, do something similar? It would give our viewers a chance to understand what goes on in the minds of some of our other viewers. It would open up a sort of mental interaction between our viewers and our guests that should make for a better understanding among all of us.

For instance, you've probably seen Dom DeLuise on our show many times. Your reaction to him must be different from some other viewer's reaction, especially if you're Italian. But have you ever wondered what was going on in Dom's mind when he was, as one correspondent described it, "putting on an act." In the first place, that's what he saw as his job—to "put on an act," to be amusing. To make people laugh. So much for that. Have you ever thought about what he might have felt while "putting on an act" for your entertainment? Probably not. So here's a letter from Dom:.

Dear Mike,

I couldn't let the joyful week I had with you go by without telling you how I feel.

I just got back to California from my tour and several things happened to me that made me feel very special and wonderful. One of them was working on your show. You all made me feel really super.

I do a lot of television and I can tell you from the bottom of my heart that your attitude, being with you, your producer, your talent coordinator, your crew, your musicians, your "lady-who-gets-the-coffee" were all so supportive and zestful that the show was a "frigging" joy for me. That's a mother's prayer.

Thank you again.
Love

The letter is, of course, signed Dom and it has a post-script, "My love to your wife."

There are all kinds of self-serving things cynics can say about a letter of that kind. Your typical mother will say, "He must have had a very good mother who taught him always to write 'thank you' letters."

As for me and the staff, we love to hear that our guests enjoyed their stay with us and cherish the memory of it.

I have a special book for some of the letters I cherish. A handwritten note from Douglas Fairbanks, a very personal note from Gypsy Rose Lee. One from Ethel Merman. I appreciate people who lead busy lives but take time off and write. Also in this collection is a poem by Rod Steiger that he read on the show and gave me.

We also love to hear from those who don't go on the show, don't want to go on the show but also had mothers who taught them to write "thank you" letters. Here's one of the most unusual letters of that kind we've ever received. It is from the author of *Smart Aleck*, a biography of Alexander Woollcott.

Dear Mike Douglas;

Do you have any idea how many books an author sends out to the press and the media? A conservative fella like me will send out 100 or 150. The wilder ones will send out as many as 1,000 copies.

Do you know how many people who receive the books write and say thank you? I'm told it doesn't matter whether it's a hundred or a thousand; the numbers are always the same—one, two, maybe three people bother to acknowledge the receipt of a book.

I was touched, therefore, to receive a personal note from you telling me you'd gotten the Woollcott biography. I don't want to go on the show; I just want to thank you for promising to read it some day in the future.

You are the kindest and most considerate man I know.

Fondly
Howard Teichmann

Almost every show draws a few letters from people who tell you what you did, or what they think you did, wrong. These are helpful warning signals telling you that you're getting a little too relaxed. "Careless" is the word. They point out something you said without thinking too much about it. You can't do that on TV. You must think about everything you say and the reaction it may elicit from those within earshot.

Once I got beaten over the head with bags full of letters scolding me for wearing alligator, and all because of a story I told one day on the air apropos of goodness knows what, something that happened on a street in New Orleans.

I was strolling along, gawking like the typical tourist, when I grew conscious of a small boy—the kind often called a street urchin— keeping pace beside me. We'd gone maybe half a block together and after sizing me up he said, "Hey, mister, betcha five bucks I can tell where you got your alligator shoes."

"Okay, big shot," I said. "Where?"

"On your feet," he shot back. Then because I didn't collapse in hysterics he added, "Don't you get it?"

"I get it," I said and handed him his five.

And I really got it from our viewers who had no way of knowing that they were not new shoes. They'd been bought—in fact the incident took place—long before any action was being taken or even suggested to save the saurians.

You get long, meandering letters about nothing at all from lonely people who tell you all about themselves for no other reason than that they need someone to talk to. They take you into their hearts. And their daily meetings with you on TV in their homes make you seem to be one of their family.

All letters are, of course, a compliment, even when they blast you. It reassures you that what you're doing is not going unnoticed. But the most important letters of all are from busy people. These are most wonderful when they praise you, even better when they encourage you. But the fact that these busy folks have taken time at all to write to you is "the beauty part." Elsewhere in this book there's a letter from Nelson Rockefeller that explains what I mean. Another follows from a man who has been and done alomst everything that a man can *be* and *do* in the motion picutre business from grip, actor and film cutter to writer, director, producer and head of a studio, namely Paramount. The man's name is Robert Evans. Bob writes:

Dear Mike,

In 1957 I did "Person to Person" with Edward R. Murrow. Almost twenty years have passed and I think I have been on

100

every television interview show that one can imagine. My reason for stating the above is, though it may be a sad commentary on my talent, I have never had a more positive reaction to anything I have done in my professional career, than as a guest on your show.

From Herman Wouk to the president of Brown University, to Nancy Kissinger, to Charles Bluhdorn's family to Warren Beatty, who called me in Spain at three o'clock in the morning to tell me it was the best television interview he had ever seen. These are but a few of the calls and letters I have received expressing the extraordinary quality of our interview together. I knew you had a varied and wide audience, but I never realized just what a big "star" you really are. Thank you for gracing my offices with your presence.

If invited after the first of the year I would like to journey to Philadelphia to do your show again. Forgetting the impact your show has, the pleasure of doing it with you was unique and as the word "unique" does not apply to too many things in life, why not take advantage of it?

Please extend my fond thought to Mrs. Douglas and may I wish you and yours a healthy and happy 1977.

Best regards,
(signed) Bob

Robert Evans

Paramount Pictures Corporation
5451 Marathon Avenue
Hollywood, Ca.

As Bob Evans says, "unique does not apply to many things in life." But get a load of this letter from Mrs. Ray Henderson of Rte. #4, Cleveland, Georgia. Clipped to the top of the letter was a picture of a cute, little redheaded girl of about seven or eight. The letter follows:

Mr. Douglas,
I am enclosing a photograph of my daughter and writing to thank you for saving her life.
Do you remember some time ago (on your show) a doctor

demonstrated his new technique of saving a person from choking to death?

As a result of a sore throat, Alberta was choking on a piece of steak. Because of watching that particular show, I knew what to do. After the second attempt, the meat was dislodged.

Believe me, this is the only time I've been able to act in a calm manner during the various emergencies with the children.

We live five miles from town and it is doubtful if the rescue squad could have been in time.

Thanks again from her father, Christopher (her twin brother), Mark, Debra, Alan, Robin, Peter and Timothy and myself.

On the other hand, maybe Mrs. Henderson's experience is not unique. For here is a letter from Mrs. Thompson.

Dear Mr. Douglas,

Just a note to say thank you for helping to save a friend's life.

Some time ago I was watching your show on my day off and my husband came home early from work and we were both able to watch you demonstrate the lifesaving procedure used to help choking victims. After watching the show we tried it on each other and then told many friends about it, not thinking we would ever really need to use it.

Well, we did need to use it at a social church dinner. I was standing in the kitchen when a friend walked toward me gasping for breath and first thought was, "I know what to do," and I yelled for my husband to help and he and another gentleman and I went to work. It did work!!!

We want to thank you for this very valuable lesson. I hope you will show this procedure again so people who did not see it the first time will have the opportunity to learn how to use it.

We thank you for having the type of program you have and especially the type of things shown on the Friday we watched. We thank you, as does our friend's family.

Sincerely,
Mrs. Ernest Thompson

Okay. Two "unique" letters. But how many possible other people were saved by the demonstration who never felt the urge to write and thank someone for the knowledge that saved a human life? On the basis of the statistics in Howard Teichmann's letter I guess I got the probable total.

I suppose I could collect a book of letters tying together the reasons behind them, as I've tried to do in the few preceding letters, which are all, in the last analysis, "thank you" letters.

It is unbelievable how much that kind of communication means to those who get them: the written testimonial that something they did, caused to be done or gave away was appreciated. But rarely does a viewer sit down and write a letter that asks nothing.

Dear Mike,

I love your show. Please send me an autographed picture . . . and one for my friend.

Your fan,
Billy

The trouble with that letter was it gave no other name for Billy and no address.

Then my secretary, Lynn Faragalli, will pass along a letter like this:

Dear Mike,

I like your show a lot. Would you do me a favor? I collect autographs and trade them with my friends. If you would send me three of yours I could get a Fonzie.

Tom Reid

I sent him three.

(VIII)
THERE'S NO BUSINESS LIKE SHOW BUSINESS

I'm not only willing but anxious to give Irving Berlin full credit for originating the above quotation. If Berlin didn't say it first, he sure did more for it than whoever did. And Ethel Merman helped, too.

Whether there really isn't any other business like it, I couldn't tell you. Subconsciously, I think, my mind was set on getting into it when I made my first hit in Rafferty's saloon. Then Mom used to take me to see the stage shows at the Chicago Theater, downtown in The Loop.

All those movie palaces of the late 20's and early 30's were built to make the Taj Mahal look like a mobile home. They were equipped with two organs (which I learned to regard as I grew older as an attractive redundancy). The symphony orchestra rose from the basement as they played "The William Tell Overture." The show came on and the whole action knocked the eyes out of an impressionable little kid named Mickey.

Although they seated between 2,000 and 3,000, we always had to stand in line to get in (even though we caught the morning shows, when rates were cheaper). Then we generally had to stand in line again in the inner lobby before we could be seated. To keep the people on ths line happy there were gypsy violinists and strolling guitar players, and a three-piece jazz combo played in the upper lounge where you went when you had to go to the bathroom. In various other spots up there were fortunetellers with cards, crystal balls, tea leaves . . . or they'd just read your palm. Before you even got in to see the film you were completely satiated with the entertainment hors d'oeuvres they served. I would have sold my soul to the devil to be any part of the whole carnival. I couldn't think of any reason why anyone would want to do anything else.

Since then, and living in Philadelphia, I've learned a lot of things other than show biz. Because in Philly, while I'm in it, I'm not *really* into it. And I'm glad. There have been many suggestions that we move the show to New York or Hollywood. But I like Philadelphia. I don't think Dean Martin would like it. But Dean and I are different kinds of cats.

Doing what I do in Philadelphia has made me part of the scene. It's made it possible for me to get to know another Philadelphian, Grace Kelly, Princess Grace of Monaco, who even came on the show with me. And when the city fathers started casting around for whom to invite to meet Queen Elizabeth, when she visited us on our Bicentennial, I got a chance to meet a Queen.

Maybe I'm just a small-town boy with big ideas or a big-town boy (don't want to offend Chicago) with small ideas, but I don't think I'd ever be happy as a resident of Hollywood. New York, too, for that matter. Somehow I can't picture myself as a regular at "21." But I love being a lunch regular at the Old Original Bookbinder's, a very good eating place and famous in its own right. Dinners I like to eat at home with my family where there's no obligation to be "on" and where I can hear from Gen what everybody in the family's been up to. And where, if I start to show off, I'm told off.

Even to this day, after sixteen years, when I find myself on our show talking one-to-one with some glittering celebrity or super star—John Wayne or Ted Kennedy, Bette Davis or Walter Cronkite—I hear a little voice in the back of my head just behind my left ear whispering, "Wow! Look who's talking to whom!" (Maybe I should see a doctor about that.) But I think that little voice is a very big plus for a guy involved in my kind of work. It keeps me really speaking for my viewers.

I met the late Herb Shriner a long time ago when he was a star, and he said something I've never forgotten. It's an old Indiana saying that I've found to be true over and over again. That's why I remember it. The Hoosiers say, "One boy is a boy, two boys is half a boy and three boys is no boy at all." Think about it.

I have further found that in a conversation involving three people, two generally dominate to the exclusion of the third. When that happens on a talk show you're out of business. It's imperative that the viewer feel he's a part of the proceedings.

So you go along, you pick up a lot of facts and homespun philosophy from your guests. But in order to do this, you have to follow them, not try to lead them along the lines of some prepared script or outline that the staff has put together for you. They do great work but often it all goes down the drain because something better has bubbled up.

If your guest goes off on a tangent, brings up something unexpectedly, you've got to be ready to follow right along, hoping you're heading for a point and, if things don't go right, hoping you can save the situation by finding someplace to go.

Of course, when your guest is Nelson Rockefeller, you don't have such worries.

I was sitting with the Vice President in an empty studio. He didn't want an audience. There was no one around but the Secret Service men. I'm sure the Vice President didn't want *them*. I didn't want them either. You can make a door-knob laugh faster than you can squeeze a snicker out of one of those guys. They're afraid if they laugh they'll momentarily close their eyes and they need them for looking around at people who may have guns.

I started off in a routine way by saying, "Mr. Vice President, what you do—meaning politics—seems to me to be a lot like show business. You have to please the people or find another line of work."

He agreed.

I became expansive. "In show business there's a star and there's a second banana . . . "

He grabbed my arm. "That's exactly what I am." The Secret Service men laughed and from then on everything got more relaxed. We had a great interview, in which the Veep said he was merely what electronic engineers called a "redundancy"—something to switch to when the main circuit blows.

I thought the interview went well and apparently I wasn't the only one who thought so. A few days after we'd taped it, I received the following letter on engraved stationery of "The Vice President, Washington." And the letter said,

Dear Mike,
    I just want you to know what a great time I had during the taping, and that I'm looking forward with great pleasure to seeing the show. Your skill and sensitivity as an interviewer are fabulous! Also, my thanks to you and your wonderful staff for welcoming me with the beautiful flowers. With warm best wishes and regards, sincerely . . .
                                                            Nelson

I cherish that signature. I always thought his name was Rocky. But not only did I learn about politics from the Veep, I also learned something about manners from that letter. No one is ever too big or too busy to say thank you.

Rocky wasn't the only politician I learned something from; from Bella Abzug I learned she can play the trumpet.

"What else!" I can hear everybody muttering. She even did it on the show. But she didn't have to prove to me that she could blow her own horn.

You learn something from everybody in my business. I've had a good pre-med course from having Chad Everett as co-host. He got his education on the TV show "Medical Center." Alan Alda taught me surgery and I'm taking forensic medicine from Jack Klugman. Why, with the help of a good scrub nurse like Loretta Swit from "MASH," I can take out a splinter in less than 80 minutes, using only two pints of blood to keep the patient going. Actually, I pick up my rather wide knowledge of medicine playing golf on Wednesdays. There are a great many doctors in my club. I think they figure that anyone in my business has got to become a patient sooner or later. Truly, where I play it's almost impossible to get together a foursome without a podiatrist or psychiatrist, a gynecologist or a dentist (which is two ways of making both ends meet).

As we play around, these men of science discuss their successes and other men's failures and tell their bloody, nauseating "doctor stories" while I hum "All Alone" softly to myself. However, the information I picked up casually from these golf games enabled me to write the following medical article for *Today's Health* magazine. (I've cut it considerably, not because I think you wouldn't understand the technical aspects but because you know what they say about brevity.)

THE MASTER HOST OF TALK SHOWS TALKS ABOUT HIS
APPENDECTOMY
by Mike Douglas

It started in the middle of the night with a sore throat and a blah feeling in my stomach, like I didn't want to eat again till a week from Tuesday. Smart diagnostician that I am, I decided I had a good case of the flu. After all, I figured, half my staff had come down with it, so it seemed logical that some of the viruses had floated my way. Nicely reassured I went back to sleep. Or tried to, anyway.

In the morning I felt weak, cold and I could only swallow some orange juice. Gen, who had seen how I looked for over 30 years of mornings, didn't care for my greenish tinge.

She called our doctor, James B. Donaldson, an internist and professor of medicine at Philadelphia's Temple University Medical School. More than our family physician, Jim is our friend.

I told him I had the flu. And even after I described my symptoms to prove it, he still asked a lot of questions that were clearly irrelevant. Doctors can be awfully nosey. Finally he agreed with my diagnosis saying, "At this point it sounds like the flu."

I visualized a sign on my door, Mike Douglas, M.D. I had made a diagnosis. The only trouble was that while it was true that I was developing the flu, what it turned out I actually had was acute appendicitis. I took down my shingle.

After prescribing antibiotics for my sore throat and fever and some pills for my pain, Jim told me to rest. So I went off to the studio where we were taping two shows.

When it was time to start the second one I felt so weak and hot I stuck a thermometer in my face. It came out at 103 degrees. Some wise guy said, as they always do, "When it goes to 104, sell."

My stomach bothered me and I had a strange pain near my hip that I figured was a strain from the golf game the day before. This pain Dr. Douglas ignored.

Next morning Jim ordered me to bed. Then he started poking me in the area of the belly and asking me if it hurt and watching to see if I winced. I bit the bullet and just smiled up at him with my well-known sick puppy stare and made him try to guess whether it hurt or not.

The next day I woke up drenched with perspiration but my temperature was normal. The crisis had passed! I told myself I'd knocked out the old flu bug. I had scheduled a show with

Jackie Gleason, the Great One, down in Florida that afternoon and I started packing my bags.

Then Jim showed up and told me I looked a lot better. But,
somehow, I sensed he wasn't going to let me make my south-
bound plane when he asked, "How's your belly?"

My belly, frankly, was a bundle of pain. I was slightly nau-
seated and as for my appetite, forget it. Jim pulled up a chair,
did a little more poking and said, "When I was an intern, my
chief of surgery kept hammering one thought into all the in-
terns' minds. He said, "A dog can have lice as well as fleas." I
figured out that meant that a patient could have two different
diseases.

Jim went on to explain that in infections such as mine, the
lymph glands of the abdomen sometimes become involved, a
condition called mesenteric adenitis.

By afternoon my temperature had shot up again. A comeback of the flu, I felt. Then Jim felt. He pressed down on a
spot on my lower right side and I nearly climbed the wall.
He'd touched the McBurney point, one of special tenderness
in acute appendicitis.

From this point on Jim told me more about anatomy than I
wanted to know.

I'm cutting out a lot here because there may be women and
children present. I learned that my appendix was retrocecal,
which explained the pains in my back and means that it's
behind that portion of the main bowel called the cecum. Re-
suming with my learned piece:

Does that mean that they'll have to operate from behind?
Will I be one of the few people in the world who has to turn
around when he wants to show his scar?

Jim told me not to worry, my scar would be easily accessi-
ble when it came show time.

He took a blood count and called Dr. Lloyd W. Stevens,
head of surgery at the Presbyterian-University of Pennsylvania Medical Center. Then he said, "Okay, Mike, let's go."

I got out of bed and started to put on my pants. With an in-
fected appendix hurting all the way up to my wisdom teeth, I

was dressing up. I figured there'd be nurses who might have seen my show and I didn't want to show up looking like Jack Klugman. (He was the sloppy half of "The Odd Couple.")

I barely could get my pants buttoned across my sore belly and before any nurse could admire my sartorial elegance I was out of my trousers and into one of those hospital gowns that show a lot of cleavage in the back.

I would love to say that I was taking all this with chin-up gutsiness like John Wayne. Not so. I was scared stiff.

They gave me a spinal and I watched through a haze as masked nurses (they couldn't have been that ugly) moved quickly and quietly around the table murmuring things like "He's going soon" (going where?). Large overhead lights shone down on me. I had finally made it, Chad had gotten me a starring part in "Medical Center." I hoped the writers had worked out a happy ending. (They are frequently better at that than doctors.)

Then I felt a slight dragging sensation across my abdomen.

The scapel, I thought. My big opening, I thought, and fell asleep.

About an hour later I opened my eyes when I heard Dr. Stevens say, "Well, that's it."

I had nothing to worry about except who would be doing my shows while I was healing.

That's all the article you need to read, except that Dr. Donaldson said I made a very quick recovery because I was in such good physical condition.

As for who took care of my shows and what happened in my eighteen-day absence, we were lucky to get people like Alan Alda of "MASH" (I thought of getting him to operate) and David Steinberg and Joey Heatherton, so nobody got hurt very badly, and the bills from Dr. Donaldson, Dr. Stevens the anesthesiologist, the nurses and the pharmacy read like love letters when I was told that I actually had only beaten the big trip to that talk host heaven in the sky by about five hours.

So my message to all you people who play golf with doctors is this, don't try to diagnose your own symptoms, let them. In addition to the fact that you always know where to find a doctor when you need one, the real advantage of belonging to a club that's full of doctors (instead of actors or singers) is that even Frank Sinatra can't do as much for you when you're in pain.

But as I was saying about there being no show business in Philadelphia, there was a time when there were five talk shows in the East—five, count 'em—Johnny Carson, Merv Griffin, David Frost, Dick Cavett and ours. Four were New York-based and three of those were starting to go down the drain because there weren't enough guests to go around. So you can imagine where I stood in Philly. It was like a carousel. The available people would jump from show to show, do three in one day, two the next and be ready to go round again. And they'd tell the same jokes and stories on each show just as if each catered to a world of its own when they got to me. I began to call them on it.

A guy would begin a yarn and I'd stop him. "I heard you tell that last night to Dick Cavett." It really upset me. I told them they'd better check where the audiences were before they started dropping all of their "A" material in New York. Another rating problem was that guests were getting very cliquey talking only for their friends. And they didn't know anyone in Philadelphia.

Ratings that tell where the talk shows stand consistently place "The Mike Douglas Show" first. So I'm grateful to Philly. It's been good to me, and the fact that I associate with "civilians" mostly, instead of show people, keeps me in touch with my audience. You can easily lose your perspective living in Hollywood. I go there every so often, get some stars on tape and rush right back home before I get to thinking that I should be getting laughs from the band. It was George Burns who told me that the first law of show business is "Work to the audience, not to the band."

Philadelphia is everybody's audience.

(IX)
THEY MAKE ME KNOW IT

One of the many good things about my daily duties on the tube is that I'm afforded a chance to meet with an endless parade of people who are either successful or clearly on their way to success, achievers in all fields who are realizing their ambitions.

"The Mike Douglas Show" doesn't go out looking to book losers. They are not novelties. Every family has a few. The only interesting loser I can think of is dead. I don't even know what he looks like except for his picture on boxes of tea. My Dad and my brother Bob used to talk about Sir Thomas Lipton as a good sport. He was an English yachtsman and although Englishmen and yachting were not big things among my Father's and my brother's friends (they were probably turned off to yachting by J.P. Morgan's remark, "If you have to ask how much it costs you can't afford it"), they found Sir Thomas' persistence fascinating. He came back again and again to challenge American yachtsmen for the America's Cup with a series of racing yachts he called Shamrock: *Shamrock I, Shamrock II, Shamrock III, Shamrock IV*, and I think maybe there was a *Shamrock V.*

His constant defeat was also his success, for his yacht racing was not only a great sporting event, it was a sensational P.R. gimmick. Whatever it cost to lose, Sir Thomas got back in free publicity for the name Lipton, as his personality and his persistence even got through to little boys like me.

He won our sympathy and sold a lot of tea. In spite of this, no matter what anyone tells you, the play *Tea and Sympathy* was not about yachting but schoolboys.

There was no Mike Douglas show when Sir Thomas was racing; in fact there wasn't even a Mike Douglas as yet, just young Michael D. Dowd, Jr. But had there been, we'd have booked Sir Thomas, believe me, and if he can manage to come back, all he has to do is let us know when he's arriving. We'll send a limo for him. He was the kind of individual who makes a personal impact on his field, an impact that makes him the envy of his peers. Only yachtsmen remember all the *winners* of the America's Cup. It was impossible to be alive when Sir Thomas Lipton was futilely trying to bring the Cup to Britain and not have heard of the loser, Thomas Lipton, as I did.

I meet such dominant people day after day, and, as I do, I feel in a situation analogous to that of the plain girl who's traditionally selected by the pretty girl to be her best friend, in short, to emphasize her prettiness.

This puts me in the reverse role of a guru. Nobody comes to me to ask my advice and guidance. They come not to ask but to tell.

Yousuf Karsh, the great Canadian portrait photographer who has immortalized many important people with his camera, once said that he finds, "the higher the accomplishment the greater the vanity." My discovery is, the greater the vanity, the more willing to talk about it.

And so I benefit by what these accomplished people have ascertained about themselves, their work, their interests, their skills, their fears and their ultimate goals. So do my viewers. And these rewards go beyond my viewers and me. They also extend to my guests.

A young songwriter named Janis Ian was on our show enjoying a second success. Janis had experienced a kind of "first" success—I call it flash cash—that is all too frequent in the music business and has proven to be a sort of psychological whiplash too tough for some young people to handle.

I remember hearing a radio comedian named Walter O'Keefe say on his show, right after Frank Sinatra burst through the clouds of obscurity, "Frank's no different from any other normal American young man of twenty-one who has just made a million dollars."

Janis, coming back to our show after months of withdrawal from the business to collect herself, made me realize, from everything she said, that making too much, too soon, can be disadvantageous—like being skipped two grades ahead in elementary school: you're not ready for where you find yourself and sometimes the effort to cope overwhelms you. This is just a guess, of course.

When I was (you'll pardon the expression) a student the school never skipped me—I skipped school. Which may have delayed my ultimate success. On the other hand, when success came I knew what to do with it. Give water to a thirsty man and you don't have to teach him how to drink. At the age of 36 I looked success full in the face and said, "Be my guest."

But all this was not meant to be about me or Sir Thomas Lipton, but about Janis Ian, who really drove home to me with full force the idea that early success can sometimes mean early failure and sudden setback. It even happened to Frank Sinatra. It's a good thing for the young people coming into the business to know, and from Janis' letter, which follows, I gather they tune in our show. Maybe they'll read this and be advised. Here's the letter, short but one of the most appreciated I've ever received.

Dear Mike,
A very belated thank you for both your note and the show and a special thank you for the show where I got to meet Ms. Sarah Vaughan.
It always amazes me how many young people watch your show—almost religiously and what compliments we always get.
Looking forward to seeing you and the staff again,
Sincerely,
Janis Ian

Young musicians, their groupings and their gropings fascinate me. No sooner does a new artist or a new group begin to make a ripple than we book them and try to help them on their way. The country or some part of it is paying attention to what they're doing, their "thing," so we should! We try to find out if they really have talent or if they're merely exploiting a trend. Whichever it is, coast-to-coast exposure will determine.

To list all the upcoming groups (with their weird names) and soloists we've had would instantly turn this book into the "Yellow Pages." And to select just a few of the rising stars the show has tried to help along the road to the top (and not list others) would be unfair to all. They come. They go. The ones who don't make it go. The ones who do, come back.

We've had groups and even soloists who have elicited bales of outraged letters demanding to know how I can stand that noise. Well, the truth is, sometimes I can't.

On the contemporary scene, I like Paul Williams and Paul Simon and David Gates and you can't knock Marvin Hamlisch, and there are so many good singers besides the many I've already mentioned or undoubtedly will as this book goes on, that here again I'm afraid of letting this book turn into a directory of names.

Trend setters like Bing and Frank—these are the performers I admire most.

I've sung maybe 7,000 songs on MDS over the years and I think my true favorites are the compositions of Rodgers and Hart. But that's not to put down Gershwin and Cole Porter. I like the lyrics of Lorenz Hart and the sophisticated ones of Cole Porter. Ira Gershwin and Johnny Mercer are two more of my favorites.

But I don't want to put down the new, the different. I have no patience with anyone who scoffs at something because it doesn't appeal to him. If I don't like a thing I try to find out why. If I can't, then I leave it alone. But I'm never going to try to deprive somebody else of the chance to make his own choice. I guess it boils down to being prejudiced against prejudice. And I can't damn something as worthless, though it seems absolute nonsense to me, knowing there's always an outside chance that it may be one of the big breakthroughs of tomorrow.

The best minds in the world thought they were living on a flat surface until Pythagoras came along with the idea that they were whirling around on a sphere. I still don't know why we don't fall off.

I've had scientists on my show who tell me that they firmly believe we are under observation by creatures in Unidentified Flying Objects (UFOs). It's not implausible. What right have we to insist that our planet Earth is the only one of all the millions upon million of heavenly bodies that supports life? Maybe on some of them there are older civilizations than ours, and it's not too tough to figure out that they may be better ones. Maybe the technology we're so proud of is just Mickey Mouse stuff to some other group somewhere out there in space.

So I go to see pictures like *Star Wars* and I ask questions. I ask, as so many do, if there are UFOs hovering about, why do the ones that land always do so in some remote part of the country? And why are they always discovered and explored by people whose credibility is open to question?

The answers I get are, "That's the sort of people who live in the areas where the UFOs have been said to land." And the theory for why they don't land on the top of the World Trade Center in New York or in front of the Magic Castle in Disneyland is that they would only do that if they wanted to make their presence known and they're not ready to do that. The other landings are therefore written off as accidents. At least it's nice to know these other guys aren't perfect.

But why, I ask, do they keep their activities secret? Why don't they want us to know about them? Are they afraid of what our ignorance will cause us to do to them? Or are they afraid their presence would induce some sort of world hysteria that could cause us to wipe ourselves out? It's all very fascinating, and I for one would like nothing better than to go out one night and have one of those UFOs land on my tennis court.

If they really wanted to make themselves known, they wouldn't reveal themselves to some dumb swamp-billies and take them for a ride. Maybe if they do that, and there are those who say they have, they're receiving a misinterpretation of what the poeple on earth are all about.

We dismiss them, these people who say they took a ride in a UFO, as being spaced out anyway and their whole beautiful story as an evident symptom of their disturbance. Then we ask, if they're so dumb, how come they can make up such interesting fiction? Why doesn't their imagination extend in other directions?

As I've said, I'd love to be there when a UFO lands. I'd like to take a ride with these extraterrestrials, try to communicate with them. Too many things have been laughed off as impossible that are now just everyday realities to us.

When television first came along, people said it could never replace radio because the television waves didn't conform to the contour of the earth the way radio waves do. A television beam went straight out after it hit the horizon, 20 or 30 miles away. Yet in only a few years they invented the coaxial cable to carry those waves anywhere and microwave relays and satellites that now bring direct live TV from one half of the world to the other.

I've had Gordon Cooper tell me that he and a squadron of jets chased a cluster of these flying saucers one night. Damn near burned up his aircraft, until at one point the saucers just seemed to ascend and vanish. There's too much reliable documentation to laugh off. And I'm coming to believe that the more impossible and implausible a thing sounds the more it's apt to be a fact.

No question that Mason Reese has stimulated in me some credibility for reincarnation. A seven-year-old child with the mind of a person of 40.

For example, we're on the air, actually taping. They're holding up a card for him to read. Now how many kids of seven can read with the facility needed to read cue cards? It took this child quite a while to learn. Yet Mason was not only reading what the card said but editing it on sight to suit what he really wanted to say.

I said to his father, "Isn't that a little spooky?" He said, "Not for Mason."

I definitely have to keep an open mind about supernatural powers of all kinds. It's easy to explain away spiritualism and all forms of extrasensory perception as trickery. People say, for instance, that Uri Geller is no more than a very clever magician, a sleight-of-hand performer, a prestidigitator. But a host of perfectly honest people are willing to testify that he's not.

I even believe some of the supernatural exists in Orson Welles' demonstration. For if there were no such thing as the supernatural, how could you account for Orson?

If the human mind has the power to invent a package of cookies that it takes a grown man fifteen minutes of experimentation and sheer brute strength to open, why can't it cause a spoon to bend, as Uri Geller does?

So there you are with a kaleidoscope's view of the inside of my mind—a veritable treasure of unsorted trivia born of an addiction to asking "why?" My mind is like a basket of information which if tossed in the air might leave some facts stuck to the ceiling while others fell to the floor. The ones that fell down I'd understand. The ones that stick are the ones that make me ask "why?"

So if you're looking for an on-the-job training course in journeyman philosophy and psychological perception, take on the responsibility of a 90-minute, 5-times-a-week television show. If you can do it for more than nine months without developing an ulcer, you're probably a mentally healthy man. Hang in for sixteen years and you're either a philosopher or a fool—and there are those who claim these are the same breed of cat.

(X)
THREE LUCKY LETTERS

The assumption prevails that if you're Irish and a singer you started as a choir boy. To some extent that's true. There really isn't a way out of doing some choir singing. But group singing never appealed to me. I wanted to be a soloist. It wasn't that I'm not a team player. I am. Ask my staff.

I wanted to play football and basketball in the worst way. But I was too light. Nevertheless I kept trying out for teams. But then, as now, they were looking for big men. I was lithe. I was fast. I had good coordination but I just didn't have enough brisket.

Naturally while I was concentrating on becoming an athlete, my singing was pushed to the back burner. I knew I had a good voice but it couldn't get me to first base on the ball club.

Actually I found out about my voice early in grade school. One of the nuns pulled me out of a whole class of singing kids and said, "Michael, you'll do the solos." So I did. Who was I to argue with a nun?

Then, as I think I've said, my whole ambition turned around when I was taken to see vaudeville: Eddie Cantor, Georgie Jessel, Georgie Price, Sophie Tucker, Jack Benny, Burns and Allen—George and Gracie. She got to me. I understood her. George used to say, "Gracie, if I ever get to understand you, nobody will understand me."

I loved that act.

You can imagine what a kick it was years and years later for me to interview George in his home (that had been theirs) in Beverly Hills.

When I arrived he said simply, "Hello, Mike." Then, always looking for a gag, he stopped, thought for a moment, and said, "Mike Douglas, huh? M.D. You must be the only M.D. left who makes house calls."

He had said the magic word—House Calls. Some of the best things we've ever done on the show—the best person-to-person, one-to-one things—have been taped on House Calls.

People are more relaxed, more ready to talk about themselves when they're in their own homes, surrounded by their possessions. My lights, my cameras, all the people you have to have around when you tape a show seem to fade away and the guests see around them only their own treasures, the things they live with.

The occasion was his 80th birthday, and what a wealth of show biz wisdom and human understanding flowed through the unique humor of Burns' conversation.

The roles were reversed. He wasn't my guest. I was in his home. I was *his* guest.

He was comfortable, and as my host he opened up to make me feel the same way. And what comes out is a sensible, friendly, giving conversation, not merely an interview.

Take what happened when I visited Betty Hutton in her home on one of our trips to Hollywood. It was incredible! How many times have you heard a woman say that not one of her three husbands ever loved her? And that they all contrived to find a time and place to tell her so. Can anyone imagine any woman saying that in front of a studio audience? Yet at home, comfortable, she was willing to say it for the whole world to hear.

Being in Bing Crosby's home and standing beside the piano singing with him gave me a feeling that's not to be believed. As a kid who loved music and loved to sing, I listened to all his records. As an usher, I saw all his early films. He was someone I'd like to be like and to sound like. I hope the feelings I had that day in his music room came through on the tape because it was, to me, too, too wonderful to be true. People laugh at how I stand in awe of those from whom all of us in show business have drawn so much. Well, that's the way I am.

But getting back to George Burns. When an artist of the caliber of George Burns or Groucho Marx tells you "you're good" it makes you very happy. "Great!" "Sensational!" "Terrific!" These are show biz words that have lost much of their meaning and sincerity. "Good" means . . . well . . . that you're good!

For Burns, who in my book is "good," he'll tell you himself show business was the only way to go. And it gave him three separate and wonderful careers: 1) As husband, straight man and co-star of the funniest and most lovable comedienne of our times; 2) As a stand-up comic who could stand up and dish it head-to-head with the three Bs of comedy, Benny, Berle and Bergen—not to mention the big A of ad libbers, Fred Allen; 3) An Oscar-winning motion picture actor in *The Sunshine Boys*. Then, as if all that weren't enough he got to play the title role in the movie *Oh God*.

If I ever make 80 I want to make it with the pizzazz of George Burns. But that's the future. I'm writing about a boy singer of the past, namely, me.

* * *

My brother Bob worked for a roofing company run by a man named Emery Parichy. He'd heard me sing and knew where my head was. So one day he asked Bob if he thought his brother Mike would like to sing at an affair planned for the American Legion Hall in Forest Park, Illinois, where we were living at the time.

Bob told Em he'd have to make his deal with Mike and told me I'd have to make my deal with Em. So I called him.

There wasn't a lot of dickering. Em told me the gig paid five bucks and I told him I'd be glad to take it.

That was my first professional engagement, my first paid job, and it must have gone very well because I left the hall unscarred and it led to a lot more such club dates.

It also led to my spending a lot of time away from Proviso High School trying to land a job singing on the radio. From the reception I received everywhere, I felt there must be a place for me. Nobody could tell me I didn't sing better than Rudy Vallee, and look where *he* was!

A bandleader named Bill Carlsen heard me at one of those club dates. Bill had a small band that canvassed the Middle West playing minor league night clubs, one-night stands, private parties, market openings, anything. And while still in high school I went on the road with him—Bill Carlsen and His Band of a Million Thrills.

I don't know whether it ever gave that many thrills to an audience but it sure ran something up my spine, a high school kid on the road with a bunch of seasoned musicians. Some nights they were more heavily seasoned than others. I sang under the name Mickey Dowd. What else? And Carlsen would announce. . . "And now here's Mickey Dowd to please this crowd." That lit up my best smile and I steamed on with all teeth shining. It didn't take me long to learn that a big smile was a big help. In fact, the time I put in with Bill Carlsen's group was one of the greatest learning experiences of my life.

What I mean is, the average age of the guys in the group was around 27/28. I was just under sixteen. I grew up fast.

The whole Band of a Million Thrills was recruited from my neighborhood. I knew them, their sisters, their wives. So you can bet your house I was shocked right out of my socks at the things I saw going on. I learned what a guy could count on to come his way if he was with a band. Such perquisites have ruined many a fine talent.

I loved that early experience of traveling with bands. A lot of the older guys were smoking pot then, long before most people had ever heard of it. I saw them get deeper and deeper into narcotics and dope and suddenly disappear from the scene. That's why today I feel sad hearing about all our young folks who look for highs. I know where it leads. To me just getting up in the morning is a high.

Looking for highs, sniffing coke, shooting dope, smoking this and popping that kind of pill to me is tragic.

Roaming the country was a high for me, getting to know people. It taught me that folks are mostly the same in their basic desires, hopes and fears but that there's something very different in the way they express their emotions and their reactions. The Midwesterner has different ideas from the Down Easterner because of different interests and ancestral background. The Northwest is different from the Southeast. Texans are different from Virginians. And, of course, California is different from any place.

At present, in this era of extreme permissiveness, I don't know whether the old way was good or bad, whether it's better to learn about the most important of all life forces in school or from playing doctor with a congenial friend, who is also curious about what makes girls and boys different.

With me, suddenly it was there and being a quick study, I found it a most surprising and enjoyable kind of on-the-job training.

And so I spent my high school years singing on pick-up

jobs on weekends, traveling with little bands, entertaining the ladies on Great Lakes cruises, listening to the radio and haunting the Chicago radio stations looking for a break.

People keep telling me I don't look my age. Well, I never did and you may believe me that's a great asset in show business. It lets you be around for a long while.

I must have looked awfully young and winsome—for a seventeen-year-old kid—one day up at WNBC in Chicago, where I spent a lot of time hanging around looking for auditions. The receptionist said to me, "Hey, Mickey, they're running an audition for singers in that little studio down at the end of the hall. They must be just about to call it a wrap, but I don't think they've found anyone yet. Why don't you scamper down there and give it a shot? Hurry now!"

So I grabbed up my music, and ran. A bored audition pianist was sitting in the studio, waiting patiently for someone to tell him to go home.

If anything ever comes of the few chances I've had to become a film actor, and a director happens to tell me to look bored, I'll try to copy the expression I've seen on the face of every audition pianist I've ever had the pleasure of singing against. It's classic.

There were some people in the booth that I could barely see. Not knowing what to do, I just stood there.

"Okay, kid," a voice said on the talkback, "give him your music and tell him your key, if you know it, and we'll see what you have."

So I decided to sing "Green Eyes," a kind of rangy thing, because I'd heard Bob Eberly's hit recording of it with Jimmy Dorsey and I thought Bob was great. And I was right.

Well, I got about three-quarters of the way through it, and I felt my voice getting a little tentative, because normally when you get about that far in an audition they thank you and say, "Don't call us, we'll call you." But nobody said that so I went right on good and strong to a big finish.

Instead of dismissing me with a perfunctory "thank you." the voice in the booth asked, "You got a rhythm song? Something kind of up?"

He hummed a few bars of what could either have been "I'm An Old Cow Hand" or "The Bell Song" from *Lakme* for all I could tell.

So I had a little conference with the piano player and launched into:

> Oh, bury me out
> on the lone prai-ree,
> Where the coyotes howl
> And the wind blows free,
> And when I die
> You can bury me
> 'Neath the western sky
> On the lone prai-ree.

The good thing about those Western songs is that they can all be sung at any tempo, all have the same words and all the lines are interchangeable. And what I sang was a mélange of what I remembered from hearing the song in a movie.

Fellow in the booth said, "Come on in here." When I did he said, "I'm John Prosser. John I. Prosser." I was glad he told me about that middle "I" because I didn't even know John Q. Prosser. He might have been an ex-prizefighter. His nose went in so many directions it looked as if he'd boxed the compass.

I said to myself, "Here's a guy who has a background like mine." I'd been hit in the kisser so many times I had a deviated septum way back in my ear.

"How old are you?" he asked.

"Eighteen," I lied.

"Are you free?"

"Well, I sort of like to get paid."

He laughed. "No. No. I mean free to travel."

"I don't get it. Isn't this for a job right here in Chicago? This is my home."

"Well, you'll be going a long way from home," said John I. Prosser.

"How far?" I was stalling for time.

"Oklahoma City. You'll be a staff singer at station WKY."

My reaction to this was fairly stupid as reactions go. "Oklahoma City was the farthest thing from my mind," I said, recalling that I'd played there once as the singer with a lousy five-piece band. The band was so bad it made all of Oklahoma City seem bad although I remember the gig was in a spot called the Spring Lake Garden.

Actually the people there were so friendly an nice (Y'all come back, y'hear?) that I stole a towel to remember them by. I'm so ashamed, now, for stealing the towel from those nice folks, I may send it back.

But I just dashed through the most important development of this whole thing. Get the call letters of that Oklahoma City station.

Now look at my homebase station in Cleveland and Philadelphia for the past 16 years . . . KYW. If I ever own a race horse, I'll name him WYK. It's the third combination of three letters that brought me luck.

"We can pay thirty-five dollars a week," Prosser said.

"I don't think I could make ends meet."

"How much you figure you need?"

I thought a minute. "Seventy five," I said. "I'd need at least seventy-five."

"Okay," he came back enthusiastically, "I'll give you sixty."

"I'll take it," I said before he had a chance to change his mind. I didn't realize until weeks later that the sixty I settled for was fifteen less than I told him I had to have to live on. I'd struck a great bargain.

I've never stopped wondering whether, if I'd asked for

$125, he'd have come down to $75. But I'm sure if I'd held out for the $75 I would have gotten it.

He'd been auditioning for ten days, had listened to everybody in the whole Chicago area who didn't have a cleft palate.

So off I went to my first job singing on the air, off to Oklahoma City, where I found there was more waiting for me than just that job. I even paid my own fare. And, because that's where I met my Genevieve, may I say it was a bargain.

Who wouldn't gladly buy a ticket to Oklahoma City to find a gal like her?

(XI)
LET'S MAKE A DEAL

Many of the men and women who write about television have said in varying ways that the reason "The Mike Douglas Show" attracts such a large audience is that Mike is just like his fans. As a matter of fact, many of my friends have told me the same thing and so have some of my fans in their letters.

One day out in Hollywood, where we were taping six of the greatest shows we ever did, I proved this once and for all by blurting out a line frequently heard by everyone who has had wide exposure on screen and tube. The blurter, including me, means it to be a compliment but sometimes the blurtee has reason to give it a different interpretation.

I have had it said to me by nice ladies, "Mike, I'm so excited to meet you in person, at last. I've watched you on TV ever since I was a little girl." If they weren't so excited to see me, they would stop to realize that when they were little girls, radio was in its infancy and television hadn't yet been born. In some ways neither had I.

I'm sure that line has been used on every TV performer

from Foster Brooks to Mel Brooks. It is one of those lines that seems to slip easily into the minds of those who are excited by actually witnessing someone in the flesh they have merely enjoyed watching on the TV set.

Here are a few more examples. "I know you. You're somebody."

"Will you please give me *my* autograph?"

"I'd know you in a minute but you don't look like yourself in real life."

Then there's, "Didn't you used to be Mike Douglas?"

Jack Benny loved to tell about the woman who came up to him and said, "I know who you are. You're . . . you're . . . now don't tell me, I know . . . "

After some more of that, Jack's patience began to run out and he said, "I'm Jack Benny."

The lady said, "No you're not," and went right on claiming she knew his identity, it was on the tip of her tongue.

Finally, more impatient than before, Jack said, "Madame, I'm Jack Benny."

"Now don't confuse me," the woman continued. "I saw you in . . . oh I remember . . . in . . . you're . . . "

"Jack Benny," said Jack impatiently.

"Now stop saying that. I'll get it," the woman insisted.

"Would you please tell me who *you* are?" Jack asked.

"Me? I'm Mrs. Carl Schwartz."

"No you're *not*," screamed Jack and walked away.

After Jack died, we did a show paying tribute to the man who proved that Leo Durocher's line "Nice guys finish last" was not necessarily so. And for a "nice guy" to be a successful comedian is making it the hard way. Jack didn't even really want to be a comedian. He wanted to be a concert violinist, a good one. He really did.

Joan Benny, his daughter, told us of his musical ambitions. She also told us what happened when he brought his fiddle to the White House.

Jack was on his way to visit President Truman (maybe to

play duets) when the Secret Service intercepted him at the White House gates and asked what he was carrying in his case.

It seemed such a silly question to Jack that he replied, "A machine gun. I've got a machine gun in here."

The Secret Service agent said, "Thank God. I thought you were going to play the violin."

From the repertoire of dumb things you can say to a star whom you admire, the one I selected for two of the greatest performers of our time was—you guessed it—"I used to love to see you both in pictures when I was a little boy."

Then, partially to get a laugh, partially to cover my excitement and confusion at having them on the show, but mostly to emphasize my love for them and their work, I whipped out a Mickey Mouse autograph book and asked for their signatures.

The two stars were Fred Astaire and Gene Kelly. Fred just smiled indulgently at the line he'd heard so often. Gene smiled, too, and then with the perfect timing that years in the business had given him he said, "You must have been a very old little boy."

And speaking of "very old little boys," I must again mention Mason Reese in passing. At the time he whipped onto the TV scene, Mason had the mind of a young college professor. Nobody believed he actually was the kid he portrayed in TV commercials. Some said, "They can do wonderful things with trick photography."

Mason and his dad, so it goes, were leaving a TV studio in Hollywood, having just done one of the many commercials which will put him through college. (By that time some college may be ready for him.) A motherly type rushed up to him with, "Didn't you used to be Mason Reese?"

Mason looked at her and said in his little-boy voice, "No, ma'am. I used to be Wallace Beery." More about Mason elsewhere.

One of the greatest deals I was ever part of brought me to

Hollywood to do a solid week of 90-minute shows with those two super stars as my co-co-hosts. As the first show started, the "gee-whiz" little boy in me emerged and I made my ridiculous utterance, prompted by the combination of awe and embarrassment a neighborhood kid like me might feel sitting between two of what we used to call rich kids (kids with two or more pairs of shoes). So I guess both Fred and Gene qualified. Fred was the Omaha lad whose mother sent him off to dancing school with his sister. I was the boy from the West Side of Chicago who would rather have died than attend dancing school, particularly with my sister.

Gene, if Fred will pardon my saying so here, is a little closer to my age and background than I think Fred is. Gene taught himself to dance on the streets of Pittsburgh—on roller skates. After a while he discovered dancing was easier, better and safer if you took off the skates.

In that respect I think Gene was closer than Fred to what I mean when I say "a neighborhood kid." There are various kinds. One is the kid who grew up in what I think of as the Jimmy Cagney, Pat O'Brien type neighborhood, where a lad either studied for the bar and eventually made the bench or wound up behind bars and eventually made the chair. As for the rest of the kids in the family, one became a parish priest and the other became a ward heeler.

But that's talking about slum kids. I grew up in an area just a notch above that. We had money but not much. Make that not enough. The location was the southwest portion of the town Carl Sandburg called "hog butcher to the world," and when the wind blew our way from across the stockyards we knew exactly what he was talking about.

I once asked Buddy Greco, a genuine neighborhood kid from South Philadelphia, where he was born.

He told me, "Corner 8th and Spruce."

I should have known. Every Philadelphia neighborhood kid I ever spoke to was born on a corner. It was where they met. It was where the action was.

Without thinking, I asked Buddy, "Doesn't anything ever happen in the middle of the block in Philadelphia?"

He thought for a minute and said, "Once I guess. Remember that tune Connee Boswell used to sing, "Between Eighteenth and Nineteenth on Chestnut Street"? I got the idea from the way Connee sang that tune that plenty went on there."

But Bulldog Mike Douglas pursued the question, "There must be some reason why all you kids say you come from a corner. It can't be just a coincidence."

"Maybe that's because our parents taught us the easiest thing to remember. 'If you get lost just say you live on the corner of 8th and Spruce.' They knew us little buggers wouldn't bother to remember an address. And they also knew that if brought there anyone on that corner would know us."

We kicked it around a little more and decided that the corner was the big city version of the town meeting house. Actually, the corner is sort of a municipal nuclear unit. It's an extension of the family the way "the tribe" was an extension of the family. Many a lad spends more time hanging around in the neighborhood than he does at home. The neighborhood kids are his pals, his buddies. All the rest are his enemies. At its worst, this produces street gangs, throwbacks to tribal warfare. At its best, it teaches comradeship, mutual understanding, the value of cooperation and the elements of team play that produce priests, cops, lawyers, doctors, actors, scientists and even singers.

Neighborhood kids recognize only two other groups. "Them" and "Girls." We knew we were different from "them" but we didn't know why. In the case of girls, we kept trying to find out.

The rich kids, and anyone who lived in a slightly better neighborhood than we did had to be rich, were an idealization of a childhood we secretly envied, so naturally there was nothing to do but hate them. They were sissies. What you've never met, you don't understand, you fear. It's the basis of all bigotry.

We never met any of the really posh kids who lived on the northern outskirts of Chicago or in the classy suburbs like those along Philadelphia's Main Line. We'd never even heard of places like Grosse Point, Michigan, Beverly Hills or Bel Air, the swankiest part of Los Angeles, just as Bing Crosby had to discover Hillsborough, outside San Francisco. They're the territories that come with money. And the difference in economic environment makes different kinds of kids.

For instance, the kids of the rich don't have to leave home and join a group to have fun, exercise, excitement. Their backyards are their playgrounds. They have their own swimming pools and frequently their own tennis courts. When school's out (if he doesn't actually live at school), each goes to his own compound. He may link up with one buddy, just one. It'll be them against the world. Their only problem each day will be which one goes to the other one's house.

This is generally resolved by the mother's attitude. The most lenient mothers run homes that are the most attractive to kids. That goes for all financial levels of society.

At our financial level, my mother had a tendency to fight "the neighborhood." She'd beg my brother and me to "bring home" our friends. At first it wasn't easy. Then when they got to know that good things went on at Mickey Dowd's house, it was a cinch. But at first it went like this. Mom would ask:

"Who did you play with today?"

"Joe and Herbie and Max."

"Joe and Herbie and Max who?"

"What do you mean, 'who'?"

"Don't they have last names?"

"How should I know?"

Rich kids go to boarding schools or public schools in

areas where privacy is ensured in proportion to the expensiveness of the district. Busing, of course, will change this. But slowly, I think. Decades will pass before a sound judgment of its merits can be made.

On the face of it, busing should improve the quality of a child's education and raise his social consciousness. But before that happens, a lot of kids will find themselves disoriented by after-school separatism from their classmates. They may be deprived of that process of learning, that special sort of expertise and know-how that, for lack of a better description, I'm going to have to call "Let's Make a Deal."

Making a deal is something rich kids learn from overhearing their dads talking business. Neighborhood kids have to learn for themselves that life's a succession of deals you're forced to make with yourself and with others, and that it's done by guess and by golly on the corner where you live.

That's the reason Monty Hall's great show, "Let's Make a Deal," was such a solid smash. It hit people where they live. Audiences are all ex-neighborhood kids who once had something one of their pals wanted. The only way they could get it was to "make a deal" . . . trade . . . barter . . . swap. What you called it depended on what part of the country you were in.

When a rich kid wants something, he just asks his old man to buy it for him. It's minds with that kind of training that invented conglomerates.

To a neighborhood kid, a good deal is one in which he gets the better of the other guy. Your knife for his flashlight. The other guy's old man worked nights. He had to stay home and take care of his mother and sister. He had no use for the flashlight. But the knife spelled self-defense. You figured that if you had a flashlight you could get a job as an usher on Saturday afternoons. Both of you thought you got the better of the other one, which is almost the best kind of deal you can make.

I don't know whether it was my neighborhood training in

negotiation or just luck, but I think I was a party to one of the best deals ever made. By that I mean, it did the most good for the most people. Everyone was a winner.

It was the deal the MDS made with MGM, the producers of *That's Entertainment II.* The result—we spent a week in Hollywood doing shows about the picture, with the stars who were in it. MGM got a sensational week-long plug. Our viewers got to see a lot of picture stars they might never get to see again, as themselves, informally, on a talk show. Many of the stars, some retired, got a shot in the career from the unexpected and lavish exposure.

As Sammy Davis would say, "Do the name Walter Pidgeon ring a bell with you?"

Well, one of the most charming nostalgic moments of the show was the re-teaming, for an interview, of the lovely Greer Garson and the distinguished actor Walter Pidgeon.

To Greer I managed to stammer out, "You look more beautiful than ever." But you can't say that to a man. Unless, of course, you think he is more beautiful than ever. I finally came up with one of the emptiest lines I ever ad-libbed. "It's wonderful to meet you, Walter, you're looking very well."

Pidgeon, in his late seventies, smiled at me patiently and said, "Mike, old boy, I think you need glasses."

We then had a little talk of the tell-us-about-the-good-old-days type, and Greer was charming, witty and insouciant (and I wish I'd thought of that word to say at the time). Walter used a hand-held mike the way a king wields a scepter or a priest blesses his communicants. He pointed with it, gestured with it and drew pictures in the air with it, leaving me to poke my mike in his face so that the world could hear what he was pointing, gesturing and drawing pictures about.

When both parents took me to the movies, we saw my

dad's favorites, Spencer Tracy, Jimmy Cagney, Pat O'Brien, Edward G. Robinson. Dad also liked to go and see Ann Sheridan.

There were a couple of guys I first saw in a picture called *The Road to Singapore*. I thought the one with the nose was funny but I liked the one with the big ears. I thought he was a super singer and went to see all his movies. Then I'd lock myself in the bathroom and practice my boo-boo-boo-boo-booing until Mom would hammer on the door and command, "Michael Delaney, come right out of there!" Mom's use of my middle name told me there was trouble.

When I attended a movie à la neighborhood kid "group rate," it was usually on Saturday matinees and we saw a lot of Westerns with Bill (Hopalong Cassidy) Boyd, Tom Mix, Hoot Gibson, Buck Jones, Tim McCoy and sometimes William S. Hart. By the time the singing cowboys like Gene Autry and Roy Rogers took over, I was beginning to understand what Dad saw in Ann Sheridan.

For the six great days that Fred Astaire and Gene Kelly were my co-co-hosts, I got to talk to and introduce to our audience a seemingly endless list of famous film stars I'd seen and admired when I was trying to pry my way into show business. What a kick to see Ann Miller, whom the neighborhood boys called "Legs." And there was good old reliable Bob Mitchum. The fellas called him "Sleepy Eyes."

I've had Bob on several times and every time he comes to "guest" with us, he's hit me with some spontaneous crack that gives the show an added lift.

Although I didn't remember Bob in Hopalong Cassidy pictures in spite of my intensive study of the works, and although he doesn't consider that the high point in his career, the staff dug out the truth that he'd started film work as a stunt man in the "oaters," as *Variety* called old Westerns. This was not because the horses ate oats but because the actors got paid so little that's what *they had* to eat.

We had shots of Esther Williams doing some of her great high dives to contrast with Mitchum shooting his way out of some very low dives.

I asked Bob if he'd ever heard a story I picked up a long time ago, when I was singing in saloons in the Hollywood boondocks.

The great old Western star Harry Carey actually lived on a ranch not far from the joint I was working in near Saugus. He and his wife, Ollie, who was his co-star in their early days, used to frequent that type of watering hole.

They tell me when Harry used to walk in it was pull-up-a-chair-put-your-feet-on-the-table-and-listen-to-tales-of-the-early-silent-Westerns time.

"They never told you what the scene was about, they just told you what to do," according to Harry's yarns. "You just made faces and kept your mug away from the camera if you said something 'cause what you said might not be what the subtitle said you were saying.

"Mostly we spent our days jumping on our horses, riding off and shooting. Just doing stuff like that all day gets damn dull specially when you don't know why you're doing it. So to liven things up a little the boys (who really were cowboys) would put a couple of slugs under their belts and half a dozen genuine slugs in their six-shooters. Then they'd lay back and let a couple go at the men they were supposed to be chasing. A hat would fly off with a hole in it and it sure made them dig in their spurs."

When I told this to Mitchum, he said he'd heard that they used to get their kicks shooting live ammo. Then he added, "I'm sure glad the practice went out before I came in."

Once while I was sitting there talking to Fred and Gene, in walks Tony Orlando who virtually got his start with us and has never missed a chance to show his gratitude.

Tony's walk-in is the kind of surprise thing that makes working in Hollywood, from time to time, such fun. So many big important people try to throw you by walking in on you. It's great. Stars like Gregory Peck, Bob Hope, Lucille Ball, Carol Burnett live only a few miles away, or are working in the next studio. And I enjoy it. So I'm frequently asked, "Why don't you do the show from there?"

Well, that's different. When you're just in town for a few days everyone wants to entertain you, to surprise you, to see you before you leave. You're a novelty. Not so when you're just a neighbor.

Maybe you'll find a better answer in a story an unnamed show biz reporter for one of the wire services filed after I won an Emmy in 1967. He wrote:

> Philadelphia is famous for two things, the Liberty Bell and Mike Douglas . . . they're both cracked. You can see it clearly on the bell and you can figure it out about Douglas when you learn that after winning an Emmy and very wide viewer acceptance with his aftenoon show, he chose to remain in Philadelphia instead of heading for Hollywood where the well-spring of stars is constantly a-bubbling.
>
> In Philly, which has long been the elephant's burial ground of bad plays trying out for the Big Apple, he has to rely for guest talent on those unhappy actors who have seen the notice pasted on the bulletin board, "Don't send out your laundry." In the old days of vaudeville that meant that you were canceled. It still does.

While that raises more questions about staying in Philadelphia than it answers, it seems to me that if you can succeed where everybody told you you'd fail, you've done something worthwhile and you shouldn't fool around with it. Just being compared to the Liberty Bell—cracked or not— isn't bad.

Actually, it got me a part in an important film with that very fine actress, whom I admire tremendously, Glenda Jackson. The film was called *Nasty Habits* and the setting, of all places, was Philadelphia. Just as they might have used the Liberty Bell as a landmark, they used "The Mike Douglas Show" to add authenticity to the locale. That's belonging.

In the film I was seen interviewing a character I had booked on the show to tell her side of the story concerning a power struggle being waged at the local convent (the film is a parody of Watergate). Of course, it was merely a cameo role and no great dramatic challenge, but then neither was the part Howard K. Smith played as a news commentator.

A lady in Miami Beach stopped me and said, "I thought you were just wonderful in *Nasty Habits,* Mr. Smith."

"Thank you," I said, "and I thought Mike Douglas was good, too."

"Which one was he?"

Reaction to my appearance in Burt Reynolds' film *'Gator* was somewhat more favorable.

Funny how I happened to do that picture. Burt and I had gone to a restaurant for dinner and while we were waiting to be served I noticed him looking at me in a strange way. Suddenly he snapped his fingers.

"I've got it," he said.

"Well, don't let it get on *me!*" Instinctively, I moved away.

"The Governor. You'd be just right for the Governor."

It turned out he was casting me for *'Gator.*

"Ahhh, now wait a minute, " I said, "I'm no actor." This was a statement I didn't believe at all. I've always thought that given a chance and the right director I could be a good actor. "And besides," I added, "I haven't time." This was to give him a chance to change his mind if he wanted to.

"It's just a cameo," he said.

"Well [big hesitation act], if you can get me out in a day," I said, my resistance crumbling fast.

"I can," he said, and he did. Boy, was everybody surprised at how well it turned out not only for the picture but for our show, because we got some great shots of Burt directing. I was even pleased that some of the critics said I was a pretty good actor. I'm glad they found out.

I've already mentioned some of the stunts we did and the people we met in Savannah, where Burt shot the film, and where I did all my research for playing my role as a politician.

First Savannah's Mayor John Rousakis came on the show and gave me a few pointers; then Lt. Gov. Zell Miller of Georgia helped me out with some of the finer details of how to play a Georgia governor. He not only did that, he joined right in with Mike Connors and me doing a mountain folk dance with a bunch of youngsters who called themselves the Bicentennial Cloggers. One of the kids happened to be a little girl named Amy, whose daddy had been a Georgia governor and who was, at that time, running for the presidency of the United States.

We even got some great shots for our show of Burt Reynolds actually directing me in one of my scenes for 'Gator. So I have Burt to thank for the fact that now TV people are sending me scripts. Maybe there's a place for me in the flicks. If so, that's a story that'll have to wait for another book.

Now I'd like to get back to Tony Orlando, who had just walked in on Fred Astaire and Gene Kelly when I went off on a tangent. First, how I discovered there was such a thing as a Tony Orlando.

Any man with a teen-age daughter knows that a great deal of record playing goes on around the house. That could be great. But it isn't—not the way the kids do it. They play the grooves off one number, at the highest possible level, until the house is rendered clean of all undesirable occupants, which, in the case of many kids, means the parents.

My daughter Kelly was leaning this way on a sound I seemed to hear every moment I was home. Finally I asked her what it was.

"That's Tony Orlando and Dawn. Everyone's crazy about him."

I didn't like being excluded from a group called "every-one."

"What's he look like?" I asked.

"He's on the cover of the album." She went and got it.

"And you like him?"

"All the kids do. He's super."

Next morning I told Vince to find out about the singer and book him. And that, I honestly believe, was what took Tony beyond the recording studios into the TV studios. And that's how we developed a very cordial relationship.

So, not knowing what heavy stars were co-co-hosting MDS shows in Hollywood, Tony decided to help me out with some real star power and barged in on us.

Fred and Gene were delighted. The bigger the star, the happier he or she seems to be to see a new young talent making it. Tony and I embraced. We wouldn't have done that if we'd been in Philadelphia. But in Hollywood if you don't hug and kiss everyone you meet they think you're strange. Fred and Gene stood up and applauded Tony along with the audience. It was quite a reception for the Puerto Rican Mitch Miller. Ray Bolger can get audiences to sing along just great but only with "Once In Love With Amy." Tony gets them singing all kinds of songs . . . and in several keys.

When Tony sat down and, for what seemed to be the first time, got a real look at my two co-co-hosts, he said, "What's a guy like me doing on a show with stars like Mr. Astaire and Gene Kelly?"

I wondered why Fred got the "mister" and Gene didn't. When I mentioned it to them, Fred just shrugged and Gene said, "I'm younger." Fred shrugged again. But in a different way.

After Tony joined us, we went into that part of our show where the audience gets to ask questions of the co-host.

The first lady to come up asked Fred if, after all his years in show business, he still got butterflies in his stomach before he went on. I was anxious to hear Fred's answer because I *don't* get butterflies in my stomach or anyplace else when I go on. This is either because I'm too dumb to realize the danger I'm in or because I'm on all the time. I live right out there in front of those cameras for four or five hours every day.

Fred thought a long time before answering. Maybe it just seemed like a long time because there was dead air and if there's anything a broadcaster hates it's dead air. Finally Fred said, honestly, "No. I don't get any kind of creatures in my stomach before I go on unless I realize I've forgotten my lines. When that happens everything that's in my stomach starts to leave."

Speaking of Gene, when we'd finished our week of shows and were preparing to fly home, he asked me, "Why did you turn down that invitation to have dinner at my house last week before the first show?"

I told him why. "You find out a lot of things about a job when you work at it for 16 years," I said. "One of the things is that you become too social, too well acquainted with a prospective co-host, particularly one you've never met before. You're apt to leave your whole damn show in the living room. In your case the dining room."

XII
GREETINGS . . .

Thanks to Stel, the receptionist at NBC in Chicago, and John I. Prosser, I got to Oklahoma a few years ahead of Richard Rodgers and Oscar Hammerstein II. Too bad. The title song of their great musical *Oklahoma!* could have been "our song" to Gen and me.

Oscar might have been writing about us in his line, "Every night, my honey lamb and I/Sit alone and talk/And watch a hawk/Making lazy circles in the sky." (Occasionally we forgot about watching the hawk.) Actually there is something symbolic about that line. There was an unseen and unknown "hawk" threatening us. It became known as World War II.

And, may I say, getting back to Hammerstein, if you've never been "where the wind comes sweeping down the plain" in Oklahoma, you've missed something beautiful and exciting.

Of course, going to Oklahoma to sing at a radio station was not exactly pioneering. Unless you mean pioneering radio. But that, too, wouldn't be exactly true. At the time it had already segued into what is now know as its "Golden Age," meaning there were unbelievably popular network shows. But in Oklahoma City things were still easy and friendly. This, and the well known Southern charm, added to the fact that I was earning what for me at the time was heavy money, made the place very attractive. I was happy.

When I had some time off, I took some university courses. But not many and not long enough to do any good. But I tried. My education has been "The Mike Douglas Show" and the people and ideas it exposes me to.

As for the Southern hospitality, there were congenial girls in the office and they had congenial friends. I actually entered a life that was new to me, a kind of open, suburban, small–city, country club–type life that bore no relation to my life in Chicago or on the road as a singer.

There was a young man at the station who wrote continuity and who appointed himself my guide and guardian, Charlie Purnell. We ate lunch together and once in a while he'd talk about his kid sister as if he were the only guy in the world who had one. I never heard a man so gone on his sister, with the possible exception of me.

Charlie kept inviting me to the house to meet her. But she was still in high school and I had other interests at the time and kept making excuses. Finally he came up with an offer I couldn't refuse. Thanksgiving dinner.

Nobody, and I mean nobody wants to eat Thanksgiving dinner in a lunchroom, alone, in Oklahoma City. Thanksgiving dinner is to be eaten with your family. If you can't do that, eat it with someone else's family. So guess who came to dinner at the Purnells'?

When we arrived, Charlie opened the door, took my coat and ushered us in to where I could see a young girl putting the final touches to setting the table. "Hey Sis," he called.

She turned around just as Charlie said, "This is my sister."

That was it, brother. The moment I laid eyes on Genevieve Purnell, I knew there would never be anyone else for me.

That sounds self-serving, fatuous and phoney but that's how it was. Take it from Mrs. Dowd's little boy Mickey, there is such a thing as love at first sight, even though for various reasons it's sometimes a secret kept by each party from the other.

"Gen, this is Michael Dowd. He sings at the station."

She smiled, gave a little half wave and said, "Hi, Michael."

I stammered something and she went back to fixing the table.

I didn't get the impression that I'd swept her off her feet. But I knew quite well she had swept me off mine. It's a strange sort of indescribably delectable elation.

"Come on into the kitchen and meet my mother," Charlie said, leading the way.

Mrs. Purnell was basting a turkey, which is a nice friendly way to find your future mother-in-law . . . when she's too busy doing something important to pay much attention to you. Besides, she certainly wasn't thinking in terms of a son-in-law for a daughter who was still in high school.

But it was a very very slow start. Gen and I smiled at each other a lot across the table. But to me, no matter what my visceral reaction was, she was just a kid, and I was in show business, a professional singer, a man of the world, eighteen going on thirty.

Despite that, as I put my mom on the train to go home, she said to me, "You know, I have a feeling that the Purnell girl we met is the girl you're going to marry someday."

So I continued to date the congenial gals who worked at the station, and to eat lunch with Charlie. Gen dated her high school friends. It wasn't that I didn't think about her. I thought about her a lot. But she seemed a little unattainable to me; a little too young is what I mean. I acted out the lyric of a song Yip Harburg was to write some years later for *Finian's Rainbow*—"When I'm not near the girl I love, I love the girl I'm near."

Then, about two weeks after Thanksgiving, Charlie said his mother and father liked me, and they didn't think it was right for such a nice boy to be alone on Christmas so they hoped I could have Christmas dinner with them.

Two days later I got a letter from Mom saying that Dad thought the family should be together for Christmas, even though they were not *all* together in the same place. The way he solved it was to have Mom come and have Christmas dinner with me while he and Helen had dinner with Bob and his wife.

I told Charlie I wouldn't be able to join them because my mom was coming to visit her son, the wandering minstrel.

Fortunately, Oklahoma City isn't exactly in the snow belt. All its citizens are eligible to extend Southern hospitality to one and all. So Charlie said, "You still come to dinner with us and your mother comes too."

For a long time that was the happiest Christmas holiday I could remember. Some pretty dark days lay ahead not only for Gen and me but for the whole world. World War II, which put a big question mark after the ambitions of every young man darkened the future.

But a little threat like that is no problem to a kid who's in love (even if he doesn't know it) and who furthermore doesn't even realize that his Uncle Sam wants him.

I lived for a while in the euphoria of that glorious Christmas holiday. But I couldn't stop things from slipping back to the old routine. Gen continued with her education and dated big-man-on-the campus types and I remained on my regular spot on cloud nine, dividing my terrestrial time between living out the lyric of a song Yip Harburg was to write some years later for *Finian's Rainbow*—"When I'm not near the girl I love, I love the girl I'm near"—and trying to keep in top physical shape. Maybe I could become boxing champ of the Army if the war didn't end before I got the chance.

So I did some sparring regularly at the YMCA, and watched some of the townies working out, aiming to grab an athletic scholarship from one of the local colleges. I felt I might pick up a few pointers watching them and possibly give them a few.

But I couldn't devote every night to my body building. I had a job to do, and one evening I was at work in one of the sound rooms listening to a new Stan Kenton recording that had just come in. It happened to be Gen's birthday and she was celebrating it with a high school boy who worked nights as a page at the station. Doubling his date with his job, he was showing her around when they walked into where I was listening to recordings. The page held his finger to his lips and very loudly said, "Shhhhh!" Gen shhhhh-ed, and sat down. She smiled and I smiled, and unlike the hero in all love stories I can't remember what song was playing at this magic moment. To make this good, it should have some title appropriate to what was going on. I don't suppose it did or I'd remember it.

In a minute the record ended and a lot of nothing happened. The silence was exhausting. Finally I broke it by sending the page to see if any more new recordings had arrived. It was a ruse. I didn't want more recordings. I just didn't want *him* there. But I had no plan.

The moment he left I had a plan. I knew why I'd sent him out. Now get this. As unbelievable as it sounds, I walked over, stood in front of Gen and said her name. She'd been pretending to look for something in her purse. My next words were, "When this war's over, will you marry me?"

She and I had never discussed the war or the possibility of my participating in it.

There was a long, long silence. She looked at me in a way I'd never been looked at before, in a way that, as a grown man today, I never would have guessed such a young girl could look.

Then she said, simply, "Yes, Michael. I will."

Is that wild? Can you imagine! We'd never even dated before, never been out together, and suddenly I propose marriage for some vague time after a war I'm still not quite old enough to join.

Then the page returned with some records, gave them to me and took Gen by the arm. She said, "Good night, Michael."

Her date said, "Good night, Mr. Dowd." The door closed.

I clapped my hand to my head and said to myself, "Good night!"

My mother used to clip out things she liked or related to in some way. When I was a little boy, too little to remember, there was a cartoon strip called "Skippy" by a gifted artist named Percy Crosby. I found a bunch of this Skippy stuff among the things Mom had saved. She must have seen something of me in Crosby's impish Skippy. To me, finding it years later, it had some of the qualities of Schulz's "Peanuts." When it was made into a movie it made a star of the boy who played Skippy. He's now a director and producer—Jackie Cooper.

The reason I'm recalling all this is that among her "Skippy" clippings was a cover by Percy Crosby on a humor magazine called *Judge*. To this day I take pleasure in recalling that sketch whenever I feel great about something. The subject was, of course, Skippy, done in watercolor. He's standing on a hilltop gazing out at a terrific sunset and saying, "It's so beautiful I'd like to punch somebody in the nose."

This was something I knew how to do and it was something I needed to do to work off whatever it was that was seething inside of me.

Not that I was a violent kid. It was just part of my upbringing. I was firmly convinced that fighting was manly. And lots of times I proved this to my dearest pals.

Unfortunately, I always won. None of them could really take care of me. If I'd ever been given a solid creaming, I'm sure I'd never have given a second thought to winning the

Golden Gloves or any of that resin-and-canvas glory. It was a fantasy generated by the fact that I used to do most of my scrapping with a kid named Eddie Toner. At least three or four times a week Eddie and I would tangle over something. Maybe I initiated the brawls because I knew I could win. Anyway, I always did. It built up in me a sense of great pugilistic power.

When I met Eddie after we were both full-grown men, I was glad I'd hung up my gloves. He was a brute, 6 feet 4 and all muscle. He looked at me and I looked at him, and a sort of challenging smirk came across his kisser as much as to say, "How'd you like to try me now!"

There was another kid named McNamara, also Eddie. Many's the time I brought tears to his eyes and blood to his nose. I hope he, too, didn't grow up to be King Kong and is out looking for me.

But I don't want to give the idea that I was a bully or a brawler. It was just that I was strong and God (maybe Dad) gave me great coordination. I could punch pretty hard. And Dad taught me how, when and where to do it. Add to this the fact that I never cared much for losing. I'm a born competitor.

Of course I also had what Mom called some "nice friends." Bill Kearney was into music and we used to hang out together a lot because we both had ideas about singing on the radio. But Bill didn't go into show business at all. Another one of my quieter friends, Bob Rhode is now selling real estate in Florida. His dad had died and he spent a lot of time at our house. Mom encouraged us kids to bring our friends home. Feeding them was expensive, because kids like to eat but she liked to screen them, to see who I was hanging out with.

It was a good idea, I now know. And I must say, Mom was always happy with the friends I let her meet. "Let" is the operative word there. I was careful never to bring home those I knew instinctively she wouldn't approve of. Sounds shrewd but somewhere between Chicago and Oklahoma

City I lost my shrewdness and proved it one day as I stood watching the guys train at the Oklahoma City "Y." The way it looked from where I stood, the best fighter in the room was merely a spectator. I was ready to take on any one of them. Charlie Dressen, one of the great baseball managers of all times and a man who piloted the old Brooklyn Dodgers, once said, when asked if major league baseball would ever come to Los Angeles, "Must be's are will be's," meaning if you've got it coming to you, you'll get it. That's a pretty wise observation as far as I'm concerned.

One day I'd put in some time punching the heavy bag and I'd been very fancy on the speed bag. I was doing Ali's "Float like a butterfly, sting like a bee" routine before he ever thought about it; glancing over my shoulder occasionally to see if I was making an impression on any of the kibitzing bystanders.

While I was cooling out, a guy name of Dick Smith walked over and said "I've been watching you and you look like you can really take care of yourself."

I thought of myself as a pretty punishing puncher so I just smiled modestly and said, "I think I can."

"Would you work out against me?" he asked. "My manager's coming over and I want him to see what I can do against something better than the kids around here."

I didn't know that my new friend Smith had won the middleweight championship of the State of Oklahoma, as well as the AAU championship. In a word, he was no pillow fighter. He weighed about 160 and I was only around 155 at the time. Those five pounds added up to one of my problems. Another was my complete ignorance of the fact that the world was full of people who were tougher and stronger than I was.

As I put on the headgear and other paraphernalia that's supposed to keep fighters from getting their brains and other parts scrambled when it's not for money, Smith said, "I'll pull my punches."

You've probably heard the expression "My father didn't

raise any stupid sons." Well, that wasn't true in my family. I smiled at Smith and said, "That won't be necessary." So we climbed into the ring, shook hands and squared off.

Things were going pretty well, I thought. I was satisfied with the way I was doing, so when I saw my chance, I grabbed it.

We were in a clinch in a corner and as we were coming out of it I set myself and let fly my famous left hook, which took Mr. Smith smack in the kisser. I saw his eyes close to beady slits and that's my last happy memory of that fight.

He hit me twice so fast it could have been once except that the first was on the right side of my chin and unhinged my jaw. The second was over the heart where it cracked a rib. I'd never been tagged so fast and so hard in all my life. Together those two love taps produced one very stiff amateur boxer, who fell like a goggle-eyed totem pole right into Smith's arms.

Somewhere in the distance I heard a voice saying "Son-of-a-gun! I didn't mean to do that. But you really hit me a solid shot. And, by the way, you never hit coming out of a clinch."

I remember thinking, why didn't Dad tell me that?

When I was able to talk I swore, "I'll never put these gloves on again." And I never have. Oh, I may have gone a few light rounds with my daughter Kelly when I was younger and she was a little girl. But I made her promise to pull her punches.

The first big lesson I extracted from that scrap with Dick Smith was that it's not easy to sing on the radio (or any place else) with an unhinged jaw. It's not even easy to talk. People thought I had some terrible handicap. And the cracked rib made breathing a little less than the routine thing it is to those millions who don't suffer the affliction. Eating wasn't the big treat it ought to be, either.

It took me about ten days to recover thoroughly from the damage that fight did to my body and my ego. But I'm glad it happened the way it did.

Every time I see that TV commercial for an after-shave lotion in which a man slaps himself in the face with the cologne and says, "Thanks! I needed that!" I think it's what I ought to say whenever I think of my encounter with Dick Smith.

Being an engaged man with a broken jaw and a cracked rib isn't easy. It made the first two weeks or so of our secret betrothal, as far as I was concerned, more or less a stand-off. As the days went by, the desirability of tying the knot quickly increased, but I realized that I'd set the big day for "after the war." When would that be? How long?

I decided marking time was unacceptable. It was up to me to contribute my share to the war effort. But first I had to determine my draft status. I looked around for a registration card and couldn't find one. This brought up the question, had I ever registered and if not, why?

My departure for Oklahoma City was made in such a line storm of confusion I simply could not remember. I was certain I had, but where was the proof? If I went to enlist, I reasoned, they'd ask how old I was. Then, "Do you have a draft classification? No? Why? Let's see your draft card." Bang! I'm a draft evader.

My fears were probably unfounded, but that's what I anticipated. Other considerations were the adverse effect enlistment would have on my budding career as a singer and on my income. The prospect of immediate separation from Gen gave me pause as well. The best policy was to delay as long as possible. Maybe I'd find the card . . . or the draft board would find me and mail it to me.

At the same time it was embarrassing (and maybe dangerous) to be the only male civilian under 40 minus a draft card.

Finally I made up my mind. I wrote to Chicago to inform the draft board of my whereabouts, find out my status, and await instructions. I realized there was a good chance that in Chicago they'd look at my letter and say, "Who he?" And then send a couple of MP's after me. It's just an example of the type of honesty that has frequently gotten me into trouble. I might never have been located. I heard from Chicago that they had no record of me, that they must have lost it.

As I was puzzling about my next step—register in Oklahoma City or enlist—guess what? I received another letter from Chicago that began . . . "Greetings. . . . " I'd been classified as 1-A and was told to report to Uncle Sam in Oklahoma City.

What I did next was break a leg. Not on purpose, although I knew many guys who would have done worse than that to avoid the draft. But that's an uncertain route. I heard about a fellow in Oklahoma City who actually was inducted into the Army. It was such a traumatic experience he put a rifle muzzle to his chest and pulled the trigger. The bullet went right through, just under his shoulder, never touched a muscle or a bone and went out the other side doing more damage to his uniform than it did to him. Guess how he spent the rest of the war—and more!

I broke my leg walking out of a candy store. On the sidewalk out front, two guys were beating each other soft. I, Michael Dowd, your classic neighborhood fistfighter, stepped in to separate them. As happens to most strangers who mix into fights that are none of their business, I was hit instantly. Next thing I knew there were fists and bodies flying in all directions. A big fat guy lunged at me. I grabbed at his head and cleverly pulled him down on top of me in such a way that my ankle gave. I pulled myself up, dazed and in shock, and I'm standing there on my broken limb, thinking it's just a sprain. Then in the distance I heard the familiar sound of a police siren. They always sound them loudest when on the way to stop a fight, knowing that the noise will probably break up the fracas and eliminate the necessity of getting their uniforms all mussed up. It worked. The fight splashed off in all directions and I limped five painful blocks to a doctor.

He diagnosed my problem as a sprain, just as I had

thought. But it was gorgeous, resembling an Oriental sunset painted by a nearsighted heathen with the shakes. The doc told me it would be tough to walk on and sent me to a rent-a-crutch place.

Cut to me standing on line at the draft board, waiting for my physical, slightly conspicuous by virtue of my crutches.

The line must have been two and a half miles long. And I don't know how long I could have stood there waiting if a young doctor hadn't come by, being ever so charming to a pretty nurse. He was really putting on the whole number. Why he paid any attention to me, as Groucho would say, "I'll *never* know."

But as he passed he did something I love to see done properly—a double take. Then he walked over and said, "What the hell are you doing on this line?"

"I'm 1-A. I got a call to come for my physical."

"You'll never go marching through Georgia on that gam," he said. "Come with me."

He walked me around a little, then asked what was wrong with my ankle. "The doctor told me it's sprained."

"Let's check that," he said and led me to the infirmary. The nurse followed. It was most impressive to be inducted into the Army escorted by a medical unit.

They cut off the cast, X-rayed the ankle and when the Army doc looked at the picture he said to me, "What doctor did you go to?"

"Some local guy in the neighborhood." I was afraid if I gave his name I might get him in trouble.

"This ankle isn't sprained. That guy's *head* is sprained. This is as clean a fracture as I've ever seen. You can't possibly report for a physical in this condition." So he had my ankle cared for and got me a 90-day suspension. And to this day I'm eternally grateful to that young doctor, who didn't even have the sense to give me his name when he saw I didn't have the sense to ask him what it was.

During the 90-day cooling-off period I didn't cool off a bit.

I knew that as soon as I could walk without crutches, I'd be walking right into the arms of Uncle Sam and be sent off to some place I didn't want to go.

The prospect didn't delight either Gen or me. So we were secretly married. She came home from school one afternoon, put on a neat little blue suit with a pleated skirt and her penny loafers, so no one would be suspicious about where she might be going, and off we went.

We knew what we were doing—being happy together for the past 34 years kind of proves that—so we didn't tell anyone. She was not yet 18 and I was only a little older, and even two teen-agers can figure out that if they tell their parents that they're going to be married, they'll try to stop it, because they can't remember how they felt when they decided to get married.

We both lied a little about our ages to the judge but when we got the paper home we fixed it up to show our proper ages (which may have added forgery to perjury).

As for our parents, I don't suppose the Purnells were too thrilled about Gen getting married to an itinerant singer on the brink of being drafted. On the other hand, they knew me and they liked me and they knew my mother. That helped. As for my folks, they were way off in Chicago, remote from the whole thing, and my mother probably figured, if it's all right with Mrs. Purnell, it's all right with us.

Only a couple of weeks after I swore to "love, honor and cherish," I was raising my right hand and pledging allegiance to the United States of America and marching around in bell-bottom trousers at the Great Lakes Naval Training Station near Chicago.

Gen was living with my parents in Oak Park, about 50 miles away from the base, so the Navy wasn't too bad. And as soon as they discovered that I had sung on the radio, I was doing shows for the other boots, particularly one called "Meet Your Navy." My commanding officer on that detail was a man I'd seen at the Chicago Theater and heard on the radio, Eddie Peabody. When he sat down to work, he picked the strings right off a banjo. For that he got to be a captain in the U.S. Navy.

They did things like that in World War II. The organist at the Paramount Theater in New York became Major Eddie Dunstetter in command of one of the greatest musical organizations in the service, stationed at the U.S. Army Air Corps base at Santa Ana, California.

As a result of my singing, I was advanced in the service of my country to taking a basic aptitude test. This meant that if I filled out a questionnaire saying that I'd been "on the air" in Oklahoma City, they'd put me in naval aviation.

Presumably to avoid as many foul-ups of that nature as possible, they also gave a back-up exam. I happened to be sitting next to a character who wasn't playing with a full deck. The government would have done well to trade him to Hitler for a couple of Sausage Makers, First Class.

He leaned over and, pointing to a question on the paper, asked, "What's the answer to this?"

The question was, "Which is heavier, a hundred pounds of feathers or a hundred pounds of lead?"

Being one of those hip characters who knew the answer to the question "Is Mickey Mouse a cat or a dog?" I thought he was kidding.

When I realized he wasn't, I gave him the right answer. The disbelieving boob called me a dirty name under his breath, and put down what his judgment told him to write. This qualified him to become one of the millions who worked in private industry; one of those who put rivets in wrong, or parts on upside down. With his mentality he must have become foreman in charge of snafus in some war plant.

As for me, they saw in my record that I'd taken a few college courses during my spare time while in Oklahoma City, so they figured I was a candidate for the Navy's V-12 program for producing officers in large numbers. I was delighted. It seemed a better deal than swabbing the deck of a submarine.

So I wound up at the University of Wisconsin, on the way to becoming what regular Navy men called a "90-day wonder." There is no question about it, among the men these guys eventually came to command, there was a lot of wondering.

But seriously, it's never too late to remind everyone that those "instant officers" were a mighty heavy bunch of men. Without them we'd never have been able to field a winning Navy in the time we did.

However, I never made it to Ensign. You see, I tried repeating, in Madison, what I'd gotten away with by sheer luck at Great Lakes. Gen was then living in Chicago, and every night after lights-out I'd go AWOL, sliding down the drainpipe to the ground and scooting into town to be with her, somehow managing to get back to the base undetected before reveille. The beauty part was, I never had to make my bed. It was always ready for that bouncing quarter.

Wisconsin was another matter. Gen was living in Madison and I was quartered in one of the university dormitories. This time my room was on the first floor so there was no need for the drainpipe. The problem was that the whole deal cut heavily into the time I was supposed to be cramming for my ensign's stripe. The little free time remaining quickly vanished because I was soon adding graciously to the happiness of the Navy brass by singing, at the C.O.'s request, for what he called "Happy Hour"—a cocktail party-type affair held every day in the officer's mess for "stripers" only, not candidates. Occasionally this same C.O. would give me special duty emceeing a show.

Because of all this extracurricular activity, when exam time came, I washed out. However, losing me meant losing a show emcee and someone to sing at all those Happy Hours. So I got another chance.

But, contrary to what the song says, it was not better "the

second time around." I washed out again. This might not have happened had there not been a last-minute change in C.O.'s. The new one was not so entertainment-oriented as his predecessor.

The new guy called me in. I'll never forget how impressive he looked behind his big desk, his gold braid glowing vulgarly. His face was a study in utter benevolence as he shuffled my papers in front of him, smiled benignly and then with what seemed to be his most sympathetic smile, spat out, "Dowd, what the *hell* are you doing here?"

Shocked, I stammered, "I can explain, sir. You see I'm trying to do more than one thing."

"Clearly one of them is not being a student," he said. Next thing I knew I was on my way to California, dispatched to radio school in Los Angeles. To this day I can dit-dit-dot-dot, dash-dot-dot-dash to any tune you care to whistle. This time, even though Gen followed me to the West Coast, I passed the radio school course with flying colors.

There were no Happy Hours and by this time, some seven months later, I had become an old married man. And it looked pretty silly to me for an old married man to be wearing pants that didn't have a fly in front, a middy blouse and a little white hat that could only be worn two ways. One way it looked like you were a tough guy ready for a scrap, now known as the Steve McQueen tilt. The other way you looked like Boob McNutt's retarded brother.

You would think that when they brought some sense to the uniform of the enlisted man in the United States Navy, the ABs would be getting in fewer fights with civilians—giving them more time to fight the Marines. But I understand this is not the case. The new enlistees are clamoring for the old uniforms—the bell-bottoms with the 13 buttons, the white hats and the middy blouses—and they're getting them. Lots of luck, fellas!

(XIII)
AND WHAT DID WE SEE? WE SAW THE SEA!

The above was the title song of a 1930's musical film, *Follow the Fleet*. The lyrics went like this, "We joined the Navy to see the world/ And what did we see? We saw the sea!"

The lines kept running through my head from the moment my ship put to sea, those and a few others I committed to memory when I was a little boy in grammar school.

> I must go down to the sea again
> For the call of the running tide
> Is a strong call and a sure call
> That cannot be denied.

Every time the stanza came back to me when I was at sea, I'd say to myself, "Oh, yes, it can!" That wasn't all that came back to me, those long days on the ocean . . . the memory of a firm footing would come back to me, the memory of a warm bed and decent food came back . . . and often my dinner.

I never found out why our class had to learn that poem by

Our gang—in Chicago. I'm the little guy in the middle with sister Helen and brother Bob.

Dad had his arms full with me in this early photo session. In the picture are my sister Helen and my brother Bob.

Mom was a great influence on me and encouraged my musical interests.

Kelly, our youngest, is in college and married now but here she is as a youngster getting some archery lessons from her Dad at home in Philadelphia.

It's not an old Kelly-Sinatra movie. It's for real. With me are a couple of my Navy buddies.

One of my big breaks was signing a contract to appear on Ginny Simms' radio show.

Here are Gen and I with Mom and Dad after they surprised me on our tenth-anniversary telecast. They were great. In fact, Dad stole the show.

I guess I was trying to interest the twins in music at an early age. Christine is on the left. Michele is older—by eight minutes. The setting: our first G.I. home in Burbank.

Barbra Streisand was several years away from star, let alone superstar, status when she came to Cleveland as my co-host for a week.

During the Bicentennial, we were honored to be presented to Queen Elizabeth and Prince Phillip aboard the royal yacht on their visit to Philadelphia.

Louis Armstrong visited the show a number of times—and each was a classic. Old rockin' chair got us here.

Crossing swords with Douglas Fairbanks Jr. is all in a day's work.

A sure sign of an extra special Mike Douglas Show is seeing the name of Pearl Bailey on the guest list. She's been in our green room (where guests wait to go on) as often as in the White House.

Did you ever realize how much talent there is in the name Davis? Between Sammy and Bette, you've got enough wattage to light up the whole entertainment industry.

Hollywood's all-time glamour girls like Joan Crawford have graced the Douglas show over the years. Come to think of it, there aren't many like Joan; she was an original.

When it comes to colorful personalities, Tallulah Bankhead ranked high on the list. She could always be depended on to add zest to the proceedings.

This show packed a real punch. From left: Muhammad Ali, Joe Frazier, the Philadelphia Kid, Floyd Patterson, Ryan O'Neal.

Rose Kennedy was a delightful guest and wanted to make certain she covered everything she came to talk about before she left.

On our first visit t
Miami Beach, Jack
Gleason got such
kick out of co-hostin
he agreed to stay
second week—th
only time that's ev
happened. Jur
Taylor (second fro
right) and Jane Kea
join in this routin

Whenever the late
Hubert Humphrey
appeared on the
show, it was a joyous
and inspirational
event. Muriel
Humphrey has also
brightened our show.

The one and only Groucho
Marx let the quips fly when
was a guest on our show in
Philadelphia. Some of the
barbs were aimed at his
concert accompanist and m
frequent co-host Marvin
Hamlisch, who's won all the
top awards for his music.

When Julie Nixon Eisenhower co-hosted in the fall of 1974, her husband, David, played piano for us.

Dolphins jump up for the fish lunch I'm holding in my hands and mouth at Great Adventure. Describing the action is George Hamilton, who took a dunking during our stay here.

When Peter Falk co-hosted in Philadelphia, Raquel Welch was one of the guests—and it doesn't take Columbo to figure out that a good time was had by all. Peter and I have done Easter Seals Telethons together.

Gregory Peck's got puns by the bushel, I learned when he dropped in for conversation with Roger Moore and me. I hope that, like MacArthur, he will return.

When Glen Campbell's "Rhinestone Cowboy" was riding high on the hit list, I greeted him in appropriate fashion on the stage of the Las Vegas Hilton.

Marlon Brando doesn't visit talk shows very often. I was thrilled to hear what he had to say about the hazards of filmmaking and the plight of the Indians.

What could possibly upstage such stars as Walter Matthau and Carol Burnett? Walter's dog—doing what comes naturally.

We're always pulling tricks on good sport Robert Goulet. But this time both Bob and I were being broken up by the inimitable George Burns.

I'll admit my not-so-secret desire was once to be a golf pro. That's Jack Nicklaus, only the best, giving me some tips during a taping.

You never know what to expect when you're sitting next to the bright-beyond-his-years Mason Reese.

Bringing together unusual combinations of guests is especially enjoyable for me—and viewers. Example: Robert (Baretta) Blake and the queen of television, Lucille Ball.

I'm still on Cloud 9 when I look back on the six Hollywood shows co-hosted by Fred Astaire and Gene Kelly.

Even better than the impression by marvelous Rich Little was the John Wayne done by Duke himself on our show. I'm in awe of these movie greats.

Have trunk, will travel. The elephant and me. We've been known to bring the beasts into the studios. One even got stuck in our elevator.

Having Andre the Giant on one of our shows from Miami Beach was an uplifting experience for me.

Donny and Marie Osmond say that co-hosting our show led to their getting their own series. This ice skating was done on the Osmonds' set for the Douglas show.

We made a special trip to San Francisco to tape with special people, Bing and Kathryn Crosby, in their home.

While Burt Reynolds directed me in a cameo role in his movie *Gator*, in Savannah, our cameras recorded the action. I played the role of a southern governor and used a recording of Georgia Governor Jimmy Carter's voice as a model. He went on to a bigger role.

What better way to celebrate the MDS's fifteenth anniversary than with the first visit a surprise to me—by Kay Kyser, who gave me my start and my name.

Our trip to Plains, soon after the 1976 election, brought on-camera interviews with Lillian Carter and Billy Carter and an off-camera interview with the President-elect.

Stevie Wonder proves that he's a musical genius even in the whirlpool bath where we conducted this interview.

"I've realized the highest dream of my life . . . to meet Ray Charles," Michel Legrand declared on this show. And it was a dream come true for music lovers when they performed "Georgia" together. That show won an Emmy Award for my director Don King.

I love doing sketches with Dom DeLuise—although they frequently end with pie, or worse, on my face.

Liza Minnelli has been my co-host several times, and It's been wonderful to see her develop into a superstar. Her mother, the late Judy Garland, was another guest I was honored to have on the show.

A couple of swells. Red Skelton, as Freddie the Freeloader, and I clown around during his week as co-host. What a pro!

Robert Goulet and Florence Henderson join me in welcoming back Totie Fields on our show from the Las Vegas Hilton after her remarkable recovery from surgery.

Standing on my head with yoga practitioner Yehudi Menuhin was easier than trying to match him on the violin.

A particularly satisfying part of the show has been allowing TV personalities to demonstrate that there's more to them than the characters they portray. Fonzie is a giant, but so is Henry Winkler in his own right.

I've been described as one MD who makes house calls. There's Hope for this patient. Bob, at home, was doing the laughing rather than causing it at this particular moment.

We've had great fun taping on the sets of the top TV shows in Hollywood. This late 1977 appearance by the "All in the Family" cast was their first joint television interview by Carroll O'Connor, Jean Stapleton, Sally Struthers, and Rob Reiner.

When Liberace and I played on a bill together in Chicago in 1947, our combined salaries for the week wouldn't have paid the bills for the spangles on one of the costumes he wears these days.

Princess Grace, the former Grace Kelly, was on our show in Philadelphia and Washington, but best of all was interviewing her in her own picturesque Monaco.

During a week on location in New York City, Barbara Walters was a special guest of ours. During her "Today" years, the bright, attractive person frequently was our co-host and guest. And she's always been frank and open.

Tony Orlando made his first major television appearance on our show. I consider the program on which he discussed his manic depression one of the most memorable in the history of the Douglas show.

John Masefield. There's a lot more to it. But each kid only had to memorize four lines. Then we stood in a row and said our little segments in sequence at some school ceremony, maybe Navy Day.

Anyway, I can promise you there was one guy named Mickey Dowd, who, when he was mustered out of the Navy, never wanted to go down to the sea again unless it was on someone's luxury yacht.

A common practice in World War II, when the military had to carry all its hardware and materiel halfway around the world by merchant ship, was to put a Navy gun crew aboard each of those vessels, which provided about as much protection as a bullet-proof vest made out of aluminum foil. Most of the ships were hastily built tubs called "Liberty" ships, which any enemy with its heart in its work could sink from a distance before the fourteen Navy men aboard could draw a bead.

I was a member of one of those fourteen-man Navy details. Twelve men handled the gun. The other two were radio operators. The latter was my role. May I say it wasn't the best duty the war had to offer. Anyone looking to recruit a radio man on a Navy cargo ship can overlook me. The vessel I was aboard was something like the one Jack Lemmon made believe he was on when he played Ensign Pulver in the film *Mr. Roberts,* with Jimmy Cagney, Henry Fonda and William Powell. Trouble is, we got around a lot more than they did. Their ship never left the Warner Brothers' lot in Burbank.

On my first Navy duty we moved slowly out of Long Beach harbor, then as soon as we got to sea we accelerated to what any Florida fisherman would call trolling speed. I stood on deck and thought about my future, the unknown ahead and Gen, as I gazed out across the beautiful blue Pacific (according to the doctrine of Dorothy Lamour). It wasn't blue at all. I was.

I learned later that we were on our way to Fremont, Australia, the long, slow way. The sky grew increasingly gray overhead, white caps built up with the rising wind, and it suddenly crossed the mind of Radioman Dowd that something was missing out there on that ocean.

In everything I'd seen in newsreels, or read about, cargo ships like mine traveled in convoys surrounded by destroyers belching forth smokescreens when needed, and prepared to shoot any U-boats they spotted right out of the water.

Our destroyers were conspicuous only by their absence. My ship had no companions—we were a convoy of one. With a storm brewing it's always conforting to know that there's another ship or two in the area in case you fall off yours. I could take no such comfort.

Turning to the veteran C.P.O. who was in charge of the gun crew, I asked naively, "Where's our destroyer escort?"

He took an unlit cigarette he'd been sucking on out of his mouth, flicked it into the sea and asked, "What escort? Our cargo is eighty-five percent ammunition and high explosives. If we're attacked by anything heavier than a swarm of bees, we're gonners. We've had it."

"But who'll be around to pick up the survivors?" was my next bright question.

"What survivors? Listen, son, we're on our way to Fremont the long way in order to stay as far as possible from any sort of shipping whatsoever." He put a dry Camel cigarette in his mouth and sauntered off to see that his men were taking proper care of the only chance in the world we had in case of trouble, the deck gun, which they manned night and day.

For a few moments I stood there trying to digest what I'd just heard. It was nothing to give a man a warm, secure feeling and I was hardly more than a boy. The more I thought about it, the more I thought I'd throw up.

Naturally, standing there at the rail, what I thought of most was Gen, who had gone back to Oklahoma City to be with her folks right after bidding me farewell on the dock in Long Beach. The only trouble was that after the tearful good-byes the boat didn't sail. We remained moored in Long Beach while the loading continued . . . very carefully.

One evening during this loading interval a buddy of mine named George Mather and I got a pass and took a big red interurban bus into Hollywood.

Our destination was the famous Hollywood Canteen, where a person in uniform could get a friendly greeting, a cup of coffee, a cruller and a smile from Joan Crawford and a chance to dance with Rosalind Russell . . . and then go home alone. Instead of doing that, George suggested we catch the show at Earl Carroll's Theater Restaurant, where I had a Coke and George had a few beers. Then—as such things go, he had to. At least that was his story. He left me sitting alone for a long stretch while (I found out later) he maneuvered backstage and talked, somehow, with the guy who was emceeing the show. He said his buddy was a terrific singer who was in the Navy and had entertained his buddies all over the world.

George was a helluva salesman (also a liar). But the guy he was talking to must have figured, what did he have to lose? If I turned out good, great! If not, who'd put a man down for giving one of "our boys" a chance?

So pretty soon he called my name. Surprised and a little stunned I climbed onstage in my little sailor suit, and at the risk of sounding as humble as Danny Thomas I shredded the place. I sang "When Irish Eyes Are Smiling." I thought the roof would cave in.

A lot of Navy men were in the audience, which didn't hurt my reception and I was smart enough to walk off after one number, leaving them hollering for more. I refused the encore, not wanting to push my luck.

Next thing, a character in a tuxedo comes over to George and me, saying Earl Carroll wants to see me and to follow him. So I did. I entered the office of a man I'd heard called a lecher, a tyrant and a genius, Earl Carroll. He said, "Young man, I liked very much what I heard a little while ago. I like the way you sing. This war can't last forever. So I want you to know . . . where are you from?"

"Chicago."

"I want you to know that you have a standing offer of a job here as soon as you're free to take it. You have my word."

I wrote Gen, "This is great. Join the Navy and get a job with Earl Carroll."

The reception generated a good secure feeling about the future until I heard the kind of cargo (already mentioned) we were carrying. I had to tell myself not to worry. That the ship would come through okay. I'm sure the Navy would have loved that guarantee. But I had this strong feeling that I'd come through.

Two nights before I got my orders to join ship, Gen and I had been to a movie and in the newsreel that once was a staple of every movie show, there was a shot of Clark Gable christening a new Liberty ship, S.S. *Carole Lombard.*

The ship was so named to honor Gable's movie star wife of 22 months, who had gone down in a plane crash early in the war, as she was returning from a War Bond drive.

I probably never would have given this a second thought or even remembered it, if I hadn't discovered that this was the name of the ship I was sailing on.

Years later in Philadelphia, when the famous "gangster-type" actor George Raft was my co-host, he was reminiscing about the early days of the talkies and the famous and beautiful stars who had been his leading ladies. He described Carole Lombard as, "the greatest girl that ever lived."

I did a lot of traveling with the ship *Carole* and I don't mean just "from Natchez to Mobile." I mean, as Johnny Mercer also wrote, "wherever the four winds blow," spots

like Perth, Colombo, Aden, Calcutta, Hong Kong. I met a lot
of people who hadn't played hookey as often as I did from
Garfield School in Maywood, and then from Proviso High. I
felt I wanted to know more about the world. I began to bor-
row and read books. You have a lot of time to read on a
"slow boat to China." And I guess because I saw the movie
of her christening and because *Carole* and I lived so closely
together for so many days, I felt I wanted to get to know
more about the real Miss Lombard. I asked everyone I met
about her pictures, read fan magazines about her and looked
everywhere to learn what she was all about.

The findings were unanimous that Carole Lombard was a
lovely lady.

Now I know that word "lady" is a red flag to women's lib-
erationists. I don't know why. I like it. Just as the word
"gentleman" tells me something about a man, so the word
"lady" tells me something about a woman.

There are many women who are not ladies, many men
who are not gentlemen. It is for this reason that a wire I received in December '76 means so much to me. It's from
bandleader Doc Severinsen of Johnny Carson's "Tonight
Show," congratulating me on the fifteenth anniversary of
the MDS. I have a whole book of such congratulatory wires
from the biggest names in show business and politics. Most
of them had been my guests. But Doc's wire really got to me.
He said, "To a great guy who puts real meaning into the
word gentleman."

There is another wire of which I'm very proud. It says,
"To Mike Douglas, congratulations on the 15th anniversary
of your very fine show. I'm sure that I join millions of Americans in wishing you every future success and happiness.
Sincerely, Jimmy Carter." And he sent that while packing to
move to Washington.

What better way to start off a fifteenth anniversary celebration than with a wire from a grateful peanut farmer in

Georgia, who remembers me as a father with three daughters. The Douglas family was one of the largest consumers of peanut butter in the U.S.A.

But I was on the subject of a lady named Carole Lombard. Everybody I've ever spoken to who knew her agrees she was a great comedienne. But I also gathered that there were many who would not call an actress with a working vocabulary like Carole's, a "lady." She could have given a language course in Advanced Obscenity to the crew of the ship that bore her name.

The color of a woman's speech isn't what makes her a lady. It's how she lives her life and what she stands for. How she does her job and how she relates to her fellow workers. It's integrity! Gallantry! That, I'm told, applied wholly to Carole Lombard—the lady and the ship that bore her name. I'm proud to have served aboard her. She did her job and enabled me to see a lot of the world, a whole medley of places. I saw "the dawn come up like thunder out of China 'cross the bay" . . . "Moonlight on the Ganges" . . . "the pyramids along the Nile" and "that little grass shack in Kealakekua, Hawaii."

And I sent a postcard to Bill Carlsen back in Chicago from Cairo, Egypt, to remind him of a date we played in Cairo, Illinois. I said, "The place has changed a lot. They've even forgotten how to pronounce the name. They call it Ky-ro."

Now here's another little coincidence. The incident occurred in Calcutta. Virtually the entire crew of the S.S. *Carole Lombard* had shore leave, and most of us wound up in a theater where we were lucky enough to see a French film with Hindi subtitles. When we came out every man in the crew had a different version of what the film was about. The single point of agreement was that the star was Jean Gabin.

But the star of the by-then dated American newsreel on the same bill was Clark Gable. As he's christening the *Carole Lombard*, the narrator (it might have been Lowell Thomas) declares that the ship was "destined to carry tens

of thousands of tons of cargo to our lads overseas." He did
not know and so could not mention that most of those tens
of thousands of tons were adult fireworks.

Naturally, no one aboard the *Carole Lombard* ever dared
ask, "Gotta match?"

I was glad I didn't smoke. If anything happened, as we
flew through the air I could holler, "Don't blame me."

When the war ended *Carole* and I parted. She stood
moored at the dock in Baltimore and didn't betray her emotions one bit. I turned my back and set out for Oklahoma
City and Gen so fast I could have been mistaken for the guy
with the flowing cape and the big "S" on his T-shirt.

(XIV)
BRIGHT KOLLEGE YEARS

As previously noted, Gen and I experienced some pretty glum Christmases. During the 1947 Yuletide season, I got the word that Harry Babbitt, who had left the featured vocal spot with Kay Kyser to go off on his own, had decided to return to the band, an option Kay had left open to him. Which meant that I was out.

Then, several years later, back in the fold, I experienced with Kay the cancellation of the television version of "Kay Kyser's Kollege of Musical Knowledge." Again it was Christmastime.

With no anticipation of the debacle, I experienced with Kay his second cancellation, the same season, but TV was the ax-wielder on that go-round. "How y'all?"

The reason, of course, was that Christmas customarily comes toward the end of the year, when contracts are generally about to expire. That didn't make it easier for any of us, however.

Kay wasn't canceled because he was laying an egg. He was laying an angel cake. People loved Kay and Ish Kabibble and the whole crew. But in those days, when one sponsor controlled a show, no matter what else was going on, he could wipe you out.

Why kill a winner? There were quite a few reasons, many arbitrary. Sometimes it was as simple as "My wife doesn't like it." That's the truth. Or maybe the sponsor himself got tired of it; or found something he liked better; or something he liked just as well that was cheaper.

Frank O'Connor, now an independent film producer, was then with the advertising agency that handled the Kyser show. He gave us the bad news. "I'm sorry to tell you all," he said, sadly. "I know it's going to cause you all big problems. . . ." Frank never said a truer word. For me they all had to do with caring for a wife and twin baby girls. We'd just started to settle down.

I'd gotten a G.I. loan and built us a little tract house in Burbank (actually built a lot of it myself), not far from where the NBC studios now stand. It hurts me to write that.

I used to buy the gas for my '34 Dodge from a guy named Norman Caleel, who operated a Shell station right across from what is now the front entrance to the NBC studios on Alameda Avenue. He'd talk to me a lot about how he wasn't anxious to spend his life pumping gas. He wanted to make some big money fast. As he'd heard me on radio, I somehow assumed he was thinking of getting into that line of work.

Then one day he told me about a big real estate deal he could swing if I'd come in with him for half the cash needed. He said he could buy the land across from his station for $11,000. All I needed was $5,500. It sounded great! Just one problem. I didn't have, nor could I figure out how to get, $5,500. So I missed my big opportunity to make a killing in real estate.

Not long ago I related this incident to a reporter who was interviewing me out at Burbank. He said, "Mark Twain had the same experience."

I said I didn't know Mark Twain ever was in Burbank.

The Mark Twain allusion concerns a time when Mr. Clemens had become a successful writer and lecturer, and St. Louis had become a bustling city with a busy waterfront along the Mississippi. Commenting on its growth, he said to a friend, "You know when I was a young man, I could have picked up all the land we can see in either direction on both sides of the river for a million dollars. And now, for the life of me, I don't know why I didn't."

People are always looking back and feeling sorry for themselves because, when they were broke, they couldn't afford to buy what would have made them rich.

Now, just so I don't leave my friend Caleel alone there pumping gas—he found a partner. They held the land for a little while and then sold it for $75,000 to Jim Hope Real Estate. Jim Hope has a brother who works at NBC.

Probably Caleel thinks once in a while, "If I'd only held that land a little longer."

One of the stars of Kay's group was a trumpet player named Merwyn Bogue, who handled comedy bits and for whom I played straight man. As the Kollege ding-a-ling he rose through the ranks as Ish Kabibble, the Komedian with a "k," which was about the kind of comedy we did.

The origin of our collaboration was somewhat amusing. Soon after breaking in with Kay, O'Connor, the producer, approached me with a script I didn't bother to look at, figuring all I had to do when I heard Kay mention my name was to walk to the mike and do the number we'd rehearsed. I just sat on my thumbs watching the others run through their lines when I heard O'Connor call, "Hey, Dowd! You're in this bit!"

"I don't read lines," I said. "I'm a singer."

"Read your contract," said O'Connor. At that moment a straight man was born and, automatically, a new comedy team.

So what was more natural for Ish and me (what a name for

an act, "Ish and Me"!) than to cash in on our comedy routine? We took the act on the road.

Almost immediately we discovered that we were no threat to Abbott and Costello. But we played a lot of places they didn't. Little spots, alas, in and around the Chicago area.

To give you an idea: I found an ad in one of my scrapbooks for a dive called Gussie's Kentucky on Ashland Avenue on Chicago's West Side, a break-in club for acts going nowhere. But, at least it was in Chicago and preferable to playing some little outpost between two other little outposts on the outskirts of oblivion. The two-column ad was about three inches deep and topped by a cut with Gussie's Kentucky in reverse type, white letters on black. Below that in small letters was "Tonite and every nite but Monday" . . . then . . .

"ISH KABIBBLE AND MICHAEL DOUGLAS
Kay Kyser's Graduates of Song and Comedy"

Below this on the right half of the ad was a box in which the management said, "WE APOLOGIZE! If you were among the crowds turned away from here last Saturday . . . we apologize. We have a great show, one worth waiting to see, so please come again . . . early!" To the left of the box was a list of the other stars on the bill and, incidentally, their names were in larger type than Ish's and mine. They were: "The Alibis," "Gloria Savitt," "The Castle-Aires" and Jim Olesak, who was the master of ceremonies.

Maybe the reason for the boff b.o. was a piece signed by Charlie Dawn in one of the Chicago papers. (I never seem to have sense enough to put the date and the source on the stuff I clip.) Charlie wrote:

That slick-haired, droll comedian of Kay Kyser's band is in

town for another spell of fun-making. The one and only Ish and his swell-voiced partner and pal Michael Douglas are thrilling night timers at Gussie's Kentucky with their mélange of comedy and music . . . Ish Kabibble (Merwyn Bogue to fellow home-towners of Erie, Pa.) is an expert indeed, in the art of off-hand comedy . . . with a punch.

With Douglas, he unhurriedly talks through the pick of the comedy books which vaulted him to fame with Kyser's organization.

Here's a sample of "the pick of the comedy books" that Ish and I "talked through." (Ish had long bangs cut straight across the top of his eyes.)

Me: How do you get your hair cut like that?

Ish: I freeze it and break it off.

Let me throw in here that Ish had failed to learn the one thing that every performer must know, how to handle rejection, what to do when you know you're bombing. And we did that a lot.

At the Chicago Theater, one of the few good spots we played, matters were worse than usual. And Ish, who hated to perspire, had sweat trickling down from his forehead and dripping off the end of his nose. Suddenly, following the silence that greeted one of our best gags, I heard him saying, "My partner will now entertain you for the next thirty minutes with your favorite songs." And he walked off the stage leaving me standing there, covered with my own flop sweat, and forced to struggle through a few tunes the orchestra and I had never rehearsed.

And what was worse, he had said "my partner," without mentioning my name. But what great training! Enough experiences like that and you fear nothing. Or quit the business.

Dawn's review continues: "Douglas, a Proviso man" (that translates, practically, to local boy), "shows to best voice advantage with his rendition of 'If' and 'Danny Boy.' Then comes the chatter which serves to introduce the many

Douglas song impressions such as those of Frankie Laine, Morton Downey, Tony Martin and The Ink Spots." (I cut out the Ink Spots impression because the house wouldn't pay scale for the other three guys I was imitating.) The review concludes:

> He's a grand singer and a perfect straight man for Kabibble's laugh lines. The song, music and comedy presentation of Ish Kabibble and Michael Douglas are prize winners in anybody's night life.

On the basis of that review, you'd think Ish and I should team up again and give Vegas our best shot. But he now lives in Hawaii, sells real estate and isn't interested in show business. And I never did like the act.

I don't know what became of the others on the bill: The Alibis (what a name for an act!), Gloria Savitt (I hope she changed her name and made it big as Doris Day or Peggy Lee) and the Castle-Aires (who told me they were beat out for a long run at the Roosevelt Grill in New York by Guy Lombardo). But I know all about the emcee, Jim Olesak. He lives in Waukegan, Illinois, and I received the following, undated letter from him. I hadn't the good luck to meet his wife, as I happened to be in Philadelphia when he was in Santa Ana.

Dear Mr. Douglas,

When Kay Kyser was cancelled, you and Ish took to the night club circuit. I was fortunate enough to be the emcee for your appearance at Gussie's Kentucky Club in Chicago.

I did record pantomimes to Homer & Jethro's "Over The Rainbow," Red Ingles and Jo Stafford's "Temptation" and Spike Jones' "Tennessee Waltz."

Matter of fact we saw Spike Jones, Jr., in Chicago last year and he'd never heard a recording of his Dad's "Tennessee Waltz." I was to bring him a copy of my tape but he left Chicago and I lost track of him.

My wife works with me and once or twice a year we work a banquet or Christmas party.

Anyhow, at Gussie's I took your advice, went home, got a job and raised four nice children. But after all these years my wife and I are going to get to go someplace on a vacation.

Never really traveled anywhere. We have a chance to visit some friends in Santa Ana. We are leaving 3/17 and will be there until 3/25.

Except for the ads and your autograph, my children can't believe you are the same Mike Douglas I worked with. It would really peak my trip if somehow I had a chance to introduce my wife to you.

Yours truly,
Jim Olesak, Sr.,
Waukegan, Illinois

To begin with, how do you like a guy like me, in one of the major career valleys of a barely begun career advising another performer what to do? But it shows the way my mind was running and a little later in my career, I almost caught up with it.

But all the dates I played in Chicago were not at spots like Gussie's.

Those familiar with Chicago know The Palmer House and its famous Empire Room. Well, I played that room sometime during the late summer or early fall of 1947 and I have a letter to prove it. Also proof that they paid me less than any other performer they booked.

The letter is from Merriel Abbott, who, along with Al Borde of the Central Booking Office, got five percent of my salary. That's ten percent all together out of a weekly $225.

Merriel wrote:

Dear Mike,

It was such a thrill to hear from you on my 80th birthday. Many, many thanks. In fact, the "celebration" was so great I have decided to go on and try for 90.

I love your show and watch it every afternoon and remember when you worked for me in the Empire Room. Stay successful.

I found my old booking record from 1947 of your engagement in the Empire Room and thought you would enjoy having a copy of it.

My best to you and, again, many thanks.

Most sincerely yours,
Merriel Abbott

The booking record went like this:

EMPIRE ROOM

July 10-October 1, 1947

Freddy Nagel Orchestra $2,350.00
M.C.A.
4 weeks with continuous options
37 hour week.
5% to M.A.—5% to M.C.A.

LIBERACE $900.00
M.C.A.
4 weeks-two 4 week options
1 Room
5% M.A.—5% M.C.A.

GOWER CHAMPION AND MARJORIE BELL $500.00
M.C.A.
2 Rooms
4 weeks-2 four week options
5% to M.A.—5% M.C.A.

MICHAEL DOUGLAS $225.00
Al Borde—Central Booking Office
4 weeks—two four week options
1 room
5% M.A.—5% Central Booking Office

MERRIEL ABBOTT DANCERS $720.00
    ,,   ,,   ,,   70.00
Edith Barstow 100.00

1. Acrobatic Dancer—15 years age
2. Cover girls.

There was a handwritten postscript on this, "Dear Mike, if you'll come back at this salary, I'll book you tomorrow." Liberace would be a good buy at the above price, too.

As you may have guessed, Marjorie Bell later became the "Marge" in "Marge and Gower Champion."

Now let me tell you about a guy named Kay Kyser and how I got to know and love him.

Kay was my godfather. He christened me, and I may be the only one except Kay who really remembers the birthday of Michael Douglas.

I'd been singing with the Kyser band for only a couple of days and was waiting in the wings to do a number when I was surprised to hear Kay announce, "Y'all give a nice welcome, now, to the newest member of our Kollege of Musical Knowledge, and y'ear he is, Michael Douglas."

I looked around to see who'd stolen my job. All I saw was Kay motioning me onstage to do what I was paid to do.

I did.

That was the origin of my stage name. Kay hadn't been too crazy about Michael D. Dowd, Jr. He said the moniker sounded more like that of a supreme court justice than a boy singer. "With a fancy tag like that you gotta sing twice as good as anybody, and if you did that, son, I couldn't afford you."

He didn't mind Michael. He considered that nice and earthy and Irish. But he thought the middle "D" sounded kind of "stuck-up" for his audience. "An' that Junior," he said, "thass gotta go! It sounds like some little kid is comin' on."

Then we went through the phone book for a name to re-place Dowd.

Kay liked names with two syllables. "They kinda give people a little time to listen to them," he said. "One-syllable names shoot through your ears too fast. They begin and end in the same place. They're over too soon. Half your audi-ence is leanin' forward askin' the other half, waddee say?"

I insisted that any name he picked would have to begin with D because Gen's mother had given me a bunch of beau-tiful linen handkerchiefs with the monogram M.D. on them.

"That don't matter," Kay said. "With those initials you can always sell them to some doctor."

Then, without consulting me any further, or bothering to tell me my new identity, Kay rechristened me Michael Douglas right on the air. And he always called me Michael.

Everyone followed suit. Not until I left Kyser for the sec-ond time did I shorten it to Mike, Mike sounding more ma-cho in spite of the fact that it "began and ended in the same place."

Now it's the only way people can tell the difference be-tween that guy in Philadelphia and Kirk Douglas' son Mich-ael, who co-hosted with me and had his dad on as a guest. There were so many Douglases, nobody knew what to call who. I thought of going back to Dowd.

At this point I anticipate someone thinking to herself, "How'd he get with Kay Kyser in the first place?"

A good question.

The minute the Navy turned me loose in Baltimore, I wired Gen I'd be right home. (Remember that?) No sooner had she fixed her hair than I arrived.

With some of my severance pay I bought a jalopy and drove it as if the trip was to be its last. It almost was. But they don't make cars today the way they built those old wrecks. I drove up to the Purnells', where Gen was living, with steam spurting from the car's radiator and from my ears. You never saw such a reunion! Kissing! Hugging!

Guys telling me I could have my old job back at the station and me paying no attention to them.

How were they to know anything about the job Earl Carroll had promised me one night in Hollywood, before the *Carole Lombard* sailed? Of course Gen knew. But she's no blabbermouth. And besides, she didn't believe a word the man said.

So with quiet dignity I finally informed one and all that "my lady" (as Sammy Davis calls his wife) and I were departing in our faithful chariot, which had brought me from Baltimore and was destined to carry us to fame and fortune in California.

"You can't cross the country in that crate," everyone declared in unison, as if they'd all gotten together and rehearsed. But nobody offered me a better crate. And the two essentials you had to have to tackle Hollywood, I'd read, were a car and an agent.

We had the car, the dough left from my severance pay and the naïve confidence that any agent would be glad to represent a man with a job in hand. So off we went. I believed in me, Gen believed in me and this belief led to a lot of disappointment, a lot of time living out of suitcases under roofs not our own.

One of these temporary quarters belonged to a country singer named Al Sloey. I'd met Al while knocking around in the small band business, so I looked him up. He'd come west for the same reason as I and was working at station KNX in Hollywood with a Western group called "Riders of the Purple Sage." He took Gen and me in and was swell to us. He even offered to get me an audition at KNX, which, of course, I turned down because I *had* a job.

I felt I could pick just the agent I wanted, and I wanted one with experience handling singers. So it didn't take much detective work to find out that Everett Crosby, Bing's brother, was an agent and what's more he was Bing's agent. That was good enough for me. So I managed to bull my way in to see Everett. I told him about the offer Earl Carroll had made me before I climbed aboard a load of explosives and sailed for Australia.

Crosby was immediately enthusiastic and assured me that he thought he could get me a job with Earl Carroll.

That's how agents are. Quick. Inventive. Creative.

Being a stranger in town, not up on trade gossip. I didn't know there'd been a small misunderstanding when Earl Carroll had tried to hire Bing.

Everett asked $7,500. Carroll came back with an offer of $2,500. Everett considered this to be an insult and called Mr. C. a few heavy names no agent should ever address to a producer. At that moment, Everett Crosby became persona non grata around the Earl Carroll office.

So when Ev walked in to discuss me with Mr. Carroll, he wasn't accompanied by a choir of angels. To make it better, besides saying to Mr. Carroll, "I've got a young singer you offered to pay $125 if he'd come back and see you when the war ended. . ." Mr. Crosby added, "But the kid's got to get $300 or he won't work." And Ev made his point stick. I didn't work.

The excuse he handed me was this, "Do you think I'd let a talent like you work for $125?"

"That's $125 more than I'm working for right now," I pointed out. But I sure was glad to know he considered me such a great talent. Because he'd never heard me sing. Nevertheless, it made me feel as if there was something about me he liked and I was convinced of this when he patted me on the shoulder and promised, "Don't worry, kid. I'll get you the kind of dough you deserve. I'll call you."

He didn't. So I called him. He was never in. And that's how I lost my first Hollywood job and fired my first agent.

I've often wondered what course my career would have taken if I'd gotten that Earl Carroll job. I'll never know. Things like that interest me. Some time later, broke and out of work, I was strolling along Michigan Boulevard in Chicago and met a man who steered me into the channel that ultimately led to success. What would have happened if I'd chosen to stroll along State Street?

I told Al Sloey about the collapse of the Earl Carroll job and he said not to worry, that we could square up whenever I had the dough. To help raise it, maybe, Al introduced me to some of his friends. Not long after that I landed a gig in a spot called the 52 Club. They paid me $19 (for my $300 talent). Among those who had worked there, it was called the 20-52 Club. $20 was the top money they ever paid. They told you that right at the start. What they didn't tell you was that they never paid anyone that much. They found no one worth that much. It was depressing not even to get the top dollar.

Then Al got me on one of KNX's country shows, singing songs like "Wagon Wheels" and other heavy Western ballads. I worked with Jimmy Wakely and that whole bunch of Western stars. I sang so many Western songs I began to get saddle sores on my tonsils.

One of those country and Western artists dragged me to a party one evening at Judy Canova's house. Was I impressed! Everyone was dressed as if he'd raided Gene Autry's or Roy Roger's wardrobe trunks. But the people, not the clothes, impressed me. As I looked around I said, Michael, you're really getting up in the world.

Years later we took the show down to Nashville, the World's Capital of Country Music, and as I stood on the stage of the New Grand Ole Opry House, I had the same thought. To me it was awe inspiring, like standing in The Baseball Hall of Fame in Cooperstown. The Opry has a definite place in American folk history.

Part of the stage of the beautiful New Grand Ole Opry House was the original stage of the Ryman Auditorium (renamed in 1943 the Grand Ole Opry Theater). There I stood, a talk show host and part-time pop singer from Philadelphia (by way of Oklahoma City, Chicago and Hollywood), on the same floor boards that Hank Williams, Al Dexter, Jimmy Rodgers, Roy Acuff, Minnie Pearl, Ernie Tubbs, Eddy Arnold, Fred Rose—to tick off only some of the greatest names from the rollcall—had scored from to make our country music known and loved all over the world.

We'd gone down to Nashville primarily to do segments about this city and its unique industry, not the steel and rubber produced in, say, Pittsburgh and Akron but something gentler and infinitely more pleasing to the ear—music.

Actually, when I was asked to appear on a Grand Ole Opry show, I agreed reluctantly. I didn't think the audience would take to guys who sing as I do. I soon learned that my fear was unfounded.

A delegation headed by Roy Acuff and Minnie Pearl and a Dixieland Band greeted us at the airport. They presented me with a dulcimer, a symbol of country music.

We did some great shows and had some wonderful times in Nashville. Loretta Lynn, whom I call the Queen of Country Music, sang a duet with Metropolitan Opera star Roberta Peters. The combination of Opry and opera was sensational. Nashville proved that it likes opera as well as Opry when Miss Peters received a standing ovation.

Loretta Lynn, curiously, hadn't thought singing with a Met star would be such a big deal, until, that is, she discovered that the Met star would not be Tom Seaver (now with the Cincinnati Reds).

Their shows are broken down into three one-hour segments, each emceed by a different personality. Hank Snow headed up my segment. Even after I'd okayed the deal and was waiting backstage to be introduced, I said to Hank, "I'm worried about how I'm going to be received."

I peeked out at an audience composed of country music lovers, some from different parts of the globe, making a sort of pilgrimage to this Mecca.

Hank said, in a drawl impossible to capture on paper, "Listen, Mike, those people love you. You're a real person and they know that. They identify with that and they love you. And you're going to experience something you'll never forget."

Hank was right. I did. I walked out on that stage to an ovation I'd like to get when I walk off. So I sang the only song I had ever been identified with, "The Men In My Little Girl's Life." When I finished they stamped their feet and screamed. (I didn't think I was *that* bad.) Well, it turned out they wanted more. I didn't know what to do. I mumbled a few platitudes about how great Nashville is and how proud I was to be there and—since my tears are always very close to the surface and so as not to let them spill over—I sang a pop tune. I can't even remember what it was. And all through it I kept remembering how wonderful the country music folks had been to me when I was trying to make it in Hollywood, when I was a guy who stood bugeyed, picking out all the biggies at Judy Canova's party at a time when Judy was what you might call today the Barbra Streisand of country music, capable of being both funny and vocally sensational. There were Dick Powell and June Allyson, who was then his wife, Mike Mazurki, and Cass Daley, who was never his wife. Bob Burns, who had been second banana on Bing's show, and Martha Paige, who hadn't.

Cass Daley was the first to speak to me.

"Are you in the business?"

"Yeah. I sing."

"Well, go ahead and sing. Let's hear what you've got."

When I'd sung a couple of tunes, a businesslike, stocky man introduced himself. His name was Don Sharpe. "I'm with the Frank Vincent Agency," he said, handing me a list. "These are our clients."

Frank Vincent appeared to have every star I'd ever heard of sewed up and also all those I hadn't heard of, because I didn't recognize many of the names. Not that it mattered.

Being mentioned alongside Cary Grant, Joel McCrea and Edward G. Robinson would be great. I made this roster although the jobs I got were in places like the Bar of Music on Beverly Boulevard in Los Angeles. Not great but I was working and patience was my reward.

Sharpe was talking up a deal with Tommy Dorsey, whom I wanted to work with but not if it meant going on the road. Sharpe also told me they were trying to cook up something at Republic Pictures which specialized in Westerns. And every once in a while he'd drop the name Warner Brothers. It was enough to keep me feeling something was in the works. Many times these feelings pan out.

One evening a guy from M.C.A. came rushing into the club and told me he had a job for me with Kay Kyser.

"But I think I have a job with Tommy Dorsey."

"Forget it! We're talking Kay Kyser . . . the radio!"

"Gee, I've got a wife and twins on the way. I don't want to go on the road with a band," said I.

"No road. They have to stay close to L.A. to do their radio show. You'll be home for dinner every night."

"What about records?" I asked. Look who was playing hard to get.

"Big, big record seller," Sharpe assured me.

To this day, when I'm asked, "What about your records?" all I can do is play them a medley of my *hit*, "The Men in My Little Girl's Life." That was when I still had young daughters and the problem loomed big to me. Maybe my concern was in my voice. Whatever it was, the song did very well. And maybe there was some emotion on the platter, which I say in light of a new recording I have on the charts for the first time in ten years. That's an awfully long drought for a singer.

The title of the number was "Sleep Well, My Son," and it wasn't exactly a song. When a singer gets on the charts for a record in which he hardly sings, maybe they're trying to tell him something. But I'm not listening.

"Sleep Well, My Son" wasn't written by a professional. The composer was a British real estate broker whose only son had drowned. He felt the loss very deeply and sublimated those feelings. A British announcer named Frank Topping had a musical setting made for it and the record did very well in England. We picked it up, Americanizing from the original British. Actually, all we did was change words like "telly" to "TV" and "tram" to "bus."

Here, again, was a case where the lyrics got to me. I don't have a son. But as I was recording I began to think of my father and his pain when my brother died. By the end of the fourth take I was so choked up I walked into the control room and apologized, "Sorry. I'll have to come back tomorrow and get it right." My producer just smiled and said, "Don't bother. You just cut a record. That's it. That's what we want."

Which shows why he's a producer and helps to make a case for those who say performers never know what's good for them. (See the strange case of Henry ("The Fonz") Winkler later in this book.)

It seemed odd to me that "Sleep Well, My Son" was any kind of success in England. They said the reason "The Men In My Little Girl's Life" didn't make it over there was because it was too "syrupy."

Right after "Little Girl's Life" had hit, they brought me a tune called "Old Photographs." I didn't feel any warmth at the time for snapshots. But there was one line in the lyric that caught my attention. It started, "Here's to My Maggie" or someone. I've forgotten the original name. I kept running it over in my mind till I came up with "Here's To My Jenny," which, of course, was a reference to my wife Gen. I suggested this substitution to Manny Kellam, who was trying to sell me the song and, of course, he said, "Great!" What did he care if I changed another man's lyric.

"What about the guy who wrote it?" I asked. "Won't he mind?"

Manny just laughed. "Mind? Forget it! If you'll record it after the hit you just had, you could call it 'Here's to my Laundry' and he'll pull your sleigh down Hollywood Lane in the Santa Claus Lane Parade."

Speaking of Christmas, for the 1977 holiday I recorded a number called "Happy Birthday, Jesus." I liked its message, which gets to the heart of what Christmas is all about. Apparently listeners enjoyed it too, because it was played by hundreds and hundreds of radio stations and made the country-music charts. I'll be doing it as an album for future Christmases. Music meaning as much to me as it does, it's a great kick to know that I have three recording contracts—for different types of material—going for me right now. There has been progress since the days when I was contemplating an association with Kay Kyser.

Other ambitions surfaced during my stint with Kay. After all, I was in Hollywood and that only means one thing all over the world.

"Well," I said—and here's where my head was really at— "what about motion pictures?" Across my mind there flashed a picture of the lighted marquee of the Capitol Theater on Broadway with the following billing: "Michael D. Dowd, Jr., with Kay Kyser's Orchestra in . . ." Before I could see the title, my mind went to black.

"Pictures . . . everything," the guy said.

He had me. "Talk to my manager, Don Sharpe, at the Frank Vincent Agency," I replied.

It turned out they'd already talked to Sharpe and to Kyser, who had listened to a recording of my voice and said, "I want him."

However, when I was told, "I've got you this job with Kay Kyser," that wasn't exactly accurate. Actually, they'd booked me into a tryout on "The Ginny Simms Show."

Ginny had been Kay's vocalist and a big hit with the servicemen. So CBS gave her what would now be called "a spin-off": a show of her own on which she featured as guests returning Army, Navy and Marine Corps personnel. I qualified.

Some of the other veterans on that show were a comedy team named Sweeney and March. The funny thing about them was that Bob Sweeney became a producer and Hal March a director.

Kay Kyser was actually less concerned with getting me than with getting rid of the guy he *had*, who shall go nameless. And the reason a hungry kid looked like a good quick buy was because there were complications connected with the job. When Harry Babbitt went into the service, Kay promised him that whenever he wanted to come back he could have his old job back. Actually, I think there was a law making such action mandatory. Even when Harry chose not to come back but to stay in New York and try to make it on his own, Kay reassured him that if this didn't work out, he always had a place in the Kyser organization. Shows you what kind of a guy Kay is. It also shows you that anyone who took the job that was offered to me had sort of a sword of Damocles hanging over his head.

When hiring people Kay was very fussy. He didn't want anyone who'd cause him headaches. So he asked M.C.A. to check out what kind of a guy I was. Did I drink? Did I gamble? Did I run around with women? At that time they didn't ask girls if they ran around with men.

They told him I was clean on all counts and as a bonus I didn't smoke; plus I had a pretty young wife. Kay said, "Send them out to see me."

Kay was living at that time in Coldwater Canyon in Beverly Hills, in a house he'd bought from Gene Tierney. We drove up in my vintage convertible with the shredded top and side mounts, that I'd bought from a vaudevillian named Britt Wood. The brakes were so bad I not only had to chock the front wheels against the curb; I had to put a rock under the rear wheels to keep the whole heap from taking off for Sunset Boulevard. And the paint job was so bad that if the car had taken off down the hill it would have rolled right out of the paint and left a pile of flakes in front of Kyser's.

When I rang the bell an unshaven man appeared. He seemed to be swimming in his oversized overalls.

"We came to see Kay Kyser," I said.

"Thass me, son. How y'all?"

"I'm Michael Dowd and this is my wife Genevieve."

Kay introduced his wife Georgia Carroll.

We talked a while and again he asked about my habits, which I thought at the time was a funny thing to do in front of a man's wife. I remember he used a word you don't hear very much these days, in fact, you didn't hear it very much in those days. He asked me if I was a "rounder."

Then he played some recordings by other applicants for the job.

One of them was Johnny Johnston, who made a big hit singing "That Old Black Magic" in a picture with, of all people, Bing Crosby. That's making it the hard way.

I also recognized the voice of a singer named Phil Hanna, and there was another I'm almost positive was Buddy Clark. There was no chance in the world of ever making Buddy a romantic personality. But he was sure a singer's singer. He was killed in a plane that crashed trying to make a landing right in the heart of the city of Los Angeles on Rampart Boulevard.

After each singer Kay would make a comment like, "Now that's good but not what I'm looking for." He was telling me something. But I didn't know what. Finally he came back to my record and said to Sharpe, "You know why I'm buying this man? It's because he sings clear." (An interesting use of the word, which is why I remember it.) "He means what he's singing," Kay explained. "The others are all listening to themselves, in love with the sound of their own voices. But this guy sings from the heart."

I've never forgotten that. It was a great lesson to me. And ever since I've taken great care of my heart.

Because I thought some of the singers were a lot better, I

got the idea that Kay might have been looking at me with an eye to the inevitable arrival of television. Not that I'm so pretty, but he said to Sharp, "Who does he look like?"

"He looks a little like Dennis Morgan—very Irish.

"There's two things in this world I can't stand," Kay said, "an Irish tenor and the other is kids on the screen."

I felt the job slipping away and I still don't understand that crack about kids. It was totally irrelevant.

"And another thing," Kay went on, "that name Dowd. It's a bad name for radio. People don't know what a Dowd is, or how to spell it."

I said, "It's interesting to hear you say that, sir, because I got a lot of mail when I was on the Ginny Simms Show and very few of them spelled Dowd correctly."

Kay beamed. "Thass right!" He agreed with himself.

So that's where the name-changing idea began. I said I'd like to use my middle name, Delaney.

"That sounds more Irish than Dowd," Kay said. "I don't want you to sound Irish. And I'll tell you why. I don't want you singing as high as you do. We'll bring you down about a tone and a half." He was right again. He made it so I had a better than two-octave range.

So that's how it happened that I started on radio with "Kay Kyser's Kollege of Musical Knowledge" in 1945, and lost my job on Christmas Day 1947, at a time when we had two records on the charts, Hoagy Carmichael's "Ole Buttermilk Sky" and the Charles Tobias/Nat Simon tune, "The Old Lamplighter."

Then things got really tough.

(XV)
BRIGHT KOLLEGE YEARS, REVISITED

If losing the job with Kay seemed like the end of the world, rejoining him two years later seemed like the resurrection. The twins had joined us, television was coming on as rapidly as my career was skidding into oblivion. I picked up guest shots on local TV shows for $75 or whatever the producers had left over from lunch.

I also emceed club dates, bar mitzvahs, weddings, wakes, stags, smokers, market openings and in between these great dates I sang at the Bar of Music on a regular-irregular basis.

There, at least, both the steady customers and the management liked me. I guess it follows that if the customers like you the management will. Anyway, they had a sign they put out in front every time they booked me. It said, "Special Gala Engagement." Michael Douglas Back for One Week. I never knew if it was a come-on for the patrons or a warning to me.

One evening Carl Hoff, one of the arrangers responsible for the charts for Kay Kyser's radio show, wandered in while I was on, took a seat at the bar and motioned me to join him when the set was over.

189

When I did he said, "The old man's going back to New York to do television." At that time the center of all important TV activity was New York. The West Coast saw nothing but fuzzy kinescopes and produced nothing of any importance. The coaxial cable, followed by the microwave relay, were yet to come.

Having dropped his one shoe, Carl went into a rambling thing about how the networks wanted Kay to do a simulcast, which was someone's idea of how to go on TV and still hang onto the radio audience. "The Old Professor wouldn't go for that sort of thing," Carl continued. "He knows you play differently for each medium. He just wants to stick to TV and get it right."

"Sure, sure," I threw in. I wanted to ask, "Why are you telling me all this?" but I'd learned to be a pretty good listener, a lesson I now use to good advantage on our show.

Then a light began to dawn as Carl switched to, "You know on this television thing you not only have to sing good, you have to look good. It's not that Harry's old. Hell! Kay's no kid, either. In fact the whole outfit must be pushing forty. So they need someone in there who not only sings young but *is* young."

It looked like a good spot to say the wrong thing so I held my tongue. There was a nice, long stage wait while Carl decided how to continue. Finally, he said, "Of course, right now this television doesn't pay much."

It was time for my next medley. I don't know how I stumbled through them. Television represented to *every* out-of-work performer the promised land. To those working in radio it seemed a threat, as Carl had indicated it was to Harry Babbitt. I stumbled through a few choruses and rejoined Carl. His first words were, "Kay wondered if you'd be interested."

"Television can't pay much less than I'm making now," I said. "And I'd rather be singing where I think I'm being heard, somewhere other than in a spot where I could be mired for life."

"We're talking about a hundred per week," Carl said and sort of mentally stepped back to protect himself.

"I'm doing better than that here."

"But the hundred's just for one show, just a few songs, a week."

"But a hundred a week in New York . . . you can hardly make it with a wife and kids."

"Lemme get back to you." Carl finished his beer, rose and split.

A couple of days later he dropped in and told me he'd really put the arm on the old man. "I told him a guy can't stay alive in New York with a wife and two little kids for less than two hundred," Carl reported.

Kay must have bought that argument because I got the job. But then the whole budget was only $39,000 and most of that was spent on making mistakes. I remember wondering why $39,000, why not a nice round $40,000? It seemed so much neater. Especially when it's not yours.

Quite a few years later, we were taping for "The Mike Douglas Show" in Bob Hope's Hollywood home, and while we were sitting around in his "pool parlor" waiting for the crew to get set up and place the lights so they'd make us look good, Bob was talking about his early days in TV. When I told him Kay's budget he said, "I only got $40,000 for the first TV hour I ever did." He didn't say what he gets now.

So Gen and the twins, Michele and Christine, and Mike closed their home in the San Fernando Valley, put it up for rent and headed for Manhattan, which Larry Hart called "an isle of joy" long before John V. Lindsay christened it "Fun City."

We found ourselves a little house nestled among the other little houses out on Long Island. I got a commutation ticket on the Long Island Railroad and became one of the types who knew just how late you could be and still catch the 9:18 for Penn Station. Though we did only one show a week, I ran for the train every morning because we rehearsed daily, and when we weren't rehearsing I made the rounds of the advertising agencies looking for commercial work singing a jingle or whatever was hot that week.

One agency man told me I didn't get the job because I was not six feet. So I bought myself a pair of very fashionable Adler Elevator Shoes. They made me look taller but I had trouble walking in them. Nevertheless, the next audition I walked into, tall and proud. After it was over the advertising V.P. in charge took me aside and told me my voice was great, that I almost had the job. But I didn't know how to move. He advised dancing lessons. So little by little I learned that in show biz, as in everything else, every action brings a reaction.

I learned a lot about that from Kay, too. I loved to watch him work in front of an audience. He knew how to get 'em, to hold 'em and when he felt he was losing 'em, to bring 'em back. That's a lot of know-how. It's what Milton Berle has, what Jack Benny was the master of.

There came a time, as there always did, when somebody at M.C.A. goofed and booked Kay for a series of one-nighters. Kay was sore but it meant a big break for me. He'd told me he never did one-nighters so he didn't mind putting in my contract a clause that said I'd get $100 extra for every one-nighter the band played. I was delighted. Two weeks of one-nighters meant $1,400 extra. It was more money than I'd accumulated since my release from the Navy and no one could have needed it more.

But I didn't see a cent of it until we got home. Kay didn't trust us. He didn't believe in giving people a chance to get into trouble. So you got your bread in one big loaf at tour's end.

One of the stops on that two-week excursion was a big, classy private club in Houston, Texas. And let me throw in here that nine times out of ten you're in trouble when you play for a thoroughly homogeneous audience like a club or

a ball team, any group in which the members all tend to
know each other. No one wants to be caught laughing or enjoying himself if all the rest aren't. They don't want to be
caught crying if everybody else isn't blowing his nose. So
much for a little inside show biz info.

Members of this club were on familiar terms, and they
were all well-oiled. They also all owned oil wells. In short,
they had enough money to feel they had license to be as
rude as they wanted to be.

The man who paid for our band was named Rice or Reese
or Rose or something, and he was so loaded he toyed with
the idea of buying Fort Knox and turning it into a playroom.
To further complicate matters, most of the members had
never heard of Kay Kyser. The chairman of the entertainment committee had given instructions to get the most popular band in the country to play for their dance and M.C.A.
sent us.

What's more, so this big important band wouldn't tire itself out, there was a local relief band that everyone knew
and liked. So they did most of the playing. We just got to
come on when it was show time. But it didn't get to be show
time until we got into overtime. No problem. Our mark just
bought two hours more. Everybody in the Kyser outfit wanted to have him bronzed and sent home to put on the mantel.

And when I found out that all our expenses at the hotel
had been paid I was kind of mad. I hadn't sent my clothes
out to be cleaned.

To me the most memorable part of that whole junket was
the way Kay handled that smashed bunch of oil men. He
was real klassy.

He walked out on the floor and got no more attention than
an empty music stand. The brothers were all chattering
away as if they hadn't seen each other in weeks. The general
attitude was, "Why do we have to listen to that guy? Who is
he?"

Kay didn't say a word, didn't make a move. He just stood

there—looking, the way a teacher stands and looks when she's caught a kid reading the answers to the next exam. Slowly it began to work. Little by little, the babble diminished until there was what Richard Haydn—Professor Carp of vaudeville—used to describe as "a deadly 'ush."

Then, and not until then, did Kay greet them with his famous "Evenin' folks, how y'all?" There was a burst of wild applause. Kay's familiar Southern accent got 'em. Then when he introduced himself with, "I'm the Ole Professor, Kay Kyser," bedlam broke loose. They'd discovered that standing up there was a "good old boy." They had also been made to understand that he was no one to be fooled with. He'd commanded their attention. I filed that whole scene away in the computer I carry on top of my neck for use should I ever face a similar situation.

On another occasion in Houston the famous announcer Del Sharbutt, the Texan, who used to make Campbell's Soups sound so good on radio's Club 15 show with Bob Crosby, showed me a song he'd written. We were both working at CBS in Hollywood. Del wanted me to sing the tune and if I'd had any control at all over what I sang at the time, and knew what I later found out, I certainly would have. The title of the tune was "Never Ask A Man If He's From Texas, 'Cause If He Is He'll Tell You Right Away."

Del had another one on the same subject. This one was about a riot in which a couple of hundred people were beating up on each other. Someone called the Ranger Station and one came right over. "How come they only sent one Ranger?" someone asked. The Ranger looked around and said, "You only got one riot, ain't ya?"

So much for joke time, except for a little typically Texan-type practical joke I heard about during this particular date. At the regular Saturday night country club dance, one of the members hired a group of men to drive the Cadillacs off to a quick paint shop and have them repainted another color. Expensive? Sure. But what else do you do with your money? And imagine what fun it was, a bunch of loaded Texans all looking for their Cadillacs.

Now to get back to my problem in Texas. I'd been aware that the two acts I'd introduced hadn't gotten a lot of attention. Actually, the audience seemed unaware that the show had started.

So when I came on I did the same thing I'd seen old Kay do. I just stood there and outstared them. It took a lot of very intensive staring, and I don't mind telling you it's scary. Pretty soon the chatter began to dwindle down to whispers, "What's he doin' out there?" "Who is he?"

Finally I had 'em. "Ladies and gentlemen," I said, "I want you to welcome and listen to a fine young singer, a Navy veteran of World War II" (we were already in Korea). "A man who was highly decorated, whose acts of bravery and heroism include rescuing forty survivors of a British Freighter torpedoed in the China Sea . . . and here he is now . . . Michael Douglas."

I rushed off, paused, and walked right back on, slowly, sort of like Jack Benny would have. It worked.

In my own defense I have to add that I wasn't lying when I said I'd been decorated. I had the good conduct medal, which every G.I. gets for showing up and staying out of the brig and I had all those theater of operation ribbons that make an officer's tunic full of fruit salad look like an interior decorator's dream.

When you're a radio man on a Navy cargo ship in wartime you get into every theater but those belonging to the Shuberts.

As I have said, we were living on Long Island. The Christmas season was upon us. It was heartwarming to see all the daddies climbing aboard the commuter trains for home with their arms full of Christmas gifts. But I was not one of them.

Gen had wrapped up her Christmas buying back in July

and August, a habit born of the fact that things were less expensive then. Christmas had never been the best time of the year for us. It seemed to be the time when something was always going wrong with my constantly staggering career.

So here we are in the middle of the Yuletide Season of 1950.

I'm sitting next to Kay in the Nola Studios in New York during a rehearsal for the Kay Kyser show. He preferred that I sit next to him because he liked the things I said. Or maybe because I admired him so much, I always tried to sit next to *him* and hear what *he* said. I could never understand all the people who took his dough and put him down—the way people put down Lawrence Welk—by saying he doesn't know music or is, in general, just dumb. Maybe. But both of those two guys got to be millionaires, like another fella everybody was putting down when he was getting started, a bongo player named Desi Arnaz. What technical knowledge Kay might have lacked about music, he compensated for with his uncanny awareness of what the people wanted. The same goes for Welk.

Hip musicians would say, "Kay doesn't know an upbeat from a downbeat." But I've seen Kay walk in at the completion of a recording session and everyone was packing up to go home. "Hold it a second y'all," he'd say. "Jus' lemme hear the playback of that tune." That's what he did when we recorded Hoagy Carmichael's "Ole Buttermilk Sky." We had done it in a kind of slow, sentimental tempo, the way all the other bands had recorded it. Kay made us do the whole thing over again, upbeat. And we came up with the No. 1 record in the country.

Recently, Gen was making one of her infrequent appearances along with Kelly, Michele, Kristine, my four grandchildren and my son-in-law. I introduced the song that was my first hit recording with the Kay Kyser band and went right into the number. I had only sung about four bars when Kay came rushing onstage shouting, "Stop! Stop! That ain't how you're supposed to do that. Do it just like we did it on the record."

So I gave our orchestra leader, Joe Massimino, the tempo of the old recording, and we started again. That satisfied Kay. And you know, hearing both tempos right after the other like that made me realize how right Kay had been.

His presence on the show really surprised me. The staff had arranged for him to come down from Boston to help us celebrate. And it came as a jolt when he interrupted me. This was the first time we'd been face to face in many years although we talked on the phone a lot. Whenever I needed some sound advice I'd call Kay.

He would advise me on everything when I was working for him; how to dress, how to smile when I sang a certain passage, how to stand, how to work and above all how to be sure to try to get it right. The best advice he gave me, I now pass on to one and all—"Save your money."

Then when he was finished telling me how to dress, I'd fix his collar and straighten his tie for him.

No. That's not true. That's just the kind of cheap joke you sometimes can't resist throwing in when you're in front of an audience. You hate yourself for it the minute it escapes your mouth.

But mine lacks the acerbity that made Don Rickles a star. And he wouldn't know how to hate himself. According to Bob Hope, it took Rickles just one sharp, quick line that got around very fast, to advance him in the Las Vegas pecking order from lounge to main show room.

Here's how Bob said it happened. He walked in to watch the rehearsal of a Dean Martin show. Rickles was a guest. The moment Don saw Bob, he jumped up and called, "Hold it everybody! Thank God the war is over! There's Hope!"

But back to the Nola rehearsal hall. I was glancing through Kay's *Variety* when an item jumped off the page and hit me in the eye. "Look," I said excitedly, as I pointed with one hand and clutched Kay's arm with the other, "Look! Here are the top ten TV shows and we're number five, ahead of 'Your Show of Shows.'" That was the Max Liebman blockbuster starring Sid Caesar, Imogene Coca and Carl Reiner. And it's still talked about 25 years later.

I would have read off some of the other shows we were ahead of, when a jerk with about as much class as a 35-cent blue plate cut in with, "I can tell where you'll be next month." As he said that he dropped a telegram on an open manila folder on Kay's lap. The wire said that Ford, the sponsor, had dropped us.

"The Kay Kyser Kollege of Musical Knowledge" had klosed for me for the second time and forever for everyone else.

But, as I've indicated, I keep in touch with Kay the same way some professional people like to keep in touch with a professor they admired while in college, one they felt had given them something substantial to remember, keep and live by.

Kay now has a home in Chapel Hill, North Carolina, and holds a very high position with the Christian Science Church in Boston. And that's what I call living a long way from the office.

(XVI)
THE YO-YO YEARS

When the Kay Kyser TV show flamed out, Kay hit the road for his home in North Carolina, and Gen and I headed for ours in California. Thus began our yo-yo years.

We went back and forth across the country like a couple of badminton birds. There are still ruts that we left in the highway between New York and Chicago, Chicago and Oklahoma City, Oklahoma City and Los Angeles, Los Angeles and Chicago. And vice versa.

Having had a reasonable participation in an eminently successful TV show—although not so heavy in the profits therefrom—we nevertheless had some reassuring walking-around money in our jeans. And when anyone asked what we planned to do, we just smiled enigmatically and headed for Hollywood, where it looked as if everything was going to be at, in TV, in the coming years. But on this point, opinion was divided.

New Yorkers saw their home town as television's capital of the future. Remember TV was still pretty young. Chicago was coming on big with their brand of television ("Garro-

way at Large" was so big NBC brought him to New York),
while in Hollywood the motion picture corporations that
owned the town misread the handwriting on the wall, failed
to see TV as their future salvation and fought it with all
their hearts, which is why they lost their fight—no hearts.

We headed our kids and our new Ford toward the sunset.
Our plan? To settle ourselves in a really nice place —say,
San Fernando Valley with space enough for the kids to play
and room enough for us to entertain in a manner indicative
of our new status in show business. I pictured all the Hollywood biggies lolling around our pool and me signing deals,
giving out interviews. In short, I dreamed up a glowing future in films for us.

There are three ways to drive from New York to Los Angeles, the northern way, the southern way and the fast way.
We took the last route, right through Chicago, so my folks
could see the twins. Even with that short layover, it didn't
take us long. I'm a compulsive driver.

Behind the wheel of our chartreuse-and-black Crestlin-
er—Ford Dealers had been our sponsors—I became the inspiration for all those little boys who later turned out to be
named Unser and Foyt . . . or Starsky and Hutch.

When I get going on a cross-country drive I hate to stop. I
can't sleep in motels. They look so much alike that when I
open my eyes in the morning I have no idea where I am. I
don't like feeling disoriented. So with only a few pit stops
to gas up the car and empty out the kids, we zipped across
New Jersey, Pennsylvania, Ohio and Indiana like gangsters
on the lam or the family version of Bonnie and Clyde.

The madcap pace must have been tough on Gen, but she
just smiled sweetly and dug her nails into her palms and
prayed that the scenery wouldn't zip by so fast. The kids
didn't seem to mind the trip—or any trip—at all. They were
great sleepers. We discovered early in their lives that if they
wouldn't hit the road to dreamland in their beds all we had
to do was put them in the car and drive slowly around the

block. By the time we got back to the house they were sound asleep. So on a long trip, as soon as we got going, Zap! They were out. And when we hit my folks' place in Oak Park, Zap! I was out.

To Mom and Dad our arrival was kind of a mixed blessing. They loved seeing us and their grandchildren, but in their heart of hearts they couldn't have been too thrilled at having a party of four crash in their limited quarters. Yet, in spite of our protestations of affluence and stories about our plans to hit the jackpot in Hollywood, they insisted that we be their guests. This put a heavy burden on their living space, also on their bathroom. So we made our imposition brief and then blasted off for Oklahoma City, a detour, to give Gen's parents the same kind of problems we gave mine. That's just fair play.

But I grew restless after only a few days in Oklahoma City, my fantasies of sudden stardom becoming more and more elaborate and nearer to realization.

Again we hit the road and made it to Los Angeles with only a brief pause for washing and sleeping in Gallup, New Mexico, where there isn't much else to do.

I immediately put my plan into action. We sold our house in Burbank and acquired a more pretentious one in Encino, the area where, for instance, Don Ameche lived, on an estate built by Al Jolson. I figured if he could make it from radio to pictures, why couldn't I?

Once we got the new house in shape we began entertaining. Lots of parties. Lots of new friends. Lots of promises. No jobs.

There were many street encounters with acquaintances who'd say, "Hey, Mike! Long time no see. When'd you get in town? What ya doing?"

At first I'd lie a little about the deals I had cooking, which was good for my ego but didn't do anything for my bank account nor my social standing. The conversation would end with, "Well, we gotta get together, Mike. I'll call you."

Then, as people continued to ask what I was doing, I began to respond with the truth, that I was looking for a job. They'd ask who my agent was and when I told them, it always turned out to be the wrong one.

I tried so many agents it began to look as if I'd have to hire an agent to find me an agent. And my new friends slowly drifted away, because in Hollywood nobody wants to be seen with someone who's out of work. Things went from bad to worse. The New York money was running low, and pretty soon I was singing in the same "old familiar places" that Kay Kyser had pulled me out of. And the Bar of Music pulled out their old sign "Michael Douglas Back for One Week Special Gala Engagement."

The sign was honest. Any job I got was gala. And the one week began to run into two, three, four. I didn't see this as progress.

What was worse, I was only picking up about one-third what I could get for small-time gigs in New York or Chicago. Of course, I didn't have to keep going back to the Bar of Music. I could have played La Ronde or the Black Bull or Joe Kirkwood's Bowling Alley, just to name three, but why? They didn't pay any more than the Bar of Music and the Bar of Music had that nice sign. So it became my permanent job when I was out of a job.

I got to do some voice-overs and jingles for commercials like Folger's coffee—long before Mrs. Olsen showed up—and for Exxon and Dash dog food. But none of them took off and bathed me in residuals the way I'd planned. I don't know why but I'd show up to audition and it was always Harry von Zell who got the job.

At one audition the agency producer told me I wasn't right because he was looking for a knight in shining armor. I told him I'd have worn mine but it was out at the cleaners being rust-proofed for the rainy season. I never heard from him again. This was before I heard the wise advice, "When applying for a job, if you think of something funny to say, bite your tongue." In the long run, however, I figure losing one commercial is better than losing one tongue.

Myron Cohen tells a story about a lady who came home from one of the lesser hostelries in "the Mountains," a local New York City name for resorts in the Catskills. The lady complained about the accommodations she'd had. "They were terrible. And the food," she said, "was like poison! And such small portions!"

I saw myself in the same position. Club dates were few and far between. And such short money.

Angelenos used to boast to Easterners about their weather. No sweltering summer nights. The big cliché was, "No matter how hot it gets during the day, it's cool at night."

Wilson Mizner, one of America's wits, who was in Hollywood to write a screenplay, rephrased it, "No matter how hot it gets during the day, there's nothing to do at night." L.A. has never been a late night town. Picture people, having to get up early, fall into the habit of going to bed early, exhausted. When they're not working they leave town.

I tried to figure out a way to substitute employment promises for payments on our new and more impressive house. But I couldn't even get promises.

Gen and I held a conference. We faced facts. The main one was, our plan wasn't working. Television in Hollywood was still in the nickel-and-dime stage. Good performers were getting paid off in cases of ginger ale.

Finally we decided to head back for Oklahoma City and pick up my television career, there, just as if I had learned nothing in the Kollege of Musical Knowledge.

So on a limited budget and in the Cadillac I'd gotten for the Crestline—plus a few bob—we headed east. That's a laugh. East to Oklahoma City.

At first things were great. We lived with Gen's folks until we could find our own place, and WKY-TV gave me my own show with complete control and a salary of $250 a week, awfully short money compared to what I could make in Hollywood. But compared to what I actually *did* make there, it was pretty good.

But "complete control" of my own show, I found, meant that I had to do everything but run the cameras. I had to sell advertising and sometimes write it. And I had to handle the booking of whatever guests I could find in town. The real biggies seldom happened to be in Oklahoma City. I did a man-in-the-street interview (what they now call a person-in-the-street interview). And in whatever time there was left over, I sang.

The good part was that I could sing what I pleased. I was the producer. I had complete control. So I sang the songs I liked. Unfortunately, as I should have known, I was in a part of the country where my musical taste was not widely shared. Nor did the tunes generally form the perfect lead-ins to the type of commercials that I did, for local butchers, hardware stores, druggists and discount houses.

I'd be singing a ballad that I hoped would put my Sooner listeners in a romantic mood, and the station's only announcer would come on like Howard Cosell with some strong language in favor of an Electrowave Garbage Disposal. It took me too long to realize that the tunes to sing in Oklahoma City, at that time, were cowboy songs, although there were very few cowboys around and the ones there were rode "the range," as Johnny Mercer wrote, "in a Ford V-8."

Which reminds me, when we did our remote down in Savannah, of which I've written, Mercer told me that he thought it was unforgivable that the Ford Motor Company never even wrote a letter to thank him for that plug in his hit song "I'm An Old Cow Hand." Kind, thoughtful and considerate himself, Johnny couldn't understand how even a large corporation could be otherwise.

Henry Mancini, one of our finest popular composers, who worked a lot with Johnny, said that he thinks Mercer's lyrics will be studied for years—or they should be—by aspiring young lyricists. "He had an unorthodox technique often approaching an idea obliquely before hitting it right on the nose. What's more, he never felt that what he wrote was above revision, nor that his first, second or third version of the same idea was necessarily carved in stone."

Neither Gen nor I had to have a house fall on our heads to make us realize that while it was all very comfortable in Oklahoma City, I wasn't laying down any stepping-stones to immortality with what I was doing there. Finally I said, "Let's go to Chicago. It's my home town. I've always been able to find work there, and I think the TV business offers more opportunities there." Who could argue with that? Every business, except oil, offered more chances in Chi than in Oklahoma City.

So we headed north and found a nice town house out in River Forest, from which I fared forth every morning to hunt for work.

On one of these safaris I was walking along Michigan Boulevard and met up with an old friend, Ernie Simon, whom I knew from the days when I hung around WGN hoping for employment.

We had one of those big reunions, and he asked me what I was doing in town. I gave him an evasive Hollywood answer. I said I was on my way to Cleveland. It could have been true because at that time you couldn't get to Cleveland from anywhere in the West without changing trains in Chicago. And it also could have been because I was mulling over a phone call I'd had only the day before from an M.C.A. agent named De Arv Barton. He was suggesting that I come to Cleveland. He talked about a hundred thousand bucks a year and being a big fish in a small pond. He said he knew I could make it there and that he could sell me. They'd heard me sing and they were interested.

But I'd just left Oklahoma City, and Cleveland wasn't

where my head was. It didn't seem to fit into my scheme of things. When Ernie heard me say I was going there, he said just what I wanted somebody to say. "What are you going to find in Cleveland that we haven't got better here in Chicago?" That was all I needed to hear. There didn't seem to be any more argument except that someone in Cleveland wanted me and no one in Chicago seemed to give a damn. But that wasn't true. Ernie wanted me.

"I'm starting a new show," he said, "and I'm looking for a guy who can be funny and sing. So why go to Cleveland?" It was the best news I'd had in months.

It made me think I'd been running around too much looking for success instead of sticking in one place until I won it. A guy who isn't working has a tendency to play golf a lot. And a guy who's working at something he's not crazy about, plays hookey.

A couple of years before, Paul Frumkin at WGN—he later became Irv Kupcinet's producer—told me I didn't work hard enough. What he said was, "Forget golf! Spend more time and energy on your career. You should be talking as well as singing, hosting a show. Remember this, if you haven't made it by the time you're 35, you never will."

I made it at 36, Paul.

I got in touch with Ernie and the next thing I knew I was auditioning for a script show with one of the twins. I don't know whether she was the one who'd been under contract to MGM and didn't make it or the one who wasn't under contract to MGM and didn't make it. But it was clear why she didn't make it. She read like a backward third-grader trying to cope with James Joyce.

We were stumbling along through a script when a man whose name, I found out later, was Frank Schreiber showed up in the control room. It turned out he was the manager of the station and he asked, "What's going on here?"

They told him it was an audition "for the chick" and he

said, "I'm not interested in her. Who's the guy? Hire him. I like him."

The next thing I knew I was on Ernie's show as a sort of road company Hugh Downs. I sat next to Ern and tried to throw in stuff while he was shuffling papers getting his ad libs together. He used to cut out stuff that interested him and save the clippings for when he needed them. Scraps blanketed his desk. When he couldn't locate the item he wanted, he'd whisper to me out of the side of his mouth, "You're on." Then he'd tell the audience, "Now Mike's gonna sing for you." And that's what I'd do. If he hadn't found what he wanted by the time the song was over, he'd say, "Encore, Mike." And I'd do another tune.

Of course, as soon as I had a job I began to hear from agents who wanted to sign me. Getting an agent is like borrowing money from a bank, a *Catch-22* deal. They won't lend it to you unless you have some money as security and if you have that, why do you need the loan?

For a while I was with an agent named Fred Williamson, who handled Dave Garroway. Then I found out he was too busy with Dave to have time for Mike. Another one of my temporary agents was a fella named Al Borde, who at that time was handling another piece of upcoming Chicago talent by the name of Shecky Greene.

Poor Shecky! Everything was going great for him till 1976. What a Bicentential Year he had! First he had a serious operation on his throat that placed his show business career in jeopardy. That shook him. He gave up drinking and that helped settle him down. Next his and my dear friend Totie Fields had to have her leg amputated. That shook Shecky again. Then he went on a talk show to discuss the dangers of alcoholism from the depth of his personal experience and got canceled by another program because they considered a confessed alcoholic inappropriate for their show.

Finally, to add injury to insult, on the first day he was scheduled to co-host with me in Philadelphia, he's standing in a doorway watching the run-through, with his hand in the wrong place. A country singer, a girl—I'm not mentioning her name because she felt so terrible about the accident—came through the heavy studio door and, for no reason, pushed it closed. It slammed so hard on Shecky's little finger that the tip was nearly sheared off.

Fortunately, Philadelphia's Thomas Jefferson University Hospital has one of the greatest orthopedic surgery departments in the country. Greene and the tip of his finger were rushed right into Emergency. They did such a marvelous job that Shecky can now lift his teacup with either hand, sticking out his pinky in the classic manner.

But a Shecky never forgets. As soon as his finger had healed, he came back to fulfill the co-host obligation. To cheer me up and make an entrance on the show, he arrived at the studio in an ambulance. As he got out he said, "The way things are going for me this is how I travel." He made his first appearance on stage wearing boxing gloves. "Until you take all those doors out of this joint," he said, "I'm wearing these."

That Shecky returned to make up the co-host date was a surprise and thrill to me. I personally would never have wanted to see me and my man-eating TV studio again.

Shecky is one of the few people who, during the entire sixteen years of our show, messed us up but came back to fulfill his professional obligation. A couple of others are Johnny Cash and Roger Miller.

Johnny was so spaced out the first time he was scheduled to appear with us in Cleveland that he didn't even know where he was. But, I figured, these things happen and I forgot all about it.

Sometime later I was doing a guest appearance at CBS on "The Carol Burnett Show" when I got a call from Johnny's wife. She asked if it would be all right for Johnny to visit me. I told her I'd be honored. When he arrived he said, "Mike, I owe you a show. When do you need it?" We arranged a date. But he didn't come alone. He brought his entire outfit.

It seems to me I was on the subject of agents when I got sidetracked to Shecky and missed shows. What I was really heading for was an S.O.B. agent in Chicago who used to get me club dates for union affairs and similar bookings at a hundred clams a night. Only I never saw the hundred. The agent took his commission out first and gave me his check for $90.

Then a wonderful thing happened. After I'd finished one of his gigs for the Electrical Workers union in Cicero, the head of the union came over to thank me and handed me my check. It was the first check I'd seen. And it was very interesting. I thought there was some mistake.

It was made out for $300. To show you the gall of this agent, even after he saw I was holding a $300 check for a job he told me paid only $100, he came and asked for his commission. So I gave him his ten percent of what he said they were paying me which was $10 and fired him.

I didn't like the kind of places he booked me into, anyway. That Cicero gig wasn't bad. But there was another spot in Cicero that I didn't like at all.

It was full of those characters in black suits that seemed sprayed on. And they all shared the same deformity—a big bulge under the left arm. It was here one time that I finished my act and said good night and a guy at a ringside table said, "Keep singin', kid."

I started to explain that I'd done all that I was paid for. The guy just reached inside his smooth black jacket and said, the way he thought Eddie Robinson would say it as Little Caesar, "Keep singin', kid." I kept singing. There's a fair chance I'd still be singing there if a man hadn't come in, whispered something to my fan with the artillery, and with nothing more than a nod of his head he moved out, followed by the entire audience.

There's a story known to every ex-alcoholic. In one version the drunk's wife is driving him home from a party and they pass a distillery. All the lights are blazing, steam is pouring from the stacks and she says, "See over there, you jerk, they can make it faster than you can drink it."

"I know," her husband came back. "But I got 'em working nights."

That was Ernie Simon's problem. He had 'em working nights.

So I got a show called "Hi Ladies"—and things went great. It was my first experience at being what Paul Frumkin told me I should be, a personality. Things got better and better until they got worse. WGN changed its policy. All of a sudden it was good-bye ladies for "Hi Ladies."

Also good-bye Douglas. But it turned out that there was a man named Herbuveaux, Jules Herbuveaux, at the NBC station in Chicago, WMAQ, who had been watching me. So when WGN switched from live TV to reruns of reruns of B-films and situation comedies, he brought me over to WMAQ where they tried me out as a singer on all kinds of shows, which, one after the other, failed to loop the loop! Finally George Heinemann, who is now a big wheel with the NBC network, sent down the word, "This guy's never going to make it."

But Jules Herbuveaux persuaded him to give me one more chance, and I got to be the designated singer on a new show called "Club 60," which was scheduled for an afternoon slot and in color. Everyone at the station was looking right past me to find a host for this housewives' matinee.

Don heard me fooling around on the "Club 60" set and decided that I'd make him a good straight man. And so I did. But not for long.

One morning, after signing a firm six-month contract at

$2,600 a week, Sherwood stared out of his hotel window down at the dirty snow on Michigan Boulevard and decided that the freezing Windy City was not where he wanted to be. He dressed, checked out, took a cab to the airport and flew back to California.

What NBC did about him I don't know, but they kept me on "Club 60" as co-host, first with Dennis James and then with Howard Miller. Nancy Wright was the girl singer, and the group—that was the standard cast for that type of show—was the Mellowlarks. The orchestra was under the direction of Joe Gallichio. I wonder why I go for Italian orchestra leaders with very difficult names to spell? But always Joe. Right now it's Joe Massimino.

Actually NBC needed me and shows like "Club 60" like an extra thumb. But the networks had signed a contract with James Petrillo, at that time czar of the musician's union, stipulating that every owned and operated network station had to have a full 40-piece orchestra on staff.

That's show biz. If you have to pay 23 musicians every week, you'd better find something for them to do. One of the deals they came up with was something called "Adults Only." I think Tom Mercein was the emcee and I sang the songs. The title was meant to suggest that here was a daytime show not in the soaper category and not for the kiddies.

Think what that title would mean today, with porno houses in some of the best neighborhoods in our better cities advertising "adult entertainment." The hypocrisy of *that* is that the kids today are so deeply into sex that they know more about it than most adults. So I had "Adults Only" and the old standby "Club 60." Not great! But for me they were very important milestones on the road to Philadelphia.

On those two shows I made the acquaintance of a kid named Woody Fraser. He was just out of Dartmouth and filled to the ears with ski wax. In no time he advanced from floor manager to TD to director. As I write this, he's executive producer of ABC's "Good Morning, America." He looks like a precocious baby. Has ever since I've known him. He had the enthusiasm of a hyperkinetic puppy and a towering ambition that carried him to the top of his trade.

Woody and I used to sit over his coffee and my tea, and he'd tell me about this great new kind of show he had in mind. I listened because I like to do that. That's how I learn.

But, serious as Woody was, he couldn't get anyone to work up any enthusiasm for what he was selling then.

I lacked enthusiasm for almost everything about that time. Things weren't shaping up big enough for me. I remembered, "If you don't make it by the time you're 35, you'll never make it." That worried me. I wasn't getting any younger. So finally I pulled myself together, after a little pep talk from Dad. He had a great line, "If you're ever going to become a big leaguer, you've got to play where the big leaguers play."

That spot, I knew, was not Chicago. It was Hollywood, and although I'd struck out there before, after discussing it with Gen, we decided to give it another go.

It took courage.

I don't mean it took courage to make that decision. What you have to keep in mind is that every one of those junkets that we made from New York to Chicago, from Chicago to Oklahoma City, to Hollywood and back to Chicago and back to New York and all that—all those trips were made by car, with very young kids. Now that takes courage! Anyone who's ever made a long motor trip with children can testify to that.

There's a fortune waiting for the person who works out some sort of a rhythm system for kids, some way to synchronize their little insides so that they'll both have to go to the toilet at the same time.

Where to eat is another problem. The good places are always on the wrong side of the road and it's considered cowardly to turn around. You keep looking for a spot on the right side. And it has to be one that looks clean, is not too expensive and seems to be the kind of place that won't mind youngsters. It's a game nobody has ever won. The reason for this is that by the time your wife has said, "That looked like a nice place," you've gone so far past that it would be ridiculous to go back. Picking a place to eat on a cross-country drive has resulted in more cases of starvation than poverty. And it's inspired a few divorces.

Starvation, it developed, was what we were heading for in Hollywood. Our first few months on the Coast, I picked up just barely enough each week to subsist on, playing all the same old little spots I'd staggered along in before. The Bar of Music, La Ronde, The Black Bull—how I hated that joint! People were encouraged to get up and dance while you were singing. I wasn't allowed to sing a ballad. Too hard to dance to.

Then one day I ran into Jerry Fielding, who had been one of Kay Kyser's arrangers, and he helped steer me into something I thought held promise.

KTTV, one of the top local stations in Los Angeles, was putting together a show with music for Jerry Lester and Dick Hazard, in an effort to revive the old happy-go-lucky spirit that "Broadway Open House" had when Jerry was the host. They needed a singer and straight man. Through the efforts of producer Maurice Duke, a Hollywood agent-promoter and a good friend, I was introduced to Jerry and got the job.

Unfortunately the gainful employment lasted only thirteen weeks before I was out and around again singing and emceeing shows in dreary little crossroads places I don't even care to mention. They were the kind of joints where you had to cross the dance floor to get to the toilet. Every time a man or a woman started to make the trip, all activity would cease and the drummer would give the privy-bound person a solid march beat. Big laugh for the room. Very embarrassing for the individual involved and maddening to a singer right in the middle of a love song to be interrupted by some stranger answering the call of nature.

When doing gigs like that, the time after work was the worst. I'd go to bed and lie there wideeyed, thinking and thinking. Gone were the illusions, the dream of Mike Douglas, Superstar, working in the tradition of men like Al Jolson, Bing Crosby, even Rudy Vallee.

It was one of the toughest times in all my years of duespaying. And the irony of it was playing a spot with the name that Walter Winchell had made famous all over the country. The Stork Club. Only it was in Council Bluffs, Iowa. That's very close to Omaha, Nebraska. But the Stork Club was in Council Bluffs because in Iowa they could get away with gambling.

Gen and the kids were with me, of course and, as if working in total obscurity weren't bad enough, the day the engagement ended we found ourselves snowbound and unable to get milk.

When such things happen you swear that's the finish. But I always went back and gave it another try. Come 1961. I was still at it, singing in a spot called Dick Whittinghill's. Dick was then and still is one of L.A.'s favorite disk jockeys, a member of the exclusive, and very expensive, show-biz-oriented Lakeside Country Club. Hope and Crosby at one time alternated being president. Dick is a fine example of how you can make it big in a small way, if you go about it right. I thought of Cleveland.

Which way is right no one knows and the agony of being broke in Hollywood, with success or the illusion of success all around you, can be almost unbearable.

Every person you see, or talk to, seems to be doing better than you are. And this is while you're putting on a front to make him think he has to try harder to catch up to you.

Every morning you read "the trades." These are *Hollywood Daily Variety* and *The Hollywood Reporter*. You read,

"Mike Douglas reported talking three pic film deal with big money people in Rome for films to be produced in Italy." It's ironic. You know it was planted by some P.R. guy in hopes of hitting you for a job on the strength of it. Yet you *believe* every one of the similar items in the paper.

It's strange what happens to the human mind in Hollywood. It begins to get a little flaky. That's why Philadelphia was so good for me. If it had said in one of the trades, "Strange forces are combining, without his knowledge, to bring Mike Douglas to Cleveland," I'd have known someone had been hitting the sauce a little too heavy. Yet that would have been the truth.

What a pity, when you're really down, that you're never given some idea of what's in store for you. Fate runs our lives just the way our mothers used to run our childhood. While we were being punished for some reason or other, she'd be preparing a big birthday party.

If I'd known about certain dealings that were going on in the Middle West while I was worrying my heart out over Gen and the kids and my future in California, there might not have been so much discontent, although I wouldn't have been any happier at what I was doing.

Maybe it was all part of the refining process that takes the prickly edges off a cocky kid and smooths him into a man.

(XVII)
EASTWARD HO!

I was not part of what I'm about to "remember." I'm piecing it together from fragments of what Woody Fraser has told me from time to time during the years he produced our show and the years of continued friendship since.

I say friendship, but it's more than that. Woody and I love each other like brothers. He has a childlike quality of enthusiasm and faith in himself that I find irresistible. He insists he finds that quality in me and attributes our successful association and friendship to this similarity.

It seems that shortly after I left NBC in Chicago to conquer the west, Woody found that there was nothing left at the station for him to produce. He could direct, if he wanted to, but there was nothing for him to direct but news shows.

Of course he continued to be obsessed with the idea for "that certain kind of variety show" he talked to me about so often. I guess he talked about it to everyone except the executives of NBC. If he had they'd own the idea because he was a contract employee of the network. Anything he thought of was automatically theirs. Besides, he didn't really think there was anybody there at the time who had enough vision to understand the concept.

216

So with nothing to produce and no enthusiasm for directing news shows, Woody quit NBC in Chicago.

For a few months the soles of his shoes got so thin from walking Chicago sidewalks that his socks were making contact with the pavement. And his knuckles grew sore from knocking on doors.

Then one day a mutual friend of ours by the name of Phil Bodell who knew about Woody's dream show told him that he'd picked up the word on the grapevine that the Westinghouse Broadcasting Company was looking for something different to originate from its owned and operated station in Cleveland. The Group W man to see was Ralph Hansen. Bodell said that he was in town and that Woody should go to see him.

Woody did and found out that what Bodell had told him was true, but that Hansen had no real idea what his company was looking for. There is nothing strange about that in the broadcasting business. When you're looking for a new show, you always send someone to find it who has no idea what you're looking for. The reason for this is that you don't know either.

So Woody carefully explained his concept of a 90-minute afternoon program that was to combine entertainment with information. He laid the whole thing out about alternating such guests as film and TV stars, athletes, politicians, professional people from the sciences and the arts, authors and all manner of instant celebrities, such as a guy who's trying to fly across the ocean in a balloon or a lady who's walking backwards from San Diego to Palm Beach, Florida. And Woody tied up the whole sales package with the big news that the person he needed to head up this show had to be able to do something himself and that meant to be able to sing in addition to dealing with the various personalities he saw as guests. Woody added that it wouldn't be bad if he could also dance and do a fair monologue.

Like everyone else, including me, who heard Woody's demands, Hansen told him, "It's going to be tough to find the right emcee." A multitalented catalyst who can talk comfortably to the various types of people Woody prescribed as guests, make them look good and keep his cool.

"It was like shoveling smoke," was the way Woody described it. "Like trying to sell a giraffe to someone who'd never seen such a beast. Or more like trying to sell a used unicorn to a person who knew there was no such animal."

But Woody's a pretty good salesman. He might even be able to sell me a used unicorn. In fact, I think he did once or twice. And he made a good enough impression on Ralph Hansen that Group W brought him to Cleveland to see what he could do by way of creating the product he was trying to sell—in Cleveland.

How many film and TV celebrities, authors, national political leaders, athletes and intellectuals are there in Cleveland to keep a daily 90-minute show going for more than a week?

My point is that "The Mike Douglas Show" didn't rise full-blown from the sea like Botticelli's *Venus Rising From the Sea*, on the half-shell. It wasn't just a lucky show biz stumble, like when some guys who really don't know what they're doing scramble together something good by accident, which has been known to happen.

After three months in Cleveland, Woody's mentor and backer, Hansen, the first guy who showed some faith in his idea, was fired. And to create a nice continuity of confusion Hansen's replacement lasted only three months before he too got the sack. In retrospect that three-month syndrome was probably nothing more than the customary thirteen-week cycle.

Right at that point, anyone familiar with the broadcasting business wouldn't give you a 30-second station break for Woody's chances of staying at KYW. But as Ed Wynn used to say on his 1930's radio show, "Tonight, Graham, the program is going to be different." (Graham, incidentally, was Graham MacNamee, Wynn's straight man and the first radio announcer to attain star status. Or maybe that was Jimmy Wallington who worked with Eddie Cantor.)

The difference is that instead of a new broom sweeping Woody back to Chicago, things began to happen.

Chet Collier became program manager of KYW-TV and one of his top priorities was to better the station's ratings in the early afternoon, where it ranked third and was being clobbered by the local show called "The One O'Clock Club."

Collier and Frank Tooke, the station V.P., and George Mathiesen the station manager, gave Woody some money and let him hire help in his search for the golden-haired darling whom he'd considered worthy to man the helm of a new show. For help he hired a girl named Launa Newman.

As we turn another page in the ongoing story of "Westinghouse Faces the Mike Douglas Show," we find Woody and Launa busy auditioning people, whoever was available, to see if any might meet the specifications Woody had laid down. All they came up with was run-of-the-mill singers, out-of-work disk jockeys and a guy who could play "Bye Bye Blackbird" on the piano—and nothing else.

So think about it. While I was having a discouraging time in Hollywood, Woody was having trouble in Cleveland. The auditions, however, by getting a few experimental shows on tape, did confirm the importance of the concept of a co-host.

The weekly co-host made every Monday's show sort of an "opening night" for the week. The co-host brought something new to talk about, new flint for the host's steel or vice versa, some new talent, in short freshened up the whole perspective. I think one of the things that made "The Mike Douglas Show" work from the start was the co-host idea.

So it went along, Woody producing audition after audition and Launa booking new ones as fast as each would spin out. She even booked the audiences, I'm told, to try to ensure a good reception for the auditioning artists. The idea continued to look good but the shows still looked lousy. They didn't please Woody and they didn't please the Westinghouse people, and that was bad because everyone was growing lukewarm about the whole project—and, of course, the guy who was responsible for it, namely Woody Fraser. He tried to avoid meeting people in the corridors, because people you don't meet can't tell you confidentially that you're on your way out. He didn't even dare look to see what might be lying in his In basket.

In this next episode we cut to Woody facing failure and joblessness, sitting in his office trying to wrench victory from defeat by coming up with a satisfactory master of ceremonies. The television in the office was turned on but the sound was off. A new game show was making its debut, a show called "Play Your Hunch" (an interesting title in view of what follows).

Suddenly a man came bounding out from behind a curtain, a guy Woody recognized as Mike Douglas. Ah-ha, you say, *that's* how the show started. Wrong. It was not. The person who jumped out from behind the curtain was in fact Merv Griffin. But the resemblance reminded Woody of me, so instead of picking up the phone and calling Merv, he picked up a phone and called a man who had been my manager in Chicago. That was a mistake. It cost me money. The guy did nothing more than give my number to Woody. But when I finally went on the show he insisted on his full ten percent commission for getting me the job.

And that's how it happened that the Westinghouse Group W organization and station KYW flew Mike Douglas to Cleveland to audition for a show that is essentially the one we've been doing for the past sixteen years.

I was working at the time in an L.A. spot I've mentioned before, Dick Whittinghill's. Dick gave me a day off, and I flew to Cleveland. I sat in the plane saying over and over to myself the words to a song that Marvin Hamlisch and Edward Kleban had not yet written. They probably hadn't yet written anything, and it's a safe bet that they didn't even know each other. But the lines were from the sparkling opening song of A Chorus Line—"God, I hope I get it, I hope I get it . . . I need this job, I've got to get this job."

How many times these words have been silently prayed by performers who needed money, who needed to express themselves, who needed to succeed, no one will ever know. But no line in any lyric ever written has come closer to the feelings of a person about to audition.

Some think it's much harder to perform with your mind full of apprehension. On the other hand, that's what gets the adrenaline flowing and gets you up there to do the job. That must be the correct analysis. Occasionally, before a show something will happen that gets me steamed. I'm told adrenaline comes squirting out of my ears and we have a very good show. Maybe I should arrange to have someone from Internal Revenue drop in on me just before each taping.

To end your suspense—the audition in Cleveland was a success. I didn't know this for sure when I headed home on the plane. But I felt it in my bones. Gen was optimistic, too, and I have always trusted her judgment. But good or bad, the very evening of the day I had auditioned I was back in L. A. singing at Dick Whittinghill's. The decision was not in my hands, but I had the satisfaction of knowing I had given my all.

What happened next is typical of all broadcasting procedure. Everyone liked what he saw. The Westinghouse brass were guardedly enthusiastic but the question they put to Woody was, "What do you do for an encore?"

The show wasn't just a one-shot. It was five times a week, every week in the year. They wondered if the one show I did told them enough. So they decided to bring me back to Cleveland to do some shows with widely different types of co-hosts. We actually did four. I was delighted with the results and felt that with each audition I got better. Nobody told me this, however. In fact, nobody told me anything except how much they enjoyed meeting Gen. Again we hightailed it back to Hollywood wondering about the impression we were making, while I hung on to the Whittinghill gig, hoping it would be the last of its kind I'd ever have to do.

There followed many more meetings among the Group W people, until they actually decided to have a go at the show. When this decision by Chet (who was later to become head of Group W Productions and a long-term key figure in the growth of our show) and Woody finally came down I was working in the Nevada Lodge at Lake Tahoe.

Woody was so excited I had to stand back from the phone to keep from being knocked down by the transmitted enthusiasm. He told me I had the job and the starting date was December 11, 1961. Which made '61 the year we broke the bad Christmas jinx. But Gen still shops in July or August so as not to press our luck.

I was so excited I didn't even ask how much I was going to get to do 450 minutes of TV every week.

Once again the Douglases, Gen, Michele, Christine, Kelly and a very excited Mike were off on the road to somewhere. And everything went well this time. Both Gen and I felt we were finally heading for something stable.

It wasn't Broadway and it wasn't Hollywood, but when you drive between those two places as many times as we did, you learn that there are an amazing number of people living between them and that these can be a great audience if you talk to them. Lawrence Welk found that out. These were the people we saw as our potential audience.

But rosy as everything seemed driving east, that's not how it turned out. Carmel Quinn was scheduled to be my co-host for the first week because she'd been so good in all the auditions. She was part of Arthur Godfrey's radio and TV family and had made several successful appearances with Jack Paar, so she was pretty well-known not only to the late-night show-wise viewers on both coasts but also to that vast American public that loved Arthur.

Group W ran a very well-coordinated publicity campaign that was to terminate in a party for the station personnel we were seeking to interest. After the party they were to see the taping of the first Mike Douglas show with Carmel Quinn as co-host. It never happened.

Woody got a phone call from a man in New York named Joe Higgins. He was Carmel Quinn's manager. Higgins said Quinn couldn't come to Cleveland to do the show because Arthur Godfrey needed her. What this did was to send Woody streaking to New York at the speed of sound.

At first Higgins tried to brush him off. Then, when Woody wouldn't leave the office, he threatened to call the police. Common sense and calmer judgment prevailed somewhere along the line, and after a fultile attempt to talk to Carmel, a meeting was finally arranged between Woody, Higgins and Quinn's husband, a very Irish man who ran dance halls in Dublin.

This meeting finally led to a meeting with Carmel herself, and the result was that Woody gained an audience with Godfrey, the old pro, who understood the problem and graciously agreed to tape all his radio shows on Monday and Tuesday, leaving Carmel free for the rest of the week. It was a compromise, not a solid victory, but it didn't leave us with egg all over our faces for not producing Carmel Quinn at all.

Luckily for us, *Bye-Bye Birdie* was playing in Cleveland. So we were able to get Gretchen Wyler, a good solid performer, to step in for Quinn and help us out for the first two days. She was sensational, sharp and interesting and I'm forever grateful to her.

It didn't take long for Woody to find that getting good guests for a 90-minute variety show in Cleveland wasn't easy. So we went to New York to find out why, ask some questions and try to make some arrangements. The first man he talked to was Jack Paar's manager. He explained to Woody that he had three problems, the three things talent doesn't like: 1) a week on the road; 2) one nighters; and 3) the city of Cleveland (and for Cleveland you can substitute any city in the country that doesn't bear the name New York, Washington, Chicago, Los Angeles or San Francisco). Talk shows and other developments in the business have since helped lessen this aversion. But when we started, the only other talk show was Jack Paar's. Talent agencies, book publishers, public relations people, none of these sources for guests were yet in existence for what has come to be known as "scale shows."

Nevertheless, the Midwest was not won over without a struggle. After several months on the air in Cleveland, we slowly began to attract trade attention; interest accelerated thereafter. Group W saw the time had come to syndicate "The Mike Douglas Show," which henceforth was spread to its four other owned and operated stations in San Francisco, Baltimore, Pittsburgh and Boston. Gen and I spent a lot of time on planes, flying to and from these cities promoting the syndication which, no doubt about, was the sunrise of our big break. We were on a natural high, full-time residents of cloud nine.

Along came a local union clown in Cleveland to shatter the euphoria. He seized what he thought was his chance to become a labor big shot by threatening to keep our show off the air everywhere by calling a strike unless a list of incredible union demands were met. It was a real stick-up and I'm not mentioning any names only to protect the guilty.

Naturally, the union hadn't any leverage until we came along to boost the network's earnings. The union fellow's strategy was clear—extort from the network by threatening to shut down its number-one moneywinner, namely, our show. My reaction was to apply the wisdom conveyed to me by my father on how to get along on the streets of Chicago. I stormed into the guy's offices and laid it right on the line. My real purpose was to lay something right on his nose, but better judgment prevailed. "I'm a union man, too," I pointed out. "Where do you come off keeping me off the air and putting a great bunch of people out of work just to make a name for yourself?" My language was somewhat less polite.

Whether by my action or, as is more likely, some smarter and subtler behind-the-scenes maneuvering on the part of management, the crisis passed.

The only other trouble was of my own making. As we went into syndication and the show's popularity grew by leaps and bounds, it began to penetrate my thick Irish noggin that here I was, the spark plug of what was clearly a successful enterprise, pulling in $400 a week to do five 90-minute shows, week after consecutive week, while the co-hosts brought in from New York and L.A. were earning double my salary in many cases. Again I saw red and went over the heads of everyone in the organization, making a direct appeal to Don McGannon, chairman of the board of Westinghouse Broadcasting Company.

Now a man doesn't land that kind of job unless he knows a little something about running a business and something about people, and because of this savvy, Don (he was Mr. McGannon to me at that time) saw it my way and we've been adjusting our financial arrangements together on a friendly and, to my mind, equitable basis ever since.

Maybe I should clarify what I mean by equitable. A TV station is operated to make money. A performer's worth is a measure of how much money he can bring into the till. In television this evaluation is made through ratings that tell how many people watch. A great singer may not be able to attract as large an audience as a mediocre one. Maybe it's the color of his eyes, his smile. Who knows?

The truth is, I worked for so little for so long, for so much less than I thought I was worth, simply because there was no way of telling what size audience I was capable of drawing—that when the time came to collect, I felt I was entitled. And the audience ratings bore me out. Let me give you one example of the upswing in our fortunes. Station managers began calling in to order our show *before* a salesman had even come to see them. And that's more or less the story of how a little one-station 90-minute talk show hosted by a singer who was far from a household name (excluding his own household) got started in Cleveland, Ohio.

(XVIII)
OUR SHOW IN O-HI-O

Getting on the air was a minor problem in comparison to remaining there. We'd had a forewarning of this even prior to the Carmel Quinn incident.

The agent who used the name "Cleveland" as a generic term for any place that wasn't New York or Hollywood when he said, "Actors do not want to spend a week in Cleveland," hit this problem right on the head. That's an agent's forte. His deficiency is in solving them.

Barbra Streisand's manager, Marty Ehrlichman, got a handle on the problem. Marty is said to have told Barbra right from the beginning that he would make her the biggest star in the country. And apparently he didn't tell that to all the girls—he meant it. And I'm sure our show helped get the ball rolling. We gave her the first significant, prolonged, national TV exposure, that is, during hours when the majority of viewers were awake.

I'd taken in her act on some of the late night talk shows. I loved what she did with a song. But her talk and appearance qualified her for a diploma in Advanced Nuttiness. The fact that in the early 60's she was dressing the way everybody was dressing in the late 70's was one indication. But at that time I didn't know how women (or men) would dress in the late 70's. All I knew was, there was something special about Barbra that made me want her for a co-host.

Marty said he couldn't allow her to spend a whole week in Cleveland for the money we paid. We said if we increased our scale for his client we'd be setting a precedent that could lead to bankruptcy. So we asked him if he had any ideas how our differences could be worked out. And he did. "Find her a gig for a grand in Cleveland."

So guess what! We did. We got her a week at a spot called the Chateau in Lakewood for $2,500. I think it's now defunct. How's that for a name for a night club—DeFunct?

Opening night I wandered over to see how Barbra was doing, and it was less than great. Even for a Monday night the audience was pretty thin. But why not? Nobody knew what a Barbra Streisand was. This was particularly true of a couple of drunks who were heckling her. A few personal remarks were passed, and before you could say Muhammad Ali, Marty was over at their table threatening to punch out the two of them.

I thought to myself, "Oh no. I'm not back to this. I'm not ready for this sort of stuff anymore." Nevertheless, I reluctantly sauntered over to bring my magnificent pugilistic prowess to Marty's defense. Fortunately, before it became my turn, a couple of very large representatives of the management escorted the two troublemakers to the street.

Actually, I did most of my early saloon arbitrating, between my friends and those who were not *their* friends, not so much by bare-knuckle brute force as by blarney and a lot of smiling. My drinking friends liked to have a teetotaler along as some sort of an alibi. Barbra's importance to me as a co-host lay in the fact that she was never at a loss for words. We have enough experience now to take steps to prevent freezing in a guest or co-host. But, naturally, we can't check out everyone we book for conversational response and reaction. Some of the smartest, wittiest people I know sometimes suffer from what the shrinks call a phobia. In easier terms, that's stage fright.

Once we booked a young boy who'd smuggled himself through Cape Kennedy security and almost succeeded in his insane plan to stow away on a rocket destined for the moon. He must have gone through a grueling debriefing period before he was allowed to leave the Cape and come on our show. And he was probably given elaborate instructions on what he could and could not say about his experience.

My first question was, "What gave you the idea that you could succeed in being the first stowaway to the moon?" Nothing came back. No answer. He just sat there staring at me. I could see the letters P-A-N-I-C flashing where his eyeballs had been.

He had made his appearance immediately following a commercial, so there was no sensible way I could use our emergency, last-resort device of saying, "We'll be back after these messages." It figured to have a phony ring.

So I gave the kid a good hard shove on the shoulder and said, "All right! Come on! Tell me, how long have you been a Russian spy?" This made him laugh, broke the tension and got the interview started.

That's one of the tricks I have to use occasionally. Even experienced people will sometimes freeze up and have to be shocked back to consciousness physically if they don't respond to other remedies.

One cure, if the guest happens to be from the Philadelphia area, is to ask, "How was the plane ride?" It's a surprise. It may make the person laugh. As an icebreaker, you can generally thaw out a woman by saying something flattering about her clothes, her hairdo or how much prettier she is in real life than in pictures. Which—to quote George Jessel—"reminds me of a story." A Myron Cohen story.

A Jewish bubba was wheeling her new grandchild around the neighborhood when one of her friends, seeing the kid for the first time, said "My, what a beautiful baby."

The proud grandma, treating the compliment almost as a slight, came back with, "You think this is beautiful? You should see her picture."

Among the smooth talkers who went on to talk themselves into national popularity after co-hosting with us were Bill Cosby, the Smothers Brothers, Sonny and Cher and Totie Fields, to name but a few.

For Totie, as for Barbra (and others), we attempted to find local spots to work in, although the Smothers Brothers balked at washing dishes in the kitchen of the Statler Hotel. They said it was a comedown for them. They saw themselves as working in the dining room, as busboys.

But the bait for luring co-hosts was the five days of continuous exposure. All went on to greater and greater show business heights.

Naturally we hadn't been in Cleveland very long before we started to become part of the social and cultural life of the city. It was advantageous to Cleveland to have a national TV show. It boosted the city into the show biz league, along with New York, Los Angeles and sometimes Chicago, and it gave a leg up to theater and night club operators. Every booking they made almost automatically got a plug from us, carrying a lot more sock than any paid advertising they could buy. We also offered a handy forum for politicians, charity organizations and those promoting various civic activities.

Urban planners of the future should consider making provisions for their city to subsidize (with the hope of eventual amortization of the investment) a good local talk show. It would, of course, develop more prestige and clout by going national. It would also help to reinforce the show if a ready and abundant supply of strange animals were handy, in case the supply of suitable people dried up.

I don't think anyone realized what a heavy part the fauna of the forests and jungles play as guests on a TV talk show. We guessed this might turn out to be so while still in Cleveland and began casting around for some satisfactory animal to exploit. One of the staff had been to see "The Nutcracker Suite" ballet and naturally suggested a trained bear. They're nice, big, woolly, clumsy creatures, which, if it weren't that one could hug you to death, would be real cute like a large, friendly Teddy bear. But the bear in "The Nutcracker Suite" left town before we could book it.

Then we discovered that there was no abundance of trained bears in the whole Cleveland area. Apparently the Indians had wiped them all out. And those the ball team didn't get were working for members of Bob Hope's family in some way or another.

But as the Good Book says, "Seek and ye shall find." The animal was part of a small-time vaudeville act that had been subsisting on short rations for a long stretch of time. I have to rely on memory for the name. The one that comes to mind is Bernard and his Dancing Bear. I think the bear's first name was Rudolph, but this is mere speculation as we were never formally introduced.

A quick look told you that a long period of time had elapsed since Rudolph had anything much to dance about. His coat would have made a suitable wrap for dear old "Moms" Mabley. More disturbing to me personally was that Bernard also looked a little famished. But a dancing bear was a dancing bear, and Rudolph would have to do until Ray Bolger hit Cleveland.

I can't just go skidding through a mention of "Moms." She was funny. She really grabbed me. Just the way she looked, the way she dressed, the way she moved, cracked me up. Her costumes could have been rejects from Phyllis Diller's wardrobe donated to the Goodwill people. Her garb sure helped to create goodwill for "Moms." She danced with soul and she *talked* with soul. Her outlook on life was unique, fresh and ethnic. She rates as one of my favorite co-hosts.

She was a free swinger on any topic. "I'm a hip momma," she said. "I like sports and politics and sometimes I can't tell one from the other. And just because I don't understand something don't mean I don't like it or that I'm gonna put it down. I'll try to get with it if I can. That's how you learn things. Just because I'm a woman and old and not exactly a platinum blonde don't mean I couldn't be President. If Elizabeth can run England, I could run America. What has she got that I didn't used to have and can't get again?"

She was born Loretta Mary Aikin in a little hillside town in North Carolina, but her friends called her "Moms" or Jackie. That's Jackie ("Moms") Mabley, who always had one more fan than perhaps she knew when she co-hosted "The Mike Douglas Show"—namely me.

But getting back to Rudolph. A further source of anxiety was the discovery that his specialty wasn't dancing but wrestling. Oh, well.

Anywhere in the vicinity of Rudolph could have worked perfectly as the "before" half of a demonstration for room deodorant.

Rudolph arrived in a cage, a heavy chain attached to a thick leather collar around his neck. A muzzle covered his snout. And for some reason he was in a foul mood. At least that was my impression, so I asked Bernard if everything was okay. He assured me I had nothing to worry about. Clearly, *Bernard* had something to worry about, namely getting through the show and collecting his dough.

The scenario called for Bernard to lead the bear down through the audience as if he and his companion had come to catch the show. They made an incongruous couple by most standards. Rudolph was huge and ratty. Bernard was less than huge, but he too was sufficiently ratty-looking. He was garbed in a sort of Tarzan outfit that looked as if it had served as a wall in a Siberian Turkish bath.

Their appearance evoked the anticipated female hysteria from the audience. Rudolph construed their reaction as hostile and Bernard has his hands full pulling the beast onto the stage. Once up there he still wasn't happy. His indifference to Bernard's instructions grew. Rudolph stood there, taking in the lights, the camera, the others on the stage and me—particularly me. I didn't like it. He seemed to be trying to assess from what quarter the main threat would come, and what might make a good square (or bear) meal.

Finally, Bernard keyed himself up to giving a demonstration of the art of bear wrestling. Earlier, when they were briefing me, I asked, "What happens after Bernard wrestles the bear?"

The answer was, "You wrestle the bear."

"Oh, no I won't," I said. "I don't even know that bear. He's not my type." My sadistic crew laughed, as they still do whenever I try to back away from some simple little bit that might get me killed. But I knew my protests were futile. I was already committed to going a few rounds with Rudolph.

Bernard tried to get his pet to do his thing, but Rudolph was in a funk and uncooperative. When Bernard pulled on his chain, Rudolph just pulled back—only harder.

Things were getting very dull. There hasn't been much of an audience for tugs-of-war between man and bear since those animal acts the Romans put on with men and beasts in the Colosseum. So, feeling something had to be done, I called, "Come on! Get him to wrestle with you!"

Now Bernard had probably looked on our show as his first stop along the comeback trail. But if he kept being nothing more than a stage wait, he knew he was all washed up. In desperation he pulled the chain up short and tight around Rudolph's neck and screamed, "When I say wrestle, *wrestle!*"

Still nothing happened, so Bernard hauled off and socked the brute right on the snout. Any trained fighter knows the only move you can make following that is to jump back, raise your guard and hope to hear the referee counting. That's not the way it worked out. The blow had the effect of irritating Rudolph enormously. He waved his forelegs in the air in some spastic rendition of the Hustle. A terrifying roar followed, indicating to Bernard how Rudolph felt about wrestling. He lifted the paralyzed trainer and flung him clear across the stage, his flight brought to an abrupt halt by the brick wall just beyond the curtain. Bernard crumpled in a heap of the floorboards—out! out!

The immediate result of this was a very angry bear at one end of the chain with no one holding on at the other end. As he ambled toward one of the stagehands, I hollered, with great presence of mind, "Grab the bear!" With utter disregard for the possibility of being sacked, he hollered back, "Grab him yourself! He's *your* guest!"

Fortunately, the people backstage were able to bring Bernard back to the world of reality, and groggily he grabbed the bear's chain and managed to drag him off. Bernard was a pretty husky guy. I watched as he and Rudolph passed slowly into oblivion and wondered how far Rudolph might have thrown me.

Experience is the best teacher, they say. Trouble is we never pay any attention to it. So it came to pass that about thirteen years later we had another, slightly different incident, involving a wrestling bear and Robert Goulet. But that must wait for another chapter.

Things were always going wrong, turning out differently from our plans, à la Bernard and Rudolph. Guests we anticipated might be dull proved interesting, comedians we thought would be funny bombed. But the good thing about our show lies in the fact that you can terminate any act at any time just by saying you have to break for a commercial.

Well, faced with one such crisis, I seized the chance, while the camera was on the dying act, to whisper instructions to alert the next performer that he was going on right after the commercial break.

The next act happened to be one I'm sure will bring back memories to all old vaudeville buffs, Peg Leg Bates. Mr. Bates tap-danced, in spite of the fact that one of his legs was your basic hickory type worn by the pirate Long John Silver in *Treasure Island.*

One of the talent coordinators went tearing back to his dressing room, knocked on the door and screamed, "Mr. Bates, you're on!"

From the other side of the door came the answer, "I may be on, honey, but my leg ain't."

So I did a little ad-libbing and went into another song until Peg Leg came out to dance for us.

But the most interesting and wonderful thing that happened in Cleveland was that, despite the fact that we were in the red for three years, we weren't canceled!

That doesn't happen often in the TV business.

Another rarity is for performers to take time out to give any credit for the success of a theatrical venture to management—the people who put up the money, the people who have enough faith and confidence to stick with a project. So right here and now I want to go straight down the fairway in giving an enormous amount of credit—and thanks—for the survival of "The Mike Douglas Show" to a man named Don McGannon, Board Chairman of Westinghouse Broadcasting Company. Don stuck with us and kept us going when we were losing money so fast, the government was sending over their economists to find out how we did it better than they do.

After about a year and a half of continued losses, we

edged into syndication, very slowly . . . nine stations . . . twenty stations . . . thirty stations. By the time we'd relocated to Philadelphia, I think we'd hit forty. Thus giving credence to the saying "Life begins at forty."

It took a lot of selling to get us into syndication in the first place. One of the problems was that, according to the Woody Fraser Plan, our show had an ever-varying format. No two were quite alike. A station owner, and potential buyer, would ask for a couple of tapes of our show. We'd send him three or four. But each would probably be routined differently, and the editorial focus might be entirely changed from one show to another, the reason being that we were constantly booking guests and co-hosts from all sorts of varying walks of life.

So the station owner would get back to us, asking which of the shows we sent him was the show we were selling. Then the real selling began, as we explained that our "formula" was a lack of it; that nothing was carved in stone; that we were constantly renewing ourselves.

Through all this, no hatchet man came out from New York to tell us what we were doing wrong. These expert executive types are all the same. They're very positive what's wrong, but they never have any positive ideas on what would be right.

None is ever willing to make a commitment or take a real responsibility.

It was to one of these "fixers," who recognized every mistake after he heard it, that Fred Allen said, "Where were you when the paper was blank?"

With us, most of the time there wasn't even any paper. A lot of the time even our minds were blank. Nevertheless, Don McGannon of Westinghouse had faith. There should be more like him in our business.

Come to think of it, I've had the good fortune of being associated with some truly top-notch people in a field that has its share of fly-by-night operators and its seamy side.

Vincent Andrews Sr. became my business manager around 1965. But he also became my brother, my godfather and much more. He was very special because he made everyone he came in contact with feel special. As a client, I was most appreciative not only of the deals he wrapped up but also the ones he turned down. When you've been hungry for a while, you're inclined to jump at whatever comes along. Vinnie saw that I didn't do that, tempted though I was. He also recognized Gen's astuteness and, rather than trying to separate us as some have done, made her an important part of everything connected with my career and our business interests.

His death hit us hard. Fortunately, his son, Vinnie Jr., took over the firm and we have maintained that same type of relationship through all sorts of contracts and deals and investments and involvements—everything from the TV show to the Bonaventure development in Florida's Fort Lauderdale area.

But I also think about Marvin Saltzman, who managed me when I left Kay Kyser the first time. And Tom Illius, an agent, road manager and confidant who traveled with me a lot. And Oscar Cohen, the head of Asssociated Booking who has been responsible for my first Las Vegas appearance and other dates and is a real mentor of mine. And Bobby Brenner, who has been lining up new professional outlets for me now that my TV contract gives me more time for them.

And how about Joe Petito, who used to book me for club dates in Cleveland? "Joe," I would always tell him when we were on one of those engagements, "go get the check so when I finish, we can take the loot and scoot."

(XIX)
WE MOVED

Have you ever noticed how some little unimportant thing that may have nothing whatever to do with you, may not even be directed at you, makes such an impression that it sticks with you for life? Well, here's one of mine.

Back in the days when they still had newsreels in movie theaters, there was a shot of some politician campaigning in a crowded area. Who he was made no impression on me whatsoever. What has stuck with me ever since was the picture of him picking up this little boy, holding him in his arms and asking, "Where do you live, son?"

The kid, whom I must have identified with completely, looked at the man and said sadly and simply, "We moved."

Any family that has ever moved knows the pain of it.

The kids have to change schools and link up with a whole new bunch of playmates. The mother has to make a new set of friends and connections with tradespeople and services. The father meets a new crowd he has to learn to deal with, and nothing in the new house is quite where it used to be in the old place, where you could find anything in the dark. Even the climate is generally different.

I speak from experience. We loved our first little G.I. home in Burbank, California. We all had pangs about leaving it, even though we were able to move to something nicer in North Hollywood.

With each relocation—Sherman Oaks, Encino, Cleveland—we thought we had our "ancestral home" for life. But then we had to pick up and move to Long Island, New York. It wasn't a bit easy, mentally or physically. But there's a saying in show business, "You go where the money is." It isn't an old saying but it's a well-known fact, when the money runs out, you go somewhere else.

For a while, there was a town house in River Forest, near Chicago. Then we were situated in what used to be "way out" in Encino, California, when the big break came that required us to move to Cleveland, which we grew to love. And I haven't even mentioned all the crummy places we stayed in—you couldn't call it living—which my mind paid no attention to because I knew they were temporary. Neither Gen nor I ever made plans to spend our declining years in a dump.

This is one of the sad things about show business, the moving around that has to be done and the ongoing question, "Is this the final move? Is this IT? Shall I take my wife and children or let them stay where they are, leave the kids in school, until I find out how things go?"

I don't even care to count how many times Gen and I had to weigh these matters, and her decision was always that the family is a unit, it must stay together. Separating a man from his wife and children, and vice versa, can never make any of them better or happier. And when you're in show business, unless your home life is in order the distinct possibility exists of blowing your whole career.

One offshoot of this moving around in the struggle to find your spot, separated from your family and your roots, is the reason we all hear so many stories about a man who struggles for years to "make it," and as soon as he does he dumps the wife who stood by him, stayed home and brought up the kids; stood by him through all the bread-and-gravy days only to find out that when he made it to the baked Alaska, she'd already lost him. He hooked up with a new chick he found along the way when he was lonesome and vulnerable. But enough of that sad stuff.

Maybe if "The Mike Douglas Show" ever falls apart, God forbid, Gen and I can go into business as family counselors.

None of us was happy when the news arrived that we had to leave Cleveland, neither the Douglases nor the people of Cleveland. And the strange aspect was that we were not consulted on the relocation matter.

There were possibilities of moving that we had some measure of choice about. As soon as success loomed on the horizon, talk immediately started about moving the show to New York or to Hollywood. Every argument seemed to lead logically to such a move. Both places had a greater and more constant pool of talent from which to draw. Both were considerably higher on the glamour scale.

A decision had to be made. Gen and I preferred to stay in Cleveland for several reasons. In the first place, we'd be unique! Secondly, in Cleveland we'd be king of the mountain. While Cleveland might think so, it would never occur to New York to point to me and say, "That's our boy!"

Then the Philadelphia thing happened. The F.C.C. decided, for complicated technical reasons, that the NBC station in Philly and the Westinghouse station in Cleveland should swap places. The move was, of course, a great boon for me, and we had solved for us our problem deciding between New York and Hollywood, but there's no getting away from the fact that the relocation affected a great many other people's lives adversely.

Of course, Philadelphia is neither New York nor Hollywood. It has its own character, and one big plus for us was that it was similar enough to Cleveland to allow the show to retain the same feel and atmosphere and yet be only 90 miles from the Big Apple. The small geographical distance allowed guests to come from New York and appear on our show and be back in Gotham by theater time. We had the best of the two worlds we needed.

The shift, of course, presented problems. There were big ones for some of our Cleveland crew, many of whom were born and raised in Cleveland and had to move, many for the first time, to an entirely new environment. They even had to change unions when they got to Philadelphia. So some of our people didn't come with us, and I could understand why.

As for Gen and me, pulling up stakes was no novelty—something we didn't love but had learned to accept as a fact of show biz life. We'd made some wonderful friends in Cleveland, but we'd learned that you never lose real friends and there are always new ones waiting to meet you.

The main problem of the move was that the station on Walnut Street in Philadelphia, which had suddenly become KYW, had to be completely remodeled. The whole building was only 42 feet wide. They used to build everything narrow in Philadelphia. But what it lacked in width the building fortunately made up in height. We had seven stories to fool around with. So most of our rebuilding was vertical.

First, we found that the studio had only 9 feet of head room. We figured we had to have a minimum of 13½ feet. To get that we had to lower the floor 2½ feet so that it rested right on the footings of the building, and we had to go up through a radio studio on the next floor to get the rest of the space. We only missed it by half an inch. But we still had enough room to have basketball players as guests.

Another difficulty: The building's passenger elevator. It opened right onto our studio floor. People going or coming from another floor would occasionally walk absent-minded-ly out of the elevator, thinking they were at their floor, and become surprise guests of "The Mike Douglas Show." We were compelled to eliminate that elevator entirely. This left us with the building's only other lift, a freight elevator—one of those two-way jobs that loads from the street on one side and empties into the building on the other. We needed that big one for bringing props in and out of the studio. These often included such items as dogs, horses, pigs, bears and an occasional elephant.

In the case of the elephant, the animal took one look at the elevator space he was being asked to step into and had an instantaneous and totally negative reaction. His handlers finally fooled him into thinking he was going somewhere else and crammed him into the elevator backwards. It was quite a feat. But while congratulations were being passed around, someone on another floor summoned the elevator and up they went, Jumbo and all.

Man, I'd like to have been there on whatever floor the elevator door opened and seen the expressions on the faces of those who were greeted by a glorious, full-color, live-action view of the south end of an elephant facing north. Elephants are supposed to be lucky when their trunks are up, but not when their *tails* are.

Although we got over all the production and logistical problems, that elephant was not the last one in my life. I think there is something about being a talent coordinator that marks you with strange leanings toward pachyderms. I suppose you could say booking an elephant leaves you with the gratified feeling of having done something big.

(XX)
I NEVER MET A CO-HOST I DIDN'T LIKE

I was in Las Vegas for the premiere of a mercifully forgotten film called, of all things, *The Oscar.*

I was sitting in a booth in the coffee shop at the Riviera Hotel, enjoying my usual tea and honey, when a young lady appeared wearing a very short skirt and carrying a telephone. Immediately I knew she must either be a salesman for the Bell System or a starlet whose manager told her to stay near a phone.

"Mr. Douglas," she said, as she plugged in the instrument, "this is a long-distance call for you."

I asked who it was because nobody knew where I was.

"Bob Hope," she said and handed me the phone.

Before I could say hello, Bob came on with, "Mike, I hate to bother you but . . ."

I was so astonished I interrupted to ask, "How'd you know where I am?"

"Oh, you're easy to track down," Bob said. "My people are very good at that. Sometimes they can even find me. Say, tell me something, you've had a gal on your show a lot named Phyllis Diller. In fact, I kind of identify her with your show. Can you tell me anything about her? What kind of a dame is she?"

"She is fantastic!" I said. "And what's more, lemme tell you this. If you're thinking of using her, she'd complement you just great. In fact, I think of her as sort of a female you."

"Hold it Mike," Bob said. "Hold it right there. There isn't enough room in the world for another Bob Hope—of any sex."

"Might be great," I said. "You've got the girls all sewed up, Phyllis would sew up the men. Together you'd have a lock on most of the sexes. But no kidding, Phyllis' delivery reminds me so much of you and she's a big fan of yours. And what's better than that, she's a great gal to get along with. I think the chemistry would be terrific."

"Beautiful," Bob said. "She'll be a lot of help when we send the film to the lab."

And that's how Bob Hope happened to cast Phyllis Diller as his co-star in *Boy, Did I Get A Wrong Number*.

By this time I was so curious I couldn't hang up without asking Bob how, with all the traveling he does, he had time to see my show.

"Time? How can anybody miss it? No matter where I am, at any time of day, in any time zone, when I switch on TV I get 'The Mike Douglas Show.' You get around more than I do without leaving Philadelphia. You must have a rating that would cover the national debt."

"Thanks," I said, "and by the way, if you ever need a guy in one of your pictures who can sing and dance and tell jokes while you're playing the romantic lead, I may be at liberty."

From the outset, Phyllis had been the kind of co-host I like best. I could stay home and the show would be great. That wasn't exactly the plan when the idea of having a co-host was conceived. But it's close. Everyone agreed, mainly me, that it's better to have someone handy to talk to if you're going to be on for 90 minutes.

A different co-host each week gives a new slant to the

show. More important, when one of your guests isn't giving that witty, sparkling performance you hoped for when the booking was made, you have someone else to talk to. One or two times I've felt like doing what Ish Kabibble did to me in Chicago, and saying, "My co-host will entertain you for the next 60 minutes," and walking off the set.

So the perfect co-host must be a person who knows a lot about something, talks a lot because he or she likes to talk and can sing, perform on an instrument, dance or wrestle with a bear.

In the course of a week's conversation, I find out an awful lot of strange and fascinating things about my co-hosts.

Many different types have made their singing debut with me. Generally, they will only consent to sing on the show if I accompany them. Sometimes it's tough. Because a good barroom or bathroom singer is not always that great when staying with the band, or on key and on the beat. But, with a great deal of help from Joe Massimino and his super group of musicians, it comes out all right.

Two very talented Jacksons have made their singing debuts with me—Glenda, whom I consider one of the world's finest actresses, and a Yankee Jackson named Reggie, who sang a duet with me. (In the last game of the '77 World Series, he did some great solo work and tied Ruth's record for home runs in a World Series game.)

Athletes seem to like to sing. Johnny Bench gave us a song written for him by Bobby Goldsboro. Bruce Jenner and his wife did a little warbling for us.

I guess singing is sort of a release for them just as tossing a baseball around is kind of a release for me, and nobody expects me to be good at it. That I can do it at all surprises them.

Qualifications for co-hosting, are popularity, talent, accomplishment and personality—not necessarily in that order. And if we happen to have some prior rapport with a person, it doesn't hurt. What it comes down to is people we think other people, including ourselves, would like to know more about; stars in some field, instant personalities who have just been in the news for some reason other than murder, mugging or bank robbery.

So far we haven't had any co-hosts who have been bank robbers but if we did, we'd try to book an FBI agent to create sparks. Just as when Muhammad Ali co-hosts, we try for Ken Norton, George Foreman or some other contender as one of the guests to introduce a little conflict. Or if we find that a candidate for co-host plays the bagpipes, we'd try to introduce a little harmony by booking Foster Brooks who also has a little Scotch in him. (Actually, he doesn't drink.)

Booking co-hosts generally isn't difficult. In addition to the exposure and the chance to plug a book or a film, a song or a TV show, the co-host is sure to have some laughs, and of course the pay isn't exactly chopped liver. He also gets VIP treatment, paid expenses, and a number of other perqs, as the business boys say.

When the co-host happens to be Jackie Gleason, you can be sure he'll be plugging one thing—Jackie Gleason. He's a larger-than-life guy whom I'd love to have as a permanent sidekick if the idea didn't strike me as suicidal.

Let me quickly mention Burt Reynolds and Bob Goulet as two others who can sit alongside me any time.

An actor by the name of David Groh, who'd worked in obscurity in the theater for a long while before hitting the big time as Valerie Harper's mate on the TV comedy "Rhoda," is another favorite. ("Rhoda" received such a high rating that Valerie almost suffered a nosebleed.) Following Valerie's stint on the MDS, I booked David Groh to get the other side of the story. The first day he was out operating heavy building machinery at a Philadelphia Urban Development project, the reason being that his line of work in "Rhoda" is supposed to be the house-wrecking business. So we put him into one of those big cranes that swing an iron ball against the sides of buildings to knock them down and let him have fun.

Of course, the regular operator showed him how to handle the rig, and everything was all right except he knocked down two buildings that were supposed to be left standing. No, I'm kidding. That's just a little joke I threw in there, reflexively, thinking I was doing the show.

I want to tell you, no kid who came into his sister's room on a rainy afternoon and breezily knocked down a house of cards she'd laboriously spent the day building ever had more fun than David. After all, he said as he stepped out of the cab of the crane, "You know how an actor longs to bring down the house."

One of the most consistent co-hosts I think I've ever had is Totie Fields. I'd seen her on an Ed Sullivan show and booked her right away as a co-host. I knew she'd be hot and was happy to help by giving her the first extended television exposure she'd ever had. And believe me, when you were exposing Totie at that time, you were exposing quite a lot.

The show records that this started her climb to fame and fortune. After us, she began showing up on all the other talk shows, then came Vegas and the works. Artistically, she owns Vegas.

Now that she's back on her foot again, as she might say, I can't wait to bring her to Philadelphia to resume her old job as co-host of "The Mike Douglas Show."

Back in the early days she was known to pick up one of those enormous Bookbinder's menus and ask the waiter to bring one of everything. She had to be served by two waiters because she ate enough for two, but only because she was on a diet, otherwise she would have eaten for five.

Some of my favorite co-hosts happen to be named Tony—Tony Newley, Tony Bennett, Tony Randall, Tony Quinn, Tony Martin. For instance, I like the way Anthony Newley uses his arms. Watching Tony work suggests that he may have given mime lessons to Marcel Marceau.

He seems to be playing "handies" when he sings. You not only have to listen, you must watch. I keep trying to understand what his hands are telling me. What's more I don't think his song "Teach the Children of Today to Be the Parents of Tomorrow" can be heard often enough.

Just the title says something so important that I think it should hang in every classroom in the country. And every living room. If it could be done, we'd be well on the way to reducing all juvenile delinquency. When Tony sings that song it gives me a great feeling inside.

Of course, we occasionally book someone we think will give the show a great lift and get back zilch. This is a very special type, with a very special name—"Mr.-Never-Plays-the-Mike-Douglas-Show-Twice."

To get away from show business co-hosts, one of the most forthcoming and interesting we ever had was Washington's contribution to the Bell Telephone Company, the late Martha Mitchell. Like all other co-hosts, she appeared with the full knowledge that probing questions would be asked and that these might be fielded any way the co-host chose. So some co-hosts finessed some of the questions.

Not so when Martha Mitchell was co-host. She answered the way she *had* to. The only way she knew how. Straight from the shoulder. She was a lady who spoke her mind, and when talking to the press, she let the chips fall where they might, which was all over the place.

D. D. Eisenberg of the Philadelphia *Evening Bulletin*, who interviewed her during her week of co-hosting, called her "The Scarlett O'Hara of Washington."

Watergate is now too far away and too unhappy a time to recall in detail all that Martha said (even if I wanted to go back into the file and dig out all the dirt she dished about how she was "kidnapped"). But it is proper to throw in this reminder that she was proved right about a lot of things that at the time were dismissed as simply the rantings and ravings of a sick, jealous, lonely woman.

She saw and felt sinister things going on around her involving her husband. And she reacted instinctively in a way she thought would protect him against political embarrassment and save him from himself.

She didn't like politics. She said she was unhappy with most of the people she met socially in Washington. And she left me with the impression that this aversion resulted from her perception of them as stuffy. Also she felt that most of them talked about her either openly or behind her back as if she were some sort of clown.

These were people who had reason to fear her addiction to the telephone (as well as members of the press who frequently benefited by her incessant use of Ma Bell's equipment). She said she did all that phoning around late at night to pump a little life into what she considered "stuffy Washington." This, and the inroads the problems of Watergate made on her husband's time (keeping him from her), eventually brought about an estrangement that finally led to an ultimatum she told me about.

On the telephone (how else?) from California, after she'd been trying to find out what was going on, being denied newspapers and sent off on useless trips, and getting the runaround from people trying to square a man named Mitchell, she called her husband to ask for some answers. She opened the conversation, which was pretty tense, by saying "Mitchell, this is your last warning. Either you get out of politics or I am leaving you." She added, "I called him Mitchell because as far as I'm concerned John Mitchell is dead to me." It was a very sad moment.

She explained that to most people John Mitchell was Jack, but she either called him John or John Newton.

At our first meeting, when the red light lit up on the camera I tried to strike a light note by telling her she was more attractive than the pictures and films I'd seen of her. And I asked if her dimples were hard to keep clean. (Kidding, of course.) "They're beautiful," I said. Her answer was, "They're wrinkles now, I'm afraid."

I said my daughter had one misplaced dimple, and I always told her that's where the angels had kissed her.

"That's what my daddy used to say to me," said Martha.

Summing up the matter, Martha's story of just one small, personal segment of the Watergate monster that destroyed so many lives, the details of her "kidnapping" to keep her quiet, and what we now know to be truths that were only "ugly rumors" when Martha was on MDS is, I think, an important part of contemporary American history.

And, of course, Martha's week of co-hosting was not all politics and sadness because what I saw as her natural good nature and love of people was never totaled by what had befallen her.

Dick Shawn, who was a guest on one of her five shows, saluted her with the following composition of his own creation:

> Mrs. Mitchell's a wonderful lady.
> She used to say things that were considered shady.
> Actually people thought she was nuts.
> But now we're finding out she had lots of guts.

On another day Martha co-hosted a seminar of political wives: Mrs. John Dellenback of Oregon (he's in the House); Mrs. George McGovern and Mrs. Jacob Javits, whose husbands are in the Senate; and the then-estranged wife of The Honorable Marvin Mandel, Governor of Maryland.

The ladies discussed their roles in politics, their private lives, their lack of privacy and their hopes for the future, with Martha always in the adversary position, giving the impression that while the other women were carrying the ball for their husbands, she, Martha, was carrying the ball for truth. It was quite a scrap. A tense moment arrived when one of the officeholders' wives, commenting on life in politics, remarked, "We live, eat, sleep and breathe politics."

"Together?" Martha asked.

And Richard Pryor, who was also on the show, cut in with, "She thought you were talking about an orgy."

Martha said, "Thank you, Richard."

When I had introduced Pryor to Martha, he recalled being on a train with her once. "You were on Amtrak when it first started. It went to Chicago."

Martha remembered that she'd christened that train and asked Richard, "You were on that train?"

"Yes, I was the porter."

"Did you carry my bags?"

"Yes ma'am."

I asked Richard if she'd given him a tip and he said, "Yes. Blue Boy in the fifth."

I asked Richard if he'd always laughed at himself and he said only when he wasn't crying, tears shed for the most part when he was in the Army, in which he advanced to the rank of Private First Class. Martha asked what could be under that and Richard told her not much because they killed the rank of buck private when they integrated the service. And when I asked him about the Army, he said the one thing the Army did for him was to teach him a trade. He learned to be a plumber and was sent to Germany to report to Sergeant Roll. When he arrived he called the sergeant on the phone and said, "Roll, this is Richard Pryor. I'll be reporting for duty."

"Well, it's about time," replied Roll. "I've been working with a nigger the past few years and he's driving me crazy."

"So when I reported to him I said, 'Hi . . . nigger!' "

Martha asked if that sort of blatant prejudice was common in the service.

"There was a lot of racism in Germany," he told her. "So I told my company commander my father was in the NAACP and scared him a little for about a month. Then he checked and I got shipped out. I was overseas about 14 months."

Pryor has always injected controversy into the shows he's been on, as he has continued to do in the life he leads.

I got caught in the crossfire on one occasion, when Milton

Berle was talking about a book of his that contained frank revelations of his affairs and Milton said, " . . . I told Linda Smith. I say Linda Smith and I'd better keep saying Linda Smith because I hope one of these days I don't slip and say who it really is."

"Eleanor Roosevelt?" Pryor threw in. Nobody hates to be interrupted more than Berle. He saw trouble coming and whispered to me, "Shall I go on?"

"Go ahead."

But Milton said, "Maybe I'd better tell the story another time."

I urged him to continue.

"I'm sorry, Milton," Richard said. "I was out of line."

Then, scolding himself out loud, he went on, "Richard, shut up now. The man's trying to tell a story. So shut up."

Now thoroughly steamed, Milton came back with, "Let me just tell you something, baby. I told you this nine years ago and I'm going to tell you on the air in front of nine million people . . . pick your spots, baby."

"All right, sweetheart."

"Pick your spots, all right? I'll be very glad to tell the story."

"I'm sorry, Milton. I'm really . . . honest, I'm just crazy."

"No, you're not crazy."

"I'm just having fun here. I was just sitting here and it was striking me as funny. I wasn't laughing at you. I was enjoying it with you. I've seen you in dresses, so watch it."

"I want to ask you why you laughed."

"I laughed because it's funny, man. Funny to me. It ain't got nothin' to do with you."

"Because it didn't happen to you?"

"No. It's just that the insanity of all this is just funny. You understand? And I'm funny. So I laugh and so I'm crazy. I apologize because I don't want to hurt your feelings because I respect what you do. But I don't want to kiss your ass."

So Milton said to me, "See that's why I asked you if you

want to cut here, it's okay with me. . . . That's why I asked, all due respect to ladies and gentlemen on the panel, to do this one-to-one. It would be better. Because it's a serious situation and I'd rather not discuss it anymore. Now, is there anything else you want to ask me?"

"Yeah," I said. "You started to say a moment ago, 'I never told you about my father.' How about that? Can you tell us about your father?"

So much for Richard Pryor, determined to defend his right to do and say what he thought was funny and express what was funny to him.

Like him, Martha Mitchell's heart was always singing "I Gotta Be Me," long before it was written. She clearly could have made "I'll Do It My Way" her theme song.

I think the most memorable and the most darkly significant thing she said to me was of ex-President Nixon, "I wish I'd never heard his name."

On a more psychological level she remarked, "Richard Nixon doesn't really know what Richard Nixon is really like, himself. He's a terribly private man." Then she added, smiling, "That of course I couldn't understand."

Martha Mitchell's conclusion that Richard M. Nixon is a very private person certainly didn't come as "hold-the-presses" news either to his colleagues in Washington, to the ladies and gentlemen of the media or, for that matter to the nation.

But it took his daughter Julie Eisenhower, who co-hosted with me for a week, to explain that the privacy he sought was the refuge he found in the bosom of his devoted family. "We draw strength from one another," Julie said.

This I concluded was one of the reasons she considered her father and mother to be, and I quote, "Good parents."

You can't hardly find kids today who will say a thing like that about their Mom and Dad. She said they always saw to it that she and Tricia and their sons-in-law feel very much involved in their lives, that they were making a contribution, helping.

Julie told me that Dick and Pat were not the spanking type, that they used more gentle means of reproof, like cutting off privileges. But the thing she seemed to feel was really super-super, was "I can always go to Dad with my problems. He's great about me coming and talking to him. Even more so than Mother, really."

Aren't Dads usually their daughters' favorites ?

"He comes to me with problems, too," Julie said. "And often things that are getting him down are discussed at the dinner table.

"We inevitably talk about the political maneuvering, backing and filling, backbiting and back-stabbing that became such an obsession during the heavy times of Watergate." Julie paused, then said, "I think there were many people who supported my father."

Jaye P. Morgan, the singer, who happened to be a guest on one of the shows Julie co-hosted, played a modified Richard Pryor part and replied, "Oh, I do, too. I also think there were—are a lot of people who don't."

"The reason we were completely committed to my father staying in office," Julie answered (there had been some family discussion and they had tried to talk him out of resigning), "is that he had a remarkable achievement in the foreign policy field."

"And," added Ms. Morgan, "you love him."

To relieve the tension, I jumped in and changed the subject, asking Julie if she at any time felt any estrangement from people of her own age group because of her unique position, being the President's daughter, living in the White House.

The answer was no, and she pointed out that only the month before, she'd talked to three major youth groups, and I gathered from her description that the talks were less "lectures" than seminars and less seminars than what the kids today call "rap sessions," where everybody lets it all hang out.

Julie did have one big beef about living in the White House, and I imagine the feeling is shared by all who have ever been part of the President's family. That feeling is an uneasiness about the Secret Service. "I don't think anyone has ever gotten used to having them always around, watching you. But we had it a little better. During the Roosevelt administration, the Secret Service even ate with the family."

I imagined the butler asking Eleanor, "What dishes are we using tonight, Mrs. Roosevelt? The family service or the formal service?"

And the First Lady's reply, "As usual we'll have the Secret Service."

Julie confessed that she gave them the slip once. "Now that I'm free, I can talk about it," she said. "It was when David and I were living in Massachusetts. I jumped out the window of our apartment. I was so irritated I wanted to go for a walk *alone*! I walked for about an hour and felt much better having escaped. But it was rainy and dark and I got scared and headed for home."

I'd like to hear from the Secret Service if she really did lose them for an hour, or if they were tailing her all the time and she didn't know it.

Julie and David's first spat she said was inadvertently caused by the ever-present Secret Service people. They were on their honeymoon and out on the golf course. Julie admitted that she was very self-conscious about her bad golf. "I'm a real hacker," she said, "and I didn't want them standing around staring at me as I ripped up the fairway. David said to go right ahead and play and forget them. Well, I tried until the fifth hole when I got so fed up I couldn't take it anymore and quit."

Her first memory of Washington was of being taken to her father's office, when she was four. Senator Nixon had promised to take Tricia and Julie and Pat on a picnic, but a heavy rain prevented the outing. So the family improvised, laying out a spread on the floor of the office.

I'm very proud of the fact that the records show I restrained myself from making any reference to avoiding ants.

The first time she laid eyes on the White House, Julie said, was when she was eight, at the time of the '57 Inauguration. Her parents took the children along because President Eisenhower and her father were actually sworn in on a Sunday, which must come as news to millions as it did to me. The official ceremonies were, of course, not until the following day.

"We were about to go home," Julie confessed, "when I started to cry. Mrs. Eisenhower was very concerned. She tried to comfort me and asked why I was crying. 'I don't want to go home,' I said. 'I want to have lunch in the White House.'

"So she invited us to stay, and we went upstairs and we had lunch with David and his mother. That was the first time I met David. I remember I was interested. I really didn't see that many boys. He ignored us and I guess that made me more interested. We really didn't get to know each other until we were in college. Our first date was during our freshman year."

Julie seemed pleased that she and David were not married in the White House. They felt that with the protocol and all, it would not have been private enough. (There's that Nixon need for privacy.) I think, though, what Julie meant was that it would not have been their wedding. It would have been a national event, not a personal commitment. "Besides," she explained, "we'd set the date in July [1968], everything was arranged. It would have been embarrassing to send out engraved invitations to the White House on White House stationery and then discover Daddy hadn't been elected."

When I complimented her on the free and easy manner she brought to the co-host slot, she replied that she was one of the few people in the family who feel comfortable on TV. Which was perfectly obvious. She was completely relaxed and inspired a very interesting statement from political writer William Buckley, a guest on one of the shows she did, who said he didn't think anyone would ever know the whole truth about Watergate and then philosophized that he personally never wanted to hear the whole truth about anything—his wife, his mother, his father, his son. "I think human beings are mysterious," he said. "And it's part of the human process to respect that mystery."

I wanted to say that it's part of a talk show host's job to solve it. Again, mystery of mysteries, I held my opinion to myself.

But Julie's week as co-host on MDS was not all seriousness and politics. She coaxed David to guest with her and got him to play "Canadian Sunset" on the piano. She herself got into a trick bicycle act with the Clementis. She did an improvisational bit with Kenny Rogers and The First Edition. And she drew from the Las Vegas odds-maker Jimmy the Greek the word that instead of signing his real name on checks he signed Jimmy the Greek. That way some people didn't cash them, just saved them for souvenirs. "It's a good way to make a little extra money," he said.

But believe me, I know it's a pain in the neck for your wife if she happens to handle the checkbook.

I asked Jimmy what the odds were of a woman ever becoming President of the United States.

"In the next twelve years," he said, "they're prohibitive. But in the 1990's you have a great candidate sitting right next to you."

Julie laughed and said she had no such plans but asked Jimmy if he'd be available as her campaign manager.

"I hope so," he said, "but the odds are about eight to five I won't."

It may be redundant to say at this point, but I think one of the great services television talk shows offer the people of this country is the chance to see and hear people whom they normally wouldn't meet, and who normally wouldn't meet each other, sitting discussing all kinds of things in a free and open democratic way while the whole world watches.

A good part of our audience got the chance to recall its youth the week Shirley Temple Black took time off from her duties with the United Nations Human Rights Delegation in Stockholm to co-host with me. Her efforts at the time were directed at helping the People's Republic of China gain admittance to the UN.

In talking about her work she said she loved "all the people in the world," although she hedged a bit by adding, "Of course, there are some individuals I can do without."

This love for people wasn't hard to understand because it was surely reciprocated. She admitted that no matter where she traveled there were those who remembered her as the child film star.

And when we ran some clips from her early pictures, seeing little Shirley dancing up and down the stairs with Bill Robinson not only gave us the opportunity to recall the simpler days of childhood but also to reflect on how the experience of this particular child foreshadowed the accomplishments of the woman.

But the biggest moment of all when Mrs. Black was co-hosting came during one of our Nostalgia Shows of the 20s, 30s and 40s when I got the chance to sing "I Love to Be Here With You" with Shirley. Just an old Navy man back on the bridge with the skipper of the Good Ship Lollipop. While I was singing I could see flickering on the silver screen of my imagination the kids in the old neighborhood pointing at me and hollering, "Hey! Look who's singing with Shirley Temple!"

I get a lot of that sort of flashback working with people I once worshipped from afar—afar up in the balcony. Apropos of that, when Pat O'Brien co-hosted one of our

Nostalgia Shows, he mentioned how he got into pictures and I told him how I sneaked in to see them. On another show with Pat, Edgar Bergen explained how he created the dummy Charlie McCarthy and McCarthy revealed how he made the star Bergen.

Occasionally we gamble on someone we really know nothing much about, except that he's a hit in, let's say, a TV series and often we are rewarded with a big, big bonus of entertainment. I'm thinking of Jimmie (J. J.) Walker. I'd seen him a couple of times doing a single, and while he was funny I didn't think he'd reached co-host status. Then I had to change my mind when he was a smash hit as J. J. in the TV show "Good Times." To my great joy he turned out to be a whole lot more than the shuffling, gangling, sort of misdirected character he likes to play. Still young and a big star, he's looking forward to a life of producing and directing shows, not only for himself but for others, sort of in the foosteps of other comics like Sheldon Leonard and Danny Thomas.

Danny's another type of co-host. He thinks that the "co" in front of "host" stands for Commanding Officer.

Let me insert here part of a piece written about our show by Bill Hickok for *TV Radio Talk*. It'll tell you more about what it's like to have my buddy Danny Thomas for a co-host than I ever could. Bill writes:

> The voice of Danny Thomas introduces Mike. Danny is co-host and a formidable challenge to anyone else who wants to get two cents in. He's absolutely one of the world's most devastating story tellers. His timing is flawless, his instinct perfect. His host will have to use all his craft to keep the ball in his own territory. . . .

That's how the show started. Danny and I took turns singing, and then we had one of those Q-and-A sessions where the co-host fields queries from the studio audience. Hickok continues:

. . . One lady mentions that she's from Ireland. Danny, who has been fondling an unlit cigar, waiting for an opening, begins an interrogation of her that gives the impression he had left County Cork only two days before. . . .

. . . Then after the show, Danny and Mike limo over to the old Bookbinder's to have coffee and a sandwich. They will probably have to do another show and he has about two hours to relax. You don't relax with Danny Thomas around, however. Bookbinder's happens to have some very nice people clustered about enjoying a bit of scampi or lobster. Mike has gone to his usual table in a back corner to get out of it for a little while. Not Danny. Having just come down from the men's room, he sees a group of diners. Suddenly that little voice inside him—that little show business voice that's been egging him on for all these years—says "Hey, Danny! Look! An audience!" He positions himself in front of the table area, right in front of the lobster tank, and begins: "Ladies and gentlemen, fellow Philadelphians, I'd like to say a few words about Benjamin Franklin. I'm sure you are all familiar with . . ." But he lets his audience off easily, only taking them as far as Franklin's experiments with electricity, concluding, "And that, fellow Philadelphians, is why you get an electric bill every month!"

It's an interesting contrast in personalities, two men who were children of the great depression, both consummate showmen and absolute giants in the dicey, fickle world they rule, each a super star wielding great power. Yet the difference is that when they go to Bookbinder's, Mike goes in for a cup of tea and Danny goes into his act.

If a musical comedy type of co-host like Carol Lawrence says come on and dance with me, I'll dance. You can't let a guest down. And I'll laugh when Don Rickles does a number on me but I won't lie to you. It hurts me a little. I feel like crying. But then I cry watching the laundry swish around in the washer. And when Johnny Cash, on the show, told me what a lot of work he found it, how hard he found it, to write a book, I really cried because I was just starting this one and didn't want to hear "a discouraging word."

Singing is my bag. Naturally, I like co-hosts who share my enthusiasm, people like Neil Sedaka, Paul Anka, Sergio Franchi, Petula Clark, Barbra Streisand, Olivia Newton-John, Liza Minnelli. That's where I'm at. The list is endless. Someday I hope it will include Frank Sinatra.

One of the most interesting and satisfying co-hosts I've ever worked with happens to be Ray Charles, a national treasure. Ray (and those other remarkable blind musicians, Stevie Wonder, Jose Feliciano, and George Shearing) has been nothing short of a joy. When we finished the week that Ray Charles co-hosted, I remarked to Woody Fraser, "That's it. We'll never do another week like that. Nothing will ever top it." I've often thought of that week as the highlight of my career.

The thing that makes Ray and the others unique is their inner quality, their highly sharpened sensibilities. I've been told that when you lose your sight, your other senses become more acute. It certainly proved that way with Ray.

During the shows while I was sitting back and structuring an interview, he startled me by going right to the point— zooming directly to the heart of the matter. He'd say something to make me think, "Oh, boy. That's the question I wanted to begin with. The biggie." And then he'd come forth with several equally big.

You see, before we met, I knew the man only through his music. But finding out about the person was a once-in-a-lifetime experience.

This man whom Frank Sinatra has called "the only genius in the music business" sat at a piano in our studio and said to me, "Why should I be bitter? I believe that all of us, during our life, have something happen to us that we don't really like. But that doesn't mean you stop living. Once you accept whatever it is that fate deals you, then all you have to do is adjust to it."

Ray lost his sight when he was seven. Seven years later he lost his parents.

But before his mother died she imparted a few immortal words to her son, words that should be addressed to all sightless children as soon as they're old enough to understand them. Ray's mother told him, "You're *blind*, not *stupid!* You lost your *sight*, not your *mind!*"

These are words to live by in a world of darkness. She knew that being blind was going to be a problem. So she concentrated on instilling in Ray the importance of learning how to take care of himself. And today he's trying to pass on what he's learned to others who need encouragement and guidance.

He advises blind people by telling them, "Whatever I do I try to be sure I can do it before I try it. For instance, I shave. People don't realize that when you are doing things like this, you don't go at it until you are really sure you can make it. So when I shave I rarely cut myself. And I always shave with a straight razor."

I asked him how he learns music and he told me, "People who deal with music are pretty sharp, to the point where they think they've figured it all out and got it down pat. So they say, 'Well, we can't write braille and he can't see print so we'll send him a tape.' But there is braille music. When I write music I write it in braille. The difficulty with reading music in braille is that you have to learn it a little at a time. You have to remember what you've already read. You can't read and play at the same time."

Think about that. I don't know any instrument that you don't need your hands and fingers to play.

And yet Ray's first job as a musician was in a hillbilly

band, but he said, "I was never what you'd call a Charlie Pride." He views prejudice today as something parents instill in their children. "If the parents would just leave kids alone there wouldn't be any prejudice."

I asked him if he didn't wish he could *see* his children and he said he did in his way. "I truly see my children. I'm pretty close to everything. I don't physically see them with my eyes but I have a chance to get into the inner part.

"When I like someone I'm not liking them because they're handsome or beautiful. I like them because of what they really project. If somebody said to me, 'In the morning you can see again,' I wouldn't get too excited about it."

He assigns no blame for his bout with drugs, which he discussed publicly for the first time on my show. "I started myself. I was seventeen, playing in a band with older people. During breaks they'd smoke marijuana and I wanted to be like them. They tried to talk me out of it. But I had a kid's yearning to 'belong.' It's an awful feeling to be left out of a group. I was on drugs from 1948 to 1965."

He quit because he found he had something he loved more. "My son was getting a trophy for baseball one night and I wanted to see him get it, to be there for his big moment. But I had to leave to do a recording date and he cried and cried and I got the idea that any kid who loves his father that much . . . then certainly I should do something about myself. What I do is one thing. What happens to him is another. That motivated me to say, 'Hey, now you've got somebody else who loves you so much you don't want to make him suffer.' I didn't want to run the chance that some kid would come up to him someday and tell him his father was a jailbird. So I quit."

This was all pretty heavy stuff we went through, so trying to lighten things up a little I asked about something I felt everybody who knows anyone blind is curious about, "How do you dress yourself?"

On the face of it, that's a funny question to ask a successful grown man. But unlike most of us, he can't decide to wear the brown pinstripe suit and then just look in the closet and pick it out. What would you do?

Ray said, "When I was coming up in the ranks, before I was fortunate enough to be able to hire someone to help me, I had to work out a way to do it myself. So every suit I have is a little different; the buttons, the style, the pockets, the pants. This tells me which is which."

"So all you have to do is remember that the two-button with the flap pockets is light blue. But what about the rest of the outfit?"

"If you look in my closet now you'd see that every outfit I have is complete: the shirt, the tie, the jacket, the pants."

"The socks? What about them?"

"Well, I buy brown nylon ones and black cotton ones. Each basic color has a different texture, which makes it easy. You rely on touch. And when it comes down to the absolutely ridiculous where you have two things that are identical, like handkerchiefs I just take a razor and cut a little piece off."

"But how do you remember all that stuff?"

"If you don't have to look at a lot of unnecessary things, it's easier to remember."

"Then you have no problems to speak of."

"Yeah. I'd like to speak of one problem, insurance! I could get life insurance. But I couldn't get accident or health insurance because the insurance companies seem to feel that a person who is blind is a helluva risk. But what they don't know is that blind people and anybody with any kind of handicap are far more careful. They're not apt to take chances and do things they know they can't do. You'll try to run across a street to beat the traffic. Not me."

I owe Ray for unwittingly helping me to get Michel Legrand on our show at a moment's notice.

We were in Hollywood and having booking problems. Totie Fields had to bow out and we'd built a whole show around her.

All we had solid was Ray Charles. "That's enough for me," I said. But they urged me to get another name. So I walked into the best place in Hollywood to make a spot booking, the Polo Lounge of the Beverly Hills Hotel.

The first people I saw were Mary Martin and Ethel Merman together, a pretty good parlay. But their day was all booked up. I felt like the night club comic who was bombing in a spot. When the phone rang he was so anxious to be in touch with humanity he answered. "What time is the show?" a voice asked. He said, "What time can you make it?"

Then I spotted Michel Legrand, who had told me he loved Ray Charles, considered him the greatest thing in music but that by some happenstance they had never met.

So I figured if I could talk Michel into coming on the show with Charles, it would be the greatest thing since sliced bread. And it was. Oh, boy, *was* it! And when they did "Georgia" together, it was a once-in-a-lifetime experience. The audience stood up. That sophisticated, blasé Hollywood crowd gave them a standing ovation. You seldom see that in television.

Yet it's become sort of an "in" thing in Vegas. They almost do it automatically. I dropped a handkerchief one night and when I picked it up they were all standing. It's ridiculous. I got one one night walking into Palumbo's restaurant.

Sarah Vaughan, one of Legrand's greatest fans, told me she heard me singing on a show with Michel. "Man, you really sang your ass off," she said.

Praise from people like Sarah and Ella Fitzgerald are words I treasure, because they're both great ladies, great talents and innovators. Whenever I meet Ella, she gets on my back to sing more on the show. Nice. I tell her to come on the show more and I will.

From one song writer to another, who, like Ray Charles, is out of sight but not out of mind, we move on to José Feliciano, who credits the guitar with having turned his whole life around.

"I was just one of your average, run-of-the-mill, obnoxious, mischievous kids," he told me, "until I met up with the guitar. I couldn't see it but I could feel it and hold it and make songs with it and we've been inseparable ever since."

At seventeen, José and his pal the git box ran away from home to seek their fortune and found it. Who says a blind man can't find things? Although I must say he started looking in a funny place.

"I was doing your show in Cleveland at a time when the truant officers were looking for me," he confided.

"I'm glad I didn't know that. I'd have had to turn you in or I'd probably be an accessory after the fact. But by now I think the statute of limitations has run out. You know, doing a television show is a lousy place to hide. You may not be able to see it but a lot of truant officers can."

"They didn't," he said, adding, "Ray Charles was my inspiration. I liked what he did on the piano. I wanted to do it on the guitar. That soulful music influenced me."

"Ray told me that at the point in his life at which he now is, he wouldn't particularly want sight. How do you feel?"

"Well, it would be an experience. For instance I'd like to know if people look anything like they sound to me. Then everything would be straightened out in my head as to things in life."

One of the things in life that both José and I need straightening out about is the place of the "pun" in the scheme of things. We both love them. We were talking about the problems of a blind musician playing with sighted people and he said he once switched the music on all the racks. Gave all the men braille sheets.

"That," I said, "should have made them play with more feeling."

"Well, Mike, that's a touchy subject."

For some reason or other, Harcum College sent us both T-shirts and I was wearing mine but José wasn't. When I asked "Harcum you're not wearing yours?", he said, "I didn't bother to look."

He'll go way out of his way to ring in a pun. For no reason at all he said to me, "I stole a lemon once when I was a kid and got into a lot of trouble. I needed *some* AID to get out of that one."

"I guess that taught you a lesson."

"Yes, Mike, I learned to plant my own garden. It's really interesting the way the economy is going, if you grow your own vegetables you're really beeting the economy."

The laugh was very light. "You must also be in the poultry business."

"Yeah. I'm laying my own eggs."

But when it comes to punning, I don't know anyone who can top Gregory Peck. Apropos of his appearance as General Douglas MacArthur, I asked if he, Peck, would ever want to enter politics. He said he felt that he was basically too shy for that game. Actually, he said he knew nothing at all about politics except what he learned about the CIA when he was in Spain working on a film.

Peck said that a mansion Juan Peron had lived in, when he was in exile in Spain, was rented by the CIA when Peron returned to Argentina. They did this, according to the rumor, because President Thieu of South Vietnam was having a lot of trouble and might have to leave his country, and they'd keep the mansion in Spain ready for him because they felt Thieu could live as cheaply as Juan. That's my kind of pun.

In case you think I've forgotten I mentioned Stevie Wonder, no way! He, too, is one of the bona fide geniuses of music, a real international trendsetter—and so young! Always into something new.

In the many talks we've had, it's clear to me that Stevie

feels exactly the same way about his lack of sight that Ray does and lists Ray as one of the primary influences on his music when he was growing up in Chicago. As other influences on his musical growth he credits the Staple Singers, James Brown and Neil Sedaka.

I asked him when the thought first crossed his mind that he might be able to make money singing.

"It was at a family picnic," he recalled. "I got paid a quarter. That meant a lot more to me then than a dollar. I could hear that quarter knockin' around in my pocket."

He credits his start in the record business to Berry Gordy of Motown Records, who named him Little Stevie Wonder. "Of course we had to drop the 'little' when I started to grow up." Then he said, "Stevie Wonder is only the vehicle through which the Supreme Being enabled me to express the feelings of Steven Morris, which is my real name."

I was curious as to how, since he couldn't see the sun, he could write a tune like "You Are the Sunshine of My Life." And the answer was, "You can feel the warmth and brightness of the sun. I know it's red because I've been told and I know red is the color of excitement. Just the word 'red' is exciting."

The reason behind Stevie's many impromptu visits to high schools and many benefit performances is the conviction that his success carries with it a mission. "The responsibility," he said, "is a pleasure. I feel good about it. I feel thankful."

I'm very proud that one of the first TV appearances Stevie ever made was on my show. Because I draw inspiration from him and George Shearing and Ray and José. They have given hope and encouragement to thousands who see them and hear them and say to themselves, "If they can make it, why can't I." I'm proud to be a friend of each of them.

Having learned from Ray Charles how he selects his clothes I found out from another musical co-host, Johnny

Cash, how he avoids the problem of deciding what color to wear.

We were talking about Johnny's book, *The Man In The Black Suit*, and I asked him why he always wears black.

"I've never had a real good answer for that," he said. "Except that I just feel good in black."

"Must save a lot on cleaning bills."

"It started in Memphis when I did my first recording with the Tennessee Two . . . that was Marshall Grant, who's still with me, Glenn Bates and my guitarist Luther Perkins.

"That's the Tennessee *Two?*"

"Well, there was also me."

"I see."

"We did a lot of practicing. This is before we got to do any recording."

"It works out that way most of the time."

"We'd practice at night. All night long we'd practice singing everything we could think of."

"And you put on black so you wouldn't be such a good target in the dark?"

"Well, no. Some of the neighbors heard us—they couldn't help it— and they come and asked if we wouldn't do some gospel songs in the church. We were gettin' ready to do it, gettin' dressed and I thought we ought to look professional and all dress alike. So I asked what we had alike and it turned out that we all had black shirts. That sounded good for Sunday night in church so we wore 'em. I got away from black for a while but I went back to it because it got us off to a good start that night."

You know they say that behind every man there's a woman. Well, it seems that behind every successful musician there's an unusual story.

Victor Borge came to the United States from Denmark for two reasons, to seek his fortune and to avoid the coming threat of a madman named Adolf Hitler.

He was discovered by Rudy Vallee and given his first chance on the air by Bing Crosby—but not as a musician, as a comedian. It didn't come out until later that he was not only a monologist but a serious concert pianist who could also have a lot of fun with music. He's sensational. He breaks me up. Like Bill Cosby and Buddy Hackett, he's always ready with a funny fast answer. He throws away more material than most comics have.

He told me, "My sister taught me how to play the 'Minute Waltz.' Unfortunately I can only play thirty seconds of it because she was just my half sister."

When he's not noodling around at the piano he's throwing one-liners at whoever opens his mouth. And if nobody gives him a straight line he'll feed himself.

"I was doing a concert in Edinburgh," he said, "and I found out what Scotchmen wear under their kilts."

When I asked the answer to this question that has been puzzling the world, Victor said, "shoes."

His comedy is based on his absolute literalness about things. When I ask him what he's doing he says, "Talking to you."

This literalness was the basis of his first success on the air in America. He read a story giving distinct sounds to each of the punctuation marks. It's become a classic he'll still do if coaxed hard enough. Not many such routines have survived for 30 or more years as Borge's punctuation routine has.

When talking on the show with Shelley Winters, Victor was asked his opinion of women's "lib."

Before answering he asked, "Which lib? Upper or lower?"

Shelley who had taken on some weight, said, "I'm God's gift to the medical profession. You name it, I've had it checked." Victor suggested she try checking her appetite.

Another guest on the show was a handwriting expert named Robert Wasserman, who told Victor he was going to analyze his handwriting.

"I hope that's the only test you're going to make, Mr. Wasserman," said Borge.

Sometimes sheer nonsense seems to make sense when

said by Borge. To Linda Blair, who told him she was twenty-five going on sixteen, he said, "When I was your age, I was nineteen."

Then there's Marvin Hamlisch, who swept across our musical scene like a swarm of composers after he scored the movie *The Sting* and then composed the score for *A Chorus Line*. He's won enough Oscars to start their own jazz combo. And he's funny too.

The second time he co-hosted, I greeted him saying, "Welcome back, Marvin."

"*Mr.* Hamlisch, please. I've been a co-host on 'The Mike Douglas Show.'" I'm still wondering whether that was a build-up or a put-down.

Kate Smith, who is known and loved for so many things it's almost impossible to list them, has co-hosted with me. We are both adopted Philadelphians. Her singing of "God Bless America" has been a good-luck symbol for our Philadelphia Flyers hockey team, although she's never played hockey in her life. And it came out during one of her co-hostings that she had made a real contribution to the world of comedy when she discovered Henny Youngman and had him on her radio show for a long run. (Whenever Henny appears on the show he brings me some simple little gift like a dime-and-pin [a safety pin with a dime welded on it] or a tiny bank check for the man who likes to write small checks.)

Kate is virtually the only singer I know who has never tried to be a comedian. Crosby frequently topped Bob Hope, and that famous singer George Burns occasionally likes to drop a funny line.

Rather than concentrate on songs like "King of the Road" that boosted him to fame, for instance, Roger Miller goes around writing lyrics like "You Can't Roller Skate in a Herd of Buffaloes."

Come to think of it, there's a very subtle meaning contained in that title—you can't go against the crowd.

Referring back to that remote in Savannah with Johnny Mercer and Mike Connors, we did a pickup from a dock—sounds as if my co-host was the United Parcel Service—of what was then a new shipping operation. One piece of machinery really boggled the mind, a gigantic crane that loaded and unloaded containers from ship to train or vice versa. The contraption rose a couple of hundred feet into the air and looked to have sufficient power to pick up our little planet and transpose it to Mars. Far out!

Any man who tinkered with an Erector set or Meccano would see immediately the realization of his dreams in that giant derrick. Every guy without exception in our outfit wanted to sneak into its cab on the sly and operate the monster. The guy who got this plum was co-host Mike Connors. The machine was irresistible to him. We had the foreman show Mike what he was supposed to do. Then it was to be a simple matter of Mike rising up a couple of hundred feet and doing it. When I saw what he was about to do I was supposed to say, "I'll go up with you." When I was told this, I immediately said, "Oh, no, I won't," which was my standard answer to all such high climbing.

I got the feeling they were trying to repeat what they did to me in Boston. Connors didn't know what everybody on the show knew, that I suffer from acrophobia. So he kept on urging, "Come on. It must be great up there. I'll bet you can see forever."

I told him I'd rather live forever than see it. But, again, my Dad's admonition never to reject a challenge overcame my good sense. So we went up.

To me it was the last mile. But I feel responsible for my guests and I felt it was my duty to go with him, the way a captain goes down with his ship. Only I went up.

When we reached the top of the thing where the controls were, Connors operated the huge piece of machinery as easily as if it were a claw machine in a shooting gallery. When he stepped out of the operator's booth onto the catwalk and saw me standing there terror-stricken, with my eyes closed, he said, "Look, Mike. It's nothing," and he flung one leg over the rail. "Don't," I pleaded with him. "Don't *do* things like that!" I literally got down on my knees. On camera it looked like a big gag.

It's because I sometimes don't know on the show whether something is on the level or whether they're putting me on, that that same Mike Connors almost had his voice raised two or three octaves. He was co-hosting in the studio and we had a couple of parachutists demonstrating how their gear was worn and what happens when the first training drop is made. Connors got into the chute and went up for the practice drop. As his fall was stopped suddenly, he let out an absolutely ungodly scream. I don't know how anyone could have doubted that he was in pain but we all did. We seemed to think it was a gag. By the time we realized he was in earnest, he had almost fainted.

The fault was in the size of the chute straps. They were too small for him in the area where they pass from the front, between the legs, to connect with the back of the chute.

And while on the subject of co-host Connors, I might as well go the whole route. On one show we whipped up the idea to surprise him, à la Ralph Edwards' "This Is Your Life," and bring his mother in from Fresno. It was no big deal excluding the fact that Mike was in the dark. It struck us as a nice warm thing to do, and we anticipated with glee the surprise on his face when she walked in. To make it even better, we asked her to prepare some of Mike's favorite Armenian food for him just the way she did when he was a boy.

So—everything's set. I get the cue and say, "Mike, we've got a little surprise for you. We know you love Armenian food so we asked your mother to cook some and bring it to you. And here she is . . ."

A little old lady walked in and a look of utter panic crossed Connors' face. The surprise we wanted, the joy and the laughter, weren't there.

From the corner of his mouth so our audience wouldn't
see it, he whispered to me, "That's not my mother."

Now I'm just as freaked out as Connors, because my people have obviously gotten the wrong woman. Then I saw
that everyone (except Mike and me) was doubled over with
laughter. They'd just played a little practical joke on both of
us and followed it by bringing on Mike's real mother with
the real Armenian food and everything worked out fine.

Later Connors told me that he was so frightened because
there actually had been a woman in Greece who claimed to
be his mother. She claimed he'd run away from home as a
child, claimed she was starving and kept writing him, begging him to come home and save her and presumably bring
plenty of money.

"What'll we do?" I asked, "if that other little old lady's
real son calls up and complains that he and his mother were
libelously associated with an Armenian actor?"

Fooling Connors with the wrong mother was just one incident in the MDS history of dealing with stars' parents,
especially mothers. And it's absolutely remarkable how
fond those ladies all are of their successful boys. I think this
is unusual in a psychologically saturated society that tends
to base all anti-social activity of minors on their resentment
of their mothers. Either Mother was too permissive or too
strict. Whatever bad the kid does is her fault. I don't buy it.
In a nation that makes almost a national holiday of what
started out as a publicity promotion—Mother's Day—I have
to put in with the majority who believe that without Moms
none of us would be here.

I base this on the reaction I got when I sang the song
"Mother's Day" on the show for the first time. The number
came to me from its composer, Mrs. Elaine Grannum, a
Brooklyn housewife. Mrs. Grannum sent her composition to
Frank Hunter, who was then my conductor, with a note saying she felt I was the ideal person to sing it. This was probably because she heard the rumor that I revered my mother.

We've had many a Mother's Day on the MDS. There was

the time Mrs. Rose Namath Szolnoki came by to talk about her boy, some obscure football player. Mrs. S. had just written a book entitled *Namath, My Son Joe*, which revealed all about him. But the one rumor she really quashed was that all Joe does is run around painting the town each evening.

I told her that sometimes he's been known to run around right end when he gets the proper protection.

Then we got it straight from the mother's mouth that Joe vowed he would never marry until he was through playing football because he wanted his marriage to be a success. So how he fares with the Rams will doubtless have a bearing on his marital eligibility.

For some reason it didn't come as a surprise that the playboy bachelor Joe Namath as a child was "quiet and on the shy side." He comes across that way even today. His smile is more come-hither than here-I-come. Mrs. Szolnoki remarked that as a boy his "great pleasure was chewing on popcorn and celery."

He sure got some stalk of celery when he signed up with the Jets.

"But," she added, "in the last three years he's changed."

I gathered he'd changed even before that because Mrs. Szolnoki said that right after he was born and when she first laid eyes on him, she thought she'd been given the wrong baby, "he was so dark and had sideburns." He still had those when he surprised her on the show with a telephone call. (To hear any mother tell it, when she gets a call from her son it's a surprise.) He was calling from the Jets' training camp and signed off with the promise, "I'll be in touch in the next couple of days," which elicited the standard maternal reply, "Don't forget, honey."

When Marvin Hamlisch brought his mother on the show she said, "I think it was greedy of Marvin to take three Oscars. He should have left more for the others."

Of course, she was kidding but she wasn't joking when she said, "I think Marvin has accomplished a lot. And the next thing is someone should make a happy and healthy home for him. But I don't envy the girl. He's too demanding. He lives for his music. When a girl comes to the house she should just listen to his songs. She should serve him whatever he wants because he's spoiled from his mother. It's my fault. I'm old-fashioned.

Groucho Marx confirmed Mrs. Hamlisch's opinion of Marvin's romances when he said, "Marvin's a guy who can play the piano without looking at the keys. He can turn away and look at me and know where everything is, including a couple of dames."

When I asked if either she or Marvin had that right girl in mind, she said, "He doesn't date long enough for me to really get to like anyone. As soon as I get used to one girl, there's another one. But he was a very good baby. Till nine months I didn't even know there was a baby in the house."

All Marvin would say, pointing to his mother, was, "If there should be a service called Hertz-Renta-Mother, this is what they should rent out. She's perfect."

From Burt Reynolds' mother, and all the other doting mothers we've had on the show, I've discovered that along with the instincts and feelings God gives a woman when she becomes pregnant, He includes a crash course in doting as a preparation for when the male child becomes successful.

So to get the real facts we also had Burt's dad and "brother" on the show one week in Miami Beach, and we glimpsed more sides of Burt than could be shown in that *Cosmopolitan* nude centerfold that flashed him into notoriety and for which he will always be remembered by ladies with certain things on their minds.

Burt's Dad laid it right on the line saying, "Sometimes he was good and sometimes he was bad. I don't have enough time on the show to tell you about all the bad times." And the human side of my friend the "sex symbol" came out when Burt's "brother" Jim Nicholson told how he became Burt's "brother."

"We used to play football together in the park. I didn't

have much at home. So Burt took me home with him, asking his mother and father if I could stay and from then on I was Burt's brother." Jim's wife, Jo, threw in, "With support like that Jim couldn't help but win."

My next move clearly was to ask Burt, who created a brother, what kind of a father he thought he'd make. He grew very serious and emphasized that he'd made repeated efforts to become a single father through adoption. "A lot of the agencies I've been to didn't think my image was proper. But I think I'd make a terrific father. How many boys, before they're born, have their old man's image checked out? I have a lot of love to give and so much to offer a boy."

The Reverend Jess Moody, a close friend of Burt's, agreed wholeheartedly and said he was going to "help Burt all the way in this fight."

On the other side of the coin, Burt's virile image is not only attractive to girls. During an audience question-and-answer session, a teen-age boy said to him, "When you get married, can I have your little black book?"

While Burt, taken by surprise and covered with embarrassment (the only time I've seen him that way), fumbled around for words, I jumped in to try to save him with, "By then it'll be too heavy to carry."

Burt and I have spent a lot of time together. I've gotten to know all the Burt Reynoldses there are in that complicated man: 1) the sex symbol and joker; 2) the consumate professional, actor and director; and 3) the quiet, thoughtful, religious humanitarian that lives in the man who, when he was a boy, adopted another boy, Jim Nicholson, and took him for a brother.

I think I'm a little high on Burt.

We tried to induce Liberace to bring his mother on the show, but he told us she was too busy with the slot machines in Las Vegas. He said, "My mother is so crazy about slot machines, she's been known to play them for twenty-four hours right around the clock. The management offered to put one in her room right by her bed but she said she liked to be down there with all the others where the action is. For years she just played nickel machines but now with inflation and everything she's up to quarters."

No wonder Liberace feels he has to work all the time to support a mother with a habit like that.

I spoke of Liberace to Red Skelton, one of the actors I'm most proud to have had as a co-host. He was great, and one of the things that made his appearance outstanding was his pantomime. I kept thinking how wonderful he would have been in silent movies.

Red said he never wears jewelry when he's on stage. "When you're using your hands in pantomime, people tend to look at the rings and stuff instead of at you."

He is one of my idols, one of the greatest clowns we have. The week he co-hosted he not only entertained millions he entertained *us*—the crew, the musicians, the staff. When the week was over they just couldn't do enough for him. And he told us something about his craft, too, pantomime. He explained about the three different schools of pantomime that exist. Marcel Marceau's, which is, of course, the French school. Then there's the Japanese Kabuki theatre, which is dance but also pantomime. And Italian pantomime, which Red says is the kind he performs. "They tell you exactly what's going to happen and then they act it out."

I asked if he'd ever been criticized for laughing at what he is doing. He said he thought it was perfectly natural. Everybody else is laughing. Besides, if *I* don't think it's funny, why am I doing it?

Red likes to talk about his painting, as does Jonathan Winters, who is also a serious painter. And when I asked Red how much he got for one of his clowns he said it depended on how much a person liked it. "I know I was in a gallery in New York once," he said, "and saw a painting I was willing to pay three or four hundred dollars for. So I asked the price. The manager said, 'Five thousand wouldn't buy that.' I said, 'I'm one of them' and walked out."

Something Red said I try to pass on to every young performer who comes on our show.

"I don't think an actor should try to put himself above an audience. And that's what the short cut is now with off-color jokes and things. These young funny people do what they feel is funny, and get laughs. Then one show they'll throw in something a little blue and it'll get a howl. But when the audience goes out they're saying 'He's funny but why did he have to say that?' But the comic doesn't hear this and keeps the blue notes in, adding more and more things and pretty soon he's carrying a glass and lighting cigarettes and everything is a dirty joke."

One thing I'd like to plan on having for our show. Red said that Margot Fonteyn wanted him to come to England and do "Swan Lake" with her for a command performance because she'd seen him do a comedy skit on the ballet. Well, I'd like to plan on devoting a whole MDS to Margot and Red as co-hosts presenting Fonteyn in Red's version of "Swan Lake."

So much for fun and games.

I've mentioned before Mason Reese, the young star who became a national star with his commercials, particularly the one on which he attempted to say "smorgasbord." The thing that captured the curiosity of viewers was that Mason was very precocious and had a face that seemed much too mature for a child. His "fame"got him booked on many talk shows, although I think ours was the first and we booked him as a co-host. None has been better at that job than Mason nor has anyone given the show the sentimental clout that Mason brought to a Christmas show on which he closed a week of co-hosting.

Early in the week one of my guests was Ralph Nader, with whom I was having a serious talk. (Can you have any other kind with Ralph?) Co-host Mason was still a little too young to be interested in consumer advocacy and governmental regulation. He sat there and squirmed.

When we came to the next segment of the show, with Ralph gone, Mason tried to raise the laugh level a little above ground zero. In doing so he said something to me that I have now forgotten. But in saying it he called me "crazy," copying the intonation of Redd Foxx's character Fred Sanford in the TV show "Sanford and Son" to make the word almost one of endearment. I must have been preoccupied, distracted in some way for a moment, and didn't respond to Mason's little jibe in kind. It hurt Mason very deeply. And I can understand why. We had become great pals. I really loved the kid and told him so. We played together and I said he was the kind of little boy I had always wanted. Which was true. A letter I received from Bill Reese, "sometimes known as Mason Reese's father," said, "Mason has grown to love you for all those qualities you're known and liked for by your audience and for the demonstration of those qualities, and more, off camera before and after the show."

I felt very bad when the staff told me the kid was hurt and unhappy because he thought I was mad at him. I didn't want him to carry that feeling into the Christmas holiday and was racking my brains trying to think of something I could do or say to square things between us. It really mattered very much to me. I decided on a little speech I'd make just before we closed the last show of the week, our Christmas show.

But I never had time to make it. Mason handled the whole matter in his own way.

I was closing the show, getting ready for my big speech to Mason, but first I wanted to get him in the right mood. I got as far as a reference to all the Christmas decorations in the studio and said, "Doesn't it all make you feel like Christmas?"

Mason said, "Yeah, but it isn't really . . . yet."

"Well, almost. Any last thing you want to say before we

wrap this up?" I don't know just why I asked that. Maybe I thought, suspected, he had something in mind.

"Yeah. It's really like a sad thing." He pulled a piece of paper out of his pocket and began to read.

> I may have called you "crazy."
> I know that isn't true.
> I may have fussed and fooled around
> As most kids sometimes do
> But I just love to be co-host,
> To get to know you more . . .

Here he began to choke up.

> I hope that you'll forgive my faults

Here he started crying and broke up completely.

> Cause that's what friends are for.

I took him in my arms and he lay there sobbing, and all I could say was, "I love you Mason. I love you. You didn't hurt my feelings. You're my buddy. You're my pal. Have a nice holiday and come back and see me soon. And remember your pal loves you. Will you remember that?"

There was a long pause. Finally Mason got himself together and in a tiny voice said, "I'll try."

In his letter, Bill Reese wrote that "in the Green Room there wasn't a dry eye." May I add there wasn't one in the audience either—or on stage.

The flood of mail stemming from that incident was not to be believed. And many people *didn't* believe it. But there will always be those who question real sentiment and sincerity because they've never known it.

In another part of Bill Reese's letter he says that I "played an important and unique part in Mason's life. I'm not talking about Mason's career—I'm also talking about his life experience. We don't know where his 'career' will take him. But no matter what he does, the joys he experienced because of you will remain with him. Your relationship has been a tender and caring and loving one. It allowed Mason to grow in the entertainment world with the awareness that there are real people behind the faces on the tube. And although some are 'takers,' manipulators, dishonest, phoney, there are also good, gentle, considerate, warmhearted people. You are that and more, and it's been a marvelous thing for Mason to have been involved in his formative years with you. You never talked down to him nor talked to him from your height as an 'adult.' You saw Mason as a special kind of little boy—bright, quick, funny, talented—but above all with a warm and good heart. I've told Mason that it takes a man like you to reach out and touch a boy's heart. I think it's wonderful that my son has another man in his life who loves him."

It's great to know that a father's willing to share his son's love with you. Bill's letter almost made me cry. I have a very low threshold of tears.

Of course, it was something when my little girl Chris had a baby of her own. My first grandchild. And I was just as dewy-eyed for the second one.

I'll never forget twice receiving phone calls about the arrival of grandchildren. The first time I was requested to sing, "The Men In My Little Girl's Life." It never crossed my mind that I couldn't get through it. But as I sang it and thought about it and . . . well . . . I couldn't make it. Thinking about that little doll having a baby of her own. And I think there were some handkerchiefs out in the audience, too, because they had been told why I was singing that song.

It's not my job to make people cry, but with me, sometimes, it's good to get that close to them. All my life I've enjoyed being close in with my audience. That was my night club act. The owner would say, "I want forty-five minutes" and all I had was twelve. So I'd have to talk to the audience and get the feel of them for thirty-three minutes. It's one of the things I do best, I think, talking to an audience, and I don't think I really do enough of it on the show.

It was one of the things Vic Damone stressed when we had dinner together in Tahoe the day I got the news that "The Mike Douglas Show" was to become a reality, starting December 11 in Cleveland.

Vic Damone was playing at what I laughingly thought of as the competition: a beautiful, posh spot called the Cal-Neva Lodge. It was built right across the California/Nevada border. A red line ran through the lobby to show guests what state they were in—California, Nevada or the state of poverty from dallying too long in the casino on the Nevada side.

He had heard me sing in spots around L.A. and had brought people in to hear me. When he heard I was at the Nevada Lodge he came over and asked why Gen and I hadn't been to see his show. Ours went on at a time that didn't conflict with his, as if there were a conflict. I was singing to tablecloths and waiters talking among themselves.

I told him we'd love to but we just couldn't afford it. He said to come anyway and be his guests. So leaving the twins to babysit with little Kelly, we accepted Vic's offer.

During dinner I asked him if he thought I ought to take the Cleveland offer I'd first welcomed so enthusiastically and was now having second thoughts about. He asked what kind of show: "Will you have your own band? Will you have a chance to sing? Will you get a chance to talk with people?" I answered yes to all his questions.

"Take it," he said.

Before leaving the subject of Vic Damone, naturally as soon as possible after the show got started we booked Vic as a very special guest and I told our art director, at that time a man named Rocco Urbisci, to do something great in the way of a set for him.

When I walked into the studio to see it, I found Rocco standing proudly beside his creation.

I broke up. The set was two huge letters, a "V" and a "D."

When I got control of myself I asked, "Are we doing a bit on venereal disease?"

Rocco turned red and walked out without a word, totally embarrassed. And although people kidded him for weeks about his V.D. set, would you believe that some time later, when we had a guest named Billy Mackstead, the set he built was a big "B" and a big "M."

When I saw it I just looked at Rocco and asked, "B.M.?"

He threw up his hands and said, "Oh, my God, I did it again!"

Some years later, on my second go-round in Tahoe, this time to do some taping for the show, Gen and I had forgotten how cold the nights and early morning hours can be and hadn't brought the appropriate clothing.

The morning we started to work it was doubly cold. I came down with a virus, and by the time we returned to the hotel in the evening I was shaking like what Bert Lahr used to call "an aspirin leaf." I climbed into bed, asked Gen to throw everything in the room on me including the dresser to keep me warm and to call the doctor. I didn't want to cancel the next day's taping. So they sent me a medic whose specialty is the quick recovery of performers so the show can go on.

It was well into dinnertime before he showed up, in a tuxedo. His nurse, who was his wife, was in an evening gown with a very revealing neckline. It was bing-bam and I had shots on both sides of my backside. They told me they were penicillin and B-12. It must have been a whole bunch of both, if that's what it was, because in a little while I was talking about getting up and going to see some acts.

Next morning I was ready to work and we got through the whole week without any trouble. I haven't felt such chills since, but if I ever do I'm either going to get that doctor in Tahoe to fly to Philadelphia or I'm taking a plane for Tahoe.

Again, to list all the great names in show business who have been my co-hosts and to whom I owe a debt would make this book read like a who's who of show biz. The names vary from one extreme to the other and are as different as Florence Henderson is from Zsa Zsa Gabor.

There have been so many great co-hosts. Take Stiller and Meara, an excellent actor and a superb actress. Together, they make a sock comedy team as well as wonderful parents. Their commercials on radio for a certain wine company constantly make me wish I were a drinking man so that I could offer a toast to two people who not only prove that there are good, kind, honest people in show biz but, what is more important, that like the "Cohens" and the "Kellys," the Stillers and the Mearas can abide side by side, raise a family, and be happy.

We have had a regular three-ring circus of remotes, stunts, and fascinating people enlivening the MDS over a period of sixteen years. To try and list them all would turn this book into a twenty-volume set.

The luminaries from sports, Broadway, from the worlds of film and politics, science and the humanities have all stood at our microphones as the cameras rolled, and given us their stories, their dreams and a little bit of themselves.

We've had "co-hosts" that were a classification, such as "Hollywood" or "Soap Operas," and we've had "co-hosts" as abstract as "Nostalgia."

There was the occasion when "Hollywood" was the co-host. Marlon Brando, one of the film industry's greatest and most controversial actors, turned it into a 'Nostalgia" show. Sadly he directed our attention to the plight of the American Indian and looked into the past when our nation was very young and their nations were very old and proud and they trusted us.

Then, having made the point closest to his heart, he got the show back in the groove it was meant to travel by introducing Francis Ford Coppola, the director who cast him as the Godfather.

"I had no frame of reference for playing a sixty-five-year-old Italian," Marlon said. And when I asked why, if that were the case, he took the job, his answer was, "I hadn't worked in a year and a half and needed the money."

He'd taken on a lot of weight to play in *The Godfather* and the years had put some gray in his hair since I saw him playing Rod Steiger's pug brother who didn't want to take a dive, in *On the Waterfront*. To this day I never see a torn undershirt but I think of Marlon hollering for Stella in *A Streetcar Named Desire*. Speaking of his size, he pointed to Coppola and said, "He made me the pig I am," and explained that Coppola not only makes the best pictures but the best spaghetti in the whole world.

In trying to explain to me his theory of acting, he said he doesn't think it's natural for an actor to snap out lines on cue. "You don't know what you're going to say next in real life," he explained. "You have to think about it. You don't know anything about what's coming next in real life." That's why instead of learning lines, he likes to be more natural and find out about them as they come along. To do this, he has them printed on the walls, on furniture, on the backs of other actors, on the ceiling. I interrupted to ask, "Is that what you're doing when you're talking to someone and stop and look up. Is it written up there?"

"It's written everywhere," he said.

I was glad we had young people new to show biz, like Donny and Marie, on that show so they'd get some tips from a man many consider the best actor of our generation.

Gene Hackman, who, like Brando, had been directed by Coppola (*The Conversation*), came on the show with a story about my pal Burt Reynolds, who was flying in Gene's Lear jet with Gene at the controls. "He was sitting back there quietly reading poetry while I was doing all the work of piloting, so I thought I'd shake him up by going into a slow roll." The rest of the trip was strictly "white knuckle" for Burt.

I was glad to hear His Majesty the sex symbol could be shook up about something so insignificant as a falling airplane on which he was a passenger. Imagine Reynolds letting such a trite matter interrupt his poetry reading.

The pressures of show business have taken a heavy toll. So it was with sadness and concern that I read about Tony Orlando's stopping in mid-performance and announcing that he was calling it quits. A great friend ever since he made his first major television appearance on our show, Tony was the sort of person I can speak frankly to—which I did one night when Tony and his lovely and devoted wife, Elaine, were having lunch with Gen and me at the Century Plaza. I told him that the Tony Orlando I was seeing on his CBS show was not the same honest, likable, at-ease entertainer I had enjoyed in the earlier days of his series' run. Combine the eventual cancellation of his show with such tragedies as the death of his retarded sister and the suicide of his good friend Freddie Prinze and other factors—some public knowledge and some not—and the fact that Tony was suffering a general breakdown in the summer of 1977 was not surprising if no less disturbing.

By November, Tony was getting it all together and planning a return to performing. I was very pleased that he had decided to make his first television appearance, to discuss his experiences, on my show. I'll admit I was apprehensive too—until Tony, Elaine, Gen and I sat down around the Orlando kitchen table to talk prior to the interview which we were going to tape in the living room of their beautiful house in Brentwood. Here was the Tony Orlando I used to know—open, sincere, concerned about others. He was, to be sure, nervous about going back on stage and doing it alone, without Dawn. But he wanted to get his story on the air, so that others with similar problems might be encouraged to seek help.

We must have talked off-camera for more than an hour, with Tony sharing all sorts of harrowing experiences, some of which he said he couldn't possibly tell on camera. At this point I realized that the 35 minutes we had allotted on the show, which was to consist of segments with a variety of stars taped in the Hollywood area, would hardly be sufficient. Although I usually like to leave such decisions to them, I told our producers that we would have to go the full 90 minutes with Tony. That meant juggling schedules, cancelling several bookings and disrupting the Orlando household for a full afternoon (they could not have been more gracious), but we all agreed that the results were worth it.

Seated in their elegantly appointed living room, so in contrast with the razzle-dazzle of show biz, Tony proceeded to bare his soul to me and to his public. Recalling that dinner, he said, "What you saw, nobody saw but my wife. You even said, 'You looked angry, you looked slick, you looked Hollywood, you don't seem as though you are a gentleman, you looked very edgy, tense, ready to—like a cougar—jump on the audience,' and I did not know it."

Tony related the change in him to the pressures of the TV show, the tiredness that came from working 18 hours a day, seven days a week. Then the show's cancellation and a period of postdepression. He would go out into the street to find people to talk to. And when that wouldn't work, he would go into seclusion.

Additionally, Tony was shattered by the death of his 21-year-old sister, a mentally retarded cerebral palsy victim. Not only had Tony spent much of his teenage life helping his mother raise her, but she was the one on whom he first tested his talents as an entertainer. "Because my sister couldn't say my name and really couldn't communicate at all, and yet she was participating with me in music, I realized that it is the universal language and the ultimate form of communication."

All the while he was witnessing the torment and finally suicide of his buddy Freddie Prinze, who rose to stardom on "Chico and the Man."

Tony told us that Freddie definitely had a death wish. Unburdening himself of memories he had never before discussed on television, Tony described instances where Freddie had practiced suicide with an empty pistol aimed at his mouth or temple. "Sometimes he would shoot the pistol off, and if his secretary was in another room, she thought he had shot himself. He would be lying on the floor and get up laughing.

"He wanted to be a legend, like James Dean, and dying was a way to become a legend."

Tony even ticked off a list of people—Johnny Carson, Richard Pryor, David Brenner and Paul Williams—that Freddie wanted as pallbearers!

And there was the ordeal at the UCLA Intensive Care Unit, 37 hours of waiting to find out whether Freddie would survive his self-inflicted wounds.

"They kept telling us there was some hope," Tony recalled, "but the kind of hope they were talking about was not the hope that he would ever be able to get up and walk and talk and be a regular Freddie Prinze, for he really would have been a vegetable. And thank God that the Lord was kind enough to take him in His arms and out of mine."

I don't remember when I've seen a crew—those hardened technicians who have seen it all and heard it all over the years—so moved as were the men and women who were working with us that afternoon in the Orlando home. But there was much more to come.

Tony described the highs and lows of his manic-depression brought on by a biological imbalance in the blood. He admitted dabbling in drugs, using cocaine. All leading up to that night during a performance when, as he now explained, he said to himself, "There are two ways to go. There's his [Freddie Prinze's] way and there is this way. I quit."

In trying to solve his problem, Tony had himself committed to a pyschiatric institution in New York for 72 hours, a minimum period one has to agree to beforehand. What happened to him there was so chilling he had been willing to talk about it in the kitchen but didn't feel he could do so on the air. Yet when the time came, he poured it out.

The hospital, considered one of the best in the city, was so rundown that it brought back his life in the Hell's Kitchen ghetto.

Faced with the necessity of going to the bathroom, Tony proceeded to a facility shared by 103 patients.

"It never occurred to me that the rest of the patients looked at me as this star from television, Tony Orlando. I was a patient as far as I was concerned. As I sat down, in came about 12 to 14 guys who were all taunting me, 'Go, go, we want to see a star go, go, go.'

"I went back to my old show business ways and started telling bathroom jokes. I did anything I could to get a laugh, to get out of the situation. I occasionally wanted to get up and give a guy a hit."

Tony spoke of the additional indignities of that stay, the depths of his illness. And then of the therapy, the treatment with lithium and the ever-present loving care of his wife.

It seemed natural to bring on the little woman who had been such a tower of strength to Tony. Elaine was at first reluctant but then consented. To hear the two of them discuss situations that would have tested any marriage must have been inspiring to countless viewers. A little later Tony would sing "You Are Too Beautiful" and dedicate it to Elaine, who was standing by his side then as she had been through all the years of success and despair. It was a moment I shall never forget—the absolute stillness of the room save for the song, the tears of joy of not only Elaine and Tony but of everyone present, and the scene that followed when the cameras went off, Tony saying, "I love you" to Elaine as they walked off to privacy on their patio.

I am so pleased that the reaction to the program was as rewarding as it was. I'd like to feel that Tony's conversation and performance on that show—we did several numbers together, even improvising lyrics—made it easier for him to face the public in his comeback appearance a couple of weeks later. Everyone from Betty Ford to strangers on the street had words of praise. And the mail response indicated that many people out there were appreciative of the message that had been put forth about the nature and treatment of manic-depression. Satisfying as it is to hear that one's programs provide entertainment, which we hope is what "The Mike Douglas Show" is all about most of the time, it's even more fulfilling to know that we can also inform and educate and enlighten.

XXI
ANIMALS AND DIRTY TRICKS

I have written elsewhere about the doctrine my father pounded into me when I was a little boy—and I do mean pounded. Never let yourself be challenged successfully. This has led me to do some outlandish and ludicrous things on our show, consciously and unconsciously, and generally with animals.

There is, for instance, the incident with Rajah.

An amiable elephant, rather large for his species, Rajah and I met fo the first time before the cameras of KYW. This followed a lot of canoodling and finagling between my people backstage and Rajah's trainer regarding what Rajah would do to endear himself to the televiewing world.

The trainer (whom we shall call Bernard because that's the name my mind automatically attaches to any man who handles animals) and my people had huddled over what would be the best way to show Rajah's talent which, it turned out, was gentleness. He could be brutal when pressed but he preferred to be loved. So Bernard suggested that it would not only show the stuff of which Rajah was made but also what I was made of if I were to lie down and let Rajah put one foot on my head. When I was briefed on this . . . "for a finish you'll lie down on the stage and Rajah will rest his foot on your head," . . . I said, "No, I won't!" I said it with great vigor. But even as I did so, I realized that I'd been challenged. And knowing my people, who knew this secret compulsion I have to always take a dare, I didn't look forward to the show with much enthusiasm.

So the time came. Rajah made a grand entrance and did all the tricks elephants do. Then Bernard said to me, "To show you how gentle Rajah is, we would like you to lie down and let him put his foot on your head. And to prove to you that there is no danger, we will first demonstrate Rajah's gentleness with a watermelon."

From nowhere came a melon. Rajah put his foot on what is thought of as a fruit. It was immediately turned into a vegetable—SQUASH!

There was a gasp from the audience and Bernard laughed and said, "We just did that for a little joke. Now you, please, Mr. Douglas."

Well, you have only one life to give to your audience, I thought. When you've got to go you've got to go. And I went. My father's doctrine had taught me to conquer fear. I lay down, asking, "Is there a brain surgeon in the house?"

Rajah raised his enormous foot and with it he touched my soft head with the gentleness of Florence Nightingale. There was enthusiastic applause. Then Rajah stood on his hind legs and waved his trunk to the audience in acknowledgment. I got up and took a bow. But I had the awful feeling that the applause was all for Bernard's training skill and Rajah's gentleness, not for my courage.

If you've ever had the sinking feeling inside that you get when you've survived an accident but suddenly realize how close a call it was, what could have happened, you know how I felt. I sat down and said, "We'll be right back after this . . ." and on came a commercial for Excedrin.

Earlier I told you about a wrestling bear who threw his trainer against the back wall of the studio. You might think I'd have learned something about the unpredictability of trained bears. But you forget about such things. If I remembered for very long all the things that happened to me and the dirty tricks that have been played on me and my co-hosts, I'd go into a safer and more sensible line of work.

So when you hire a guy to be a talent coordinator you leave him alone and let him coordinate. When you replace one with another, you forget to tell him little things like, "Let's not get too chummy with trained bears."

Even if we had there was a difference between this one and the one who'd performed sort of a slam dunk with his trainer. The one we are now discussing was billed as a *dancing* bear.

When I first heard about the booking, my heart sank. Then I remembered the first bear and I thought, "If we're getting a dancing bear we should have booked him when Bobby Van was a co-host." We like to try to book guests who share something in common with the co-host or me. Instead, the co-host for this bear was a great singer and a wonderful friend who's sensational as a co-host because no matter what you do to him it breaks him up and everybody laughs. I am speaking of Robert Goulet.

He was perched on our "singer's stool" in the middle of the stage, the spotlight trained on him. The microphone was in his hand and he had our studio audience hypnotized. Suddenly they began to titter and then to roar. Bob thought the thought that panics all male performers. He twisted himself to the side, so the audience wouldn't get a full head-on view of him glancing down. The laughter built, as Bob continued to sing insouciantly.

Then he felt a hairy arm around his neck and a darling little chimpanzee gave him a great big kiss. Bob broke up so badly we thought we might never get him together again. He hadn't heard the chimp come in—on roller skates—because of the laughter.

I think Bob expects us to cross him up. But he never knows when or where. We asked him once if he'd do the old night club *shtick* of going into the audience and singing a love song to a girl. He was doing this to a very attractive young woman. She was being suitably embarrassed and Bob was laying it on thick. The song ended, applause, Bob bowed and thanked everyone including the attractive girl. She said, "I enjoyed it, too, Bob," in a very deep voice and took off "her" wig. But that was the end of it. They never really developed a relationship.

Now back to the dancing bear. Bernard put him (the bear) through a few little waltz steps, the foxtrot and the hustle so that everyone in the audience would be pleased. Then to demonstrate his all-around dancing skill he went for a tour jeté but didn't show anything that would cause Baryshnikov to worry.

Things seemed all on the up and up when Bernard asked Bob if he'd like to try a waltz with the bear. With no hesitation Bob approached the animal, put his arm around the bear's shoulder and started to dance. Bob's beauty or his animal magnetism or something appealed to the bear and aroused his deepest sensual impulses. When he danced, he danced! He took Bob in his arms and the next thing we knew had him on the floor and was sitting on his face. It took Bernard, the trainer and my entire stage crew to break up the affair.

To explain what happened to me one time when everyone was in a happy mood, you have to know how the show operates. The staff interviews the guest and puts some questions on cue cards, which I see and occasionally edit and frequently never read. I never rehearse these questions with the guest. So I'm always loose for whatever comes back.

They had booked a podiatrist. Why? Who knows? Possibly it was Foot Health Week. But in the event I didn't know the meaning of the word, they reminded me, "Remember, a podiatrist is a baby doctor."

I did a Jack Benny. "Now *cut* that out!" I said. Occasionally during the day someone would come to tell me something consequential about the podiatrist and to remind me that he was a baby doctor. I knew that they were trying to "gaslight" me so I was very careful. When they held up a card saying that our next guest was a famous baby doctor, I didn't go for the trick. I said it correctly—foot doctor—and thumbed my nose at everyone around, a gesture which completely baffled the audience both in the studio and in the homes.

The interview went well until the end. I'd concentrated so on "foot" instead of "baby" that I finished by saying, "Thank you very much, Doctor Foot."

There's a story something like that about a young reporter sent to interview J. P. Morgan the financier. It was a big break for the cub and he had been programmed for a week by his editors and the staff not to seem to notice Mr. Morgan's enormous nose. Just don't look at his nose. He's embarrassed by the size of his nose. It's gigantic. For two days before going to see the man his friends pounded away on the size of Morgan's schnozz.

When interview time came, he was ushered into the tycoon's office and very politely said, "Good morning, Mr. Nose."

Chimpanzees are always good for a giggle no matter what you do with them, so I worked out a little stunt that landed me in plenty of trouble.

I appeared outfitted in a gorilla suit for an interview with a chimp. Matters might have proceeded better had I done a little research on the compatibility of chimpanzees and gorillas. I quickly became a love object for my guest, who gave signs of possessing a powerful sex drive. He began stroking the gorilla's paw (beneath which was my own hand) and my suspicions about his romantic inclinations were increased when the primate let out a cry very similar to those I recall hearing in Tarzan movies as a boy, so loud and shrill that it parted my hair and rattled my back teeth. Thinking it would calm him, I too began to vocalize.

I must have communicated something totally unacceptable and offensive—an invitation to something beyond the bounds of all decency—because my love mate gave me one long horrified look, swung off into the audience and proceeded to dismantle the studio.

Pandemonium followed and I realized the seriousness of the matter when the quivering trainer said to me—me!— "Why don't you go out there and bring him back?"

"Why don't you? You're the trainer," I demanded, but he just shrugged and gave a nervous giggle.

Before we could get a ruling on whose job it was to corral my berserk playmate, the chimp had swung out of the studio and into the newsroom, hooked a finger under one of those great, big I.B.M. electric typewriters and flung it straight through the wall.

The fire and police departments were called, but it took an employee from the city zoo to calm down my enraged inamorata. I still wonder whether it was the gorilla suit that got him or whether he loved me for myself alone?

On another show, when Carol Burnett and Walter Matthau were guests, Walter brought a guest of his own, his dog, one of those amusing-looking English sheepdogs who can't see where they're going.

Incidentally, Carol had been my guest before and had invited me, right on the air, to be a guest on her first television show. It's a mutual admiration society between us. She's such a talented lady.

Well, she and Walter and I were discussing Walter's latest picture when suddenly the dog took the play away.

He rose, stretched himself slowly, yawned and mean-
dered off behind the sofa on which we were sitting, where
there was a grouping of ornamental shrubs. This got a laugh
and inspired Walter to say, "Don't worry. He's perfectly
trained."

Carol glanced over to where the dog had strayed and
asked, "To do what?"

I said, "Don't worry. They're artificial plants."

"Really?" said Walter. "That's wonderful. They've started to grow."

We had a group of guys on one show with specialized
functions in pictures—stunt men, marksmen, acrobats who
double for the stars. Among them was an archer.

In the morning briefing, I was told that I was to play a
scene from *William Tell*, in which I was going to be his son,
from whose head Mr. Tell had to shoot an apple.

My reaction was immediate and positive. "No, I'm not!"
The idea that I was to be the pedestal from which an apple
was to be sliced into a Waldorf salad by some Hollywood
Robin Hood with a bow and arrow did not appeal to me one
iota.

So they went through the business of showing me how
this sharpshooter never missed. They set up the dummy
that he employed in his usual act. The William Tell bit was
to be the grand finale.

Our star notched an arrow, took careful aim at the apple
on the head of the dummy (later to be me) and "Twang!" He
hit the dummy right in the tummy. (Maybe just a little low.)
Very funny!

I smelled a setup, something like the old elephant and the
watermelon bit. And again I couldn't resist a challenge. So
we tried the trick, and of course it worked. And again I
paused to wonder why I do such nutty things.

Maybe the reason is that every man requires some adventure in his life, a respite from the routine, and there isn't an
awful lot of time for that in mine. There is the daily and de-

manding chore of putting together the show. The finished product may appear smooth to the viewer, but as Señor Wences so cleverly put it, "Easy for you, difficult for me."

Earning a vacation requires a double effort, doing one extra show a week. So if I let my staff talk me into doing what appear to be daffy things, for me they are no daffier than it is for a banker or a shipping clerk to take time off to scale a mountain or stalk lions in deepest Africa with nothing but a sling shot and a yo-yo (a relatively new sport in which the sling shot is used to capture the lion's attention and the yo-yo hypnotizes the beast into coming home with you for breakfast).

I tell you all this because, although I should have seen it coming, I submitted myself to the delicate skill of a man whose main job was instructing Hollywood performers on the gentle art of using a whip as a weapon of either defense or attack, not on an animal but upon a human enemy. You must have seen these jokers in circuses and state fairs who take a long bull whip, ask some drunk from the audience (the sober wouldn't volunteer) to put a quarter in his mouth and allow the whipster with one flick of his whip to change it into two dimes and a nickel, or two bus tokens and five pennies. My mother always told me never to put money in my mouth.

Our guest had not only performed all these tricks but had demonstrated his ability to take a whole loaf of bread and in a few snaps of the whip completely slice it into pieces of sandwich thickness. Comes now the time when good old Mike is asked to put a card in his mouth, preferably a ten of diamonds and let the man with the whip cut it into two five-of-spades.

The first thing was to have me close my eyes. Open-eyed, seeing what was happening, they told me, I might flinch and do myself an injury. Notice how, if anything happened, it would be my fault, not the guy's with the whip. So, blindfolded, I was told to face the audience. This, so that the whipster could be brought down front and allow those in the studio a full view of what was happening.

The card was placed in my mouth. The man with the whip remained upstage. Then he did his trick. He never touched the card. Instead he flicked this long, lethal weapon in such a way that it wound around my head and the tassel at the end draped itself artistically over one of my eyes, like the tassel on the mortarboard of a newly graduated college student. There was a gasp, applause and a voice which I knew was mine but I don't know who was operating it, that said, "We'll be back after this brief pause."

You see they lie to me. They have to in order to get the effects (from me) that they want and, naturally, I want. Because of that I accept the lies—and pray a lot.

All of the foregoing, of course, has nothing to do with my voluntary entrance into a large plexiglass tank filled with water, while the underwater demolition expert who'd given me scuba lessons stood outside the tank and watched.

I don't like to put my head under water. I didn't like it when I agreed to play with a water polo team we had on the show. I made up my mind never to do it again. Then I changed my mind because the show must go on, even if I go crazy.

The real reason I don't like to put my head under water, I see as my parents' fault. We didn't have our own swimming pool for me to practice in. But, as I've tried to make clear, there's a lot of the "I'd die for dear old Yale" in me. So there was the tankful of water, the scuba gear and me. I donned it, trying to remember everything the man told me to do and bravely climbed in and began swimming around under water. As I'd been told (although it sounded ridiculous), it was not only easy, it was fun.

I began smiling broadly, remembering that laughter could mean instant drowning, and waving to the audience. But plans had been made behind my back to add a surprise element to the submarine excursion. The prop man had been instructed to procure a harmless water snake. The plan was to introduce this into my wet environment to find out what I'd do. Paramedics were standing by off stage with life-saving gear in case I fainted. But little chance of this was considered as the only kind of water snake my people had ever seen or heard of was about a foot long.

The floor manager checked with the prop man. "Got the snake?"

"In the bag" was the answer, pointing to a plain brown grocery bag, a larger version of the type which some men carry and drink from that often contains a whole bottleful of snakes.

"Go!" said the floor manager.

The prop man emptied the bag into the tank as I was swimming away from him, waving and smiling. I was having the time of my life. Then I turned to swim back.

There before my very eyes was the Loch Ness monster. In less time than it takes to write that the prop man had been given a very large water snake, the daddy of all water snakes, enormous but harmless, I was out of the tank. There were no steps, no ladders, no EXIT signs.

"You went right over the top without touching the sides," I was told. "It was beautiful! You must have taken wall-scaling when you were in the Navy."

"Naturally," I said, having recaptured my calm, sophisticated charm. "Haven't you ever read, 'a wall of water was approaching the ship'?"

Now for the big explosive finish to this chapter of guile and deception. Many of you may have seen on David Frost's *Guinness Book of Records* show a gentleman modestly billed as "The Human Bomb."

This gentleman's incredible act consists of placing sticks of dynamite in his belt, stuffing himself into a box, activating the explosive, and somehow emerging alive.

I was tempted to ask him, before he performed his feat, "What happens if you don't come out? Does your widow take a bow?" But I knew, as Nixon said, "That would be wrong."

At the urging of a couple of card-carrying sadists in my employ, men who will stop at nothing (assigning the job to someone else, of course) to get a good effect, Mr. Human Bomb added a couple of sticks of dynamite to his normal load so that we'd get more bangs for our bucks.

So, when the time was at hand and he activated the charge and blew himself out of his box, he almost blew the first two rows of our audience into the next county. When the debris had settled and the smoke had cleared, we ran over to inspect.

"Are you all right?" I asked in a trembling voice.

He looked at me, smiled bemusedly and said, "I'm all right, David."

The relief at hearing that he didn't hold *me* to blame was enormous.

(XXII)
PARTING IS SUCH SWEET SORROW

On one of our trips to Hollywood, I got to talk to a young actor named Winkler, who was at that time enjoying sensational success. He couldn't show his face in public without being mobbed. When he walked into a bank, they declared a dividend.

Henry, that's his first name, reran for me his version of that old show business axiom, a conviction held by all directors and producers, that actors don't know what's good for them. He said his agent had to almost shanghai him to Hollywood to get him to give up what was then a very limp career on Broadway.

Because *sic transit gloria mundi* . . . also Tuesdi . . . Wednesdi . . . Thursdi . . . Fridi . . . Saturdi . . . and Sundi . . . it is important to note that at the time we talked, Winkler was the sensation of the top television show "Happy Days." He was my guest and his presence on any TV show poured beaucoup digits on the rating numbers. Although it hadn't really been planned that way, he had become the runaway favorite of the series in the part of a street-smart punk with a heart and an irresistible desire to do good that he couldn't overcome—Arthur Fonzarelli, "The Fonz."

There can be little doubt that it was Winkler's handling of the Fonz part that made it a skyrocketing hit. Even the most expert producer or director can't tell when or why such a thing happens. Even the writer doesn't know.

The actor follows his instinct and creates a character that charms audiences. Yet had he followed his instinct, his feeling that it would be better to stay in New York on Broadway, Henry Winkler would never have attained a popularity as an actor that threatened to lose him his identity as a person (and his privacy) and turn him permanently into "The Fonz." It's typecasting after the fact, and I have a feeling it's on the way out.

Henry fights it every inch of the way, playing any role he can get on stage or in a picture, when he has time, if it's different from the Fonzarelli role. And it's a tribute to Winkler the actor that he's as different from "The Fonz" as a dish of pasta fazool is from a well-done brisket of beef. Except for one thing. Both the actor and the character know all the answers. When they don't, they make them up. But each in his own way.

Winkler's is the way of a man who graduated from Emerson College and received his master's degree from Yale. "The Fonz" graduated from the streets and mastered a big Harley.

The only reason I'm getting into all this is because all the celebrities, all the superstars I've met (and I've met nearly all of them) develop a similar problem and each has to solve it in his own way to survive. To fail to solve it could lead to disaster.

Another young actor who went the same route Winkler traveled is a young comedian, Jimmie Walker. I've already mentioned that he complained about his loss of privacy and freedom to do what he wants to do. "So I stay home a lot," he said. "It don't make sense! Your popularity is your prison. And the same goes for your whole family. Your success is theirs. Your dog can even pick up a few extra bones wagging its tail for Puppy Pudding or something."

It's true. Winkler told me about his mother being asked to go on a TV talk show. Proudly, she announced to the whole neighborhood, "Look who is going on the teevee."

Most of the people she said this to probably managed to see her but not her son, Henry. He was on a trip and was in the air while she was *on* the air. So he missed his Mom. When she asked him how she was, did she have a future, he couldn't answer. He hadn't seen the show.

As luck would have it, the show happened to be "Good Morning, America," so I was able to tell Henry that the producer was an old friend of mine. I said that I was sure I could get him a videotape of his Mom's triumph. You see, the producer of "Good Morning, America" was none other than my dear friend Woody Fraser, ex-producer of "The Mike Douglas Show."

Why an "ex-producer"? Those things happen. Even blood brothers can have their differences. Remember those two fellas named Cain and Abel?

But unlike those two characters, Woody and I always seemed able to work things out. Unfortunately, even a good thing like that can't go on forever. Fortunately, dear friends can have violent differences of opinion and still remain friends.

Maybe that's what Erich Segal meant when he said that much-quoted and kidded line, "Love means never having to say you're sorry."

There comes a time, however, when the difference of opinion widens too far and the solution is to stop working together. Then the difference disappears and the friendship remains.

Our problem narrowed down to this—the booking of the

shows. Not what kind of people to book but how many per show.

His idea was to set a fast pace, never leave anyone on long enough to get tiresome. Well, there's a lot to be said for that strategy. But the guy who's chatting with those guests must feel that he has a little time to operate. If each appearance is so limited, the result is inevitably something bland, speed having been substituted for substance. The point of contention was simple: I preferred fewer guests whereas Woody liked to pack the show so tight I sometimes had to sit on it to get it closed. So I finally chose to sit on Woody.

I felt hemmed in by his express train schedule. One little adlib that might lead off at a tangent to a totally new subject and open up a whole new train of thought became out of the question because it might take up too much time. Woody's argument was that the timing on our show is complicated enough without going out of your way to create problems.

I finally lost my temper and said that Mussolini was always defended because he made the trains run on time. That was mean and uncalled for. On the other hand, if you're up there in front of the cameras you can't talk with your tongue on a stopwatch,

Here's what I mean.

Mel Tillis, the great country and western singer, was making an appearance. We were the first to book him. Everyone else had shied away because Mel has this problem— he stammers. The networks feared an adverse response from viewers who might assume the entertainer was mocking people with speech impediments.

Mel didn't stammer when he sang, which is not unusual. Lou Holtz, one of the great vaudeville monologists and radio stars, only stammered when he was *off*-stage. After Mel had opened with a song, I tried talking to him in such a way as to conceal his "handicap." When he had trouble getting something out, I would anticipate and supply the missing word, which resulted in a sort of echo routine, me throwing in the word and Mel repeating it. What became slowly clear to me was that Mel couldn't care less if people were aware that he stuttered, making my assistance a mistake.

Finally, having cast caution to the winds and gone through this whole bit getting a lot of laughs along the way, the time came for him to depart. I said good-bye to Mel by telling him, "If I'm ever standing before a firing squad, I pray for only one thing—that you're the guy who has to say, 'Ready! Aim! Fire!'"

Naturally it was a yell. It came right off the top of my head. And that'll give you an idea of what's up there. But coming at the end of a long adlib routine with Mel, the roar of laughter and the applause threw the whole timing of the show out of kilter. We had to cut one segment completely.

In fact, the bit ran so long it wound up several weeks later, when Glen Campbell was co-host, starring guess who—Mel Tillis. Mel had won the Country Music Award as Entertainer of the Year. So naturally we had him on again and again he led me into an adlib that a four-year-old couldn't have missed—obvious, corny and yet you couldn't let it go by or people for weeks would be stopping and asking you, "In that talk with Mel Tillis about the bull, why didn't you say . . . ?"

We were talking about his hobby, cattle breeding. What else would a country and Western star be interested in? Who else could afford it? It's an expensive hobby. Mel told me he'd just paid $15,000 for a bull.

Anyone in the world hearing that line simply had to say, "Man, that's a lot of bull!" I didn't try to buck a trend.

But another thing Mel did, and this is what got us off our schedule for the second time with him, he repeated his acceptance speech when he received the award.

He said, "This has been a great year for the handicapped. I won and I can't talk. Stevie Wonder won an' he can't see.

So I'm glad to accept this award for all the handicapped people in this country who have made it. And those who are qualified and haven't been given a chance have every right to think that maybe it's not them but the country that's handicapped."

Getting back to Woody, it's one thing to love a man like a brother and be grateful for all the ways he's helped you, but there comes the moment of realization that your friendship must be separated from your business for the survival of both. This doesn't mean you love the man any less. It just means that you love freedom more. So after trying to resolve our differences, after going round and round, Woody got off.

Woody headed for California where he produced "The Della Reese Show" and others and then got a big job as head of program development for RKO.

Remember in those old silent movies when they wanted to bridge a passage of time they'd flash on a subtitle that said, "Sometime later"? In the TV business we say the same thing this way, "We'll be back after these brief messages." But we'll skip that.

A man named Barry Sand was producing our show and doing a fine job. But I didn't want to lay too much of a load on him so when I had to come up with an outside segment for an Easter Seal telethon, I looked around for someone else to produce it. As luck would have it I heard Woody Fraser was in the East. Everybody has a tendency to rely a little bit on whoever it was who first helped him get started on the road to where I am. So I called Woody, who said he'd be glad to help.

Well, we were sitting around watching a tape of one of my shows and little by little it got kind of nostalgic out.

"Barry's doing a great job," Woody said.

"Yeah. All the guys who came after you did a good job. But you're not easy to follow."

Woody shrugged.

"I don't know, Woody," I said. "I've just never been as happy with another producer as I was with you. It's some kind of . . . I don't know . . . I can't describe it!"

Have you ever noticed that when someone says he can't describe something he then goes ahead and tries to describe it? Well, that's me.

"It's some kind of chemistry, I guess. You've always been able to come up with ideas and I've been able to make them work for you. I mean, the fact that this is true must mean the ideas were good for me," and on and on and on until it got a little sickening. Finally I said, "Do you like what you're doing now?"

He asked the natural question "Why?"

"Would you like to come back?" I blurted out.

"Are you serious?"

"Try me!"

And so Woody came home. But don't think I didn't have trouble selling him to Westinghouse. They knew him. He worked for them before I did. They knew he was brilliant. But they also knew that he didn't even know how to spell the word budget. And no one could convince him that it was more important to do a job at the right price than simply to do it right!

One of the rules of business is that you can hate a person only until he becomes necessary to you. Well, I didn't hate Woody at all, but I began to feel he was necessary to me. And I made that necessity clear to Westinghouse. So Woody and I were reunited.

But here's a funny thing. If you're good, you're good, and it gets around and if you're good and successful it gets around even faster. Well, maybe it isn't funny. Maybe it just makes sense.

Pretty soon I was picking up rumors that ABC was romancing Woody. They wanted him to come and produce their "Good Morning, America" show. But what no one knew was that at the same time they were trying to get

Woody they were also waving bouquets at me. I guess maybe they thought we were a package and if they could get either one, they'd get the other. It's cheaper that way, sometimes. They finally got David Hartman, who's great.

Well, when the whole thing came into the open, I told Woody I wouldn't stand in his way if he wanted to take the new challenge and go with ABC.

It was nothing, really. Just good business on everybody's part. Woody had raised his baby ("The Mike Douglas Show") to a solid success and his mind started working in other creative directions. He felt he'd given our MDS everything he could think of. So he passed the production reins to Jack Reilly and only comes to Philadelphia to help me do my part in the annual Easter Seal telethon and to stay a couple of nights at the house with Gen and me. Then we sit and talk about his promise to give my production company first crack at the next great show idea that hits him.

XIII

IN CLOSING

I thought a long time before deciding to include what follows.

I offer it as a tribute not only to Mom but also to Dad.

I had reservations because I didn't want my father to think that I was in any way putting him down. I could never do that. The very foundation of my love for him was his firm belief in being a strong competitor. It was that alone that gave me the motivation to stick in show business when it really looked as if I was stuck with it. Dad, I think I've indicated, like all of us, was never perfect. Nor was Mom. They were both human, very human beings with hopes and ideals that they instilled in me.

When you put them both together, they were two sensational parents, and I hope Mom carried with her to the grave thoughts of me as loving and proud as the one I know she must have held for my brother Bob. I know Dad has those same loving thoughts.

There is no use repeating that I have never taken a drink. As is often the case with us teetotalers, there is a reason. I had an aunt who adored me. She used to grab me, hug me and kiss me so often and so fervently that I had a hangover the next morning.

Among her many problems was that she couldn't remember—sometimes she couldn't *say* Michael. I had yet to become Mike. I called her Auntie and she called me Skeezix after the character in "Gasoline Alley." The name Skeezix seemed to come easy to her, like a sneeze, or a snort. She was my mother's sister.

Dad drank quite a bit when he needed to hide from himself. Fortunately, he was not an alcoholic. His drinking was his pleasure, not a disease. But it was a pleasure he took refuge in when he felt ashamed of himself. His problem was gambling. On occasional paydays his craving for a game (perhaps it was partly his competitive spirit) overcame his good judgment, his love for Mom, us kids and everything.

The result was that he sometimes arrived home having blown the rent money as well was what was to have handled the outstanding tabs from the friendly butcher and grocer who gave us credit, and charged us heavily for it.

There has to be that final straw that breaks the back of tolerance in any intolerable situation. This came one payday when Dad showed up morose, remorseful, loaded with apologies, guilt and John J. Jameson. Yet his apologies for what had happened (to those who knew him) were like a kid apologizing for getting the measles, whooping cough or something else he didn't know how to avoid.

He couldn't cure what he had but Mom figured out a way.

It was the same way the United States used in wiping malaria out of the Isthmus of Panama so the canal could be built without losing hundreds of people to disease. Find the cause and get rid of it. The cause was mosquitoes and we did.

Mom knew the cause of what she had to deal with. She knew where it came from and she took action.

Gangsters were pretty heavy in our area of Chicago at that time. Which meant it did no good to complain about them to the police. But Mom knew the spot where the action was. Everybody did. A lot of wives suffered from the same problem Mom had.

So she organized a raid—her own kind. She took Bob, Helen and me and marched right over to the spot where Dad had dropped his bundle—two weeks' pay. By sheer strength of personality and the persuasive power of three frightened-looking kids she got in to see the head man.

It may have been because Italians are very sentimental people, very fond of children. Whatever it was, she got in and told the two-for-a-quarter Godfather who ran the establishment (and most of the men in the neighborhood who were in hock to him) just what he was doing to her and a lot of mothers just like her. It made the capo cry. We all cried. Mom had made the most eloquent speech I had ever heard.

What she did was one of the bravest acts I've ever seen for two reasons. Brave to go against that hoodlum. But even braver to tempt the anger she knew it would inspire in the man she loved. She braved the blow to a man's pride to save everything he held dear to him.

But she challenged the hood and she won. He not only gave her back every cent Dad had lost, he promised her he'd never let Dad in his joint again.

How Mom and Dad worked it out between them when she told him what she had done, naturally, I have no way of knowing. But they must have. A thing like that in a family is like the crisis in a case of pneumonia—there's a point at which you either recover or succumb.

I'm forever grateful to both of my parents for that incident. For Mom's courage in doing what she did and Dad's wisdom and understanding while learning a lesson that made him an even better father.

If anything has come out of this book at all, I hope it is my complete and entire admiration and love for two parents who gave me so much that I needed before I knew I needed it. And gave me so much support when I found out how *much* I needed it.

The world would be a wonderful place if all parents were like mine, when all people can say that and mean it as I do.

Index